THE FILMS OF
JOHN HUSTON

THE FILMS OF
JOHN HUSTON

by John McCarty

CITADEL PRESS • *SECAUCUS, NEW JERSEY*

Designed by Paul Chevannes

Published by Citadel Press
A division of Lyle Stuart, Inc.
120 Enterprise Ave., Secaucus, N.J. 07094
In Canada: Musson Book Company
A division of General Publishing Co. Limited
Don Mills, Ontario

Queries regarding rights and permissions should be
addressed to: Lyle Stuart, 120 Enterprise Avenue,
Secaucus, N.J. 07094

Manufactured in the United States of America

Library of Congress Cataloging-in-Publication Data

McCarty, John, 1944-
    The films of John Huston.

    Bibliography: p.
    1. Huston, John, 1906-   —Criticism and
interpretation. I. Title.
PN1998.A3H799   1987   791.43'0233'0924   86-32685
ISBN 0-8065-1020-X

For Cheryl—who likes
Moby Dick almost as much
as I do.

Acknowledgments

I wish to express my gratitude to the following people and organizations for their many kindnesses and invaluable cooperation in helping me put together this work on the films of John Huston: Dominick Abel; American International Pictures; Eric Caidin (Hollywood Book & Poster Company); Columbia Pictures Industries; Mary Corliss (Museum of Modern Art); Pam Elder (KCET); Ken Hanke; Mike Hawks (Larry Edmunds Bookshop); Jerry Ohlinger's Movie Material Store; Irv Letofsky (*Los Angeles Times,* Sunday Calendar Editor); Christopher McCarty; Dave McDonnell; Metro-Goldwyn-Mayer; Paramount Pictures Corp.; Tom Phillips (Paramount); Mark Ricci (The Memory Shop); Scott Rudnick (Collector's Bookstore); 20th Century-Fox; United Artists Corporation; Universal Pictures; Tise Vahimagi (National Film Archive); Warner Bros. Inc.; Allan J. Wilson (Citadel Press).

Photo Credits

Warner Bros. Inc.
Allied Artists Pictures Corp.
Long Road Productions
Mitzi Trumbo
Loew's Inc.
United Artists Corporation
20th Century-Fox
Universal International
Metro-Goldwyn-Mayer, Inc.
Warner Bros.—Seven Arts
Columbia Pictures
National General Pictures
New Line Cinema
Paramount Pictures
Lorimar Productions, Inc.
Columbia Pictures Industries, Inc.
Universal City Studios, Inc.
ABC Motion Pictures, Inc.
American International Pictures
Cinerama Releasing Corp.
Dino DeLaurentiis Cinematografica S.p.A.
Long Road Productions
NBC
Avco Embassy Pictures
The Ladd Company

Contents

John Huston—circa 1950.

Introduction

JOHN HUSTON is one of the last of that breed of second generation directors—those who followed the pioneers—whose body of work continues to entrance audiences and influence aspiring directors all over the world. At age 80, he is still going strong.

A recipient of the American Film Institute's Life Achievement Award for a career that has "stood the test of time," Huston remains what he has always been, a globe-trotting maverick who prefers to live and work away from Hollywood. He chooses his own material even if he has to wait years to get it made—as was the case with *The Man Who Would Be King* (1975), a long-cherished project he'd once hoped to star Humphrey Bogart and Clark Gable. His most recent film, the iconoclastic black comedy *Prizzi's Honor* (1985), has garnered him the kind of critical accolades one usually associates with the debut of a promising beginner.

Poet, painter, prizefighter, gambler, bullfighter, soldier, filmmaker: Huston has been all of these. And he has imbued his work with echoes of all of his various lives. To watch a John Huston film is to gain an insight into the mind and make-up of the man himself. Huston's films, no matter how disparate their subject matter, are unified not so much by a unique style as by a distinct way of looking at the world. In his autobiography, he writes of his early years as a down-and-out screenwriter suffering from a malaise called bad luck: "The sources of bad luck reside in the unconscious. We inflict it on ourselves as a kind of self-punishment. At the time, I only thought of myself as unlucky—under a dark cloud—but that fuming dark cloud undoubtedly emanated from my own spirit." One can see in this early self-description the not so vague outlines of such future Huston protagonists as Sam Spade (Humphrey Bogart) in *The Maltese Falcon* (1941), Fred C. Dobbs (Humphrey Bogart) in *The Treasure of the Sierra Madre* (1948), Henry Fleming (Audie Murphy) in *The Red Badge of Courage* (1951), Toulouse Lautrec (José Ferrer) in *Moulin Rouge* (1953), as well as many others. Each is his own worst enemy, and his struggle to defeat that enemy, which is the core of each film, ends, as often as not, unsuccessfully.

In *The Maltese Falcon,* for example, Spade's amatory weakness for the conniving, murderous Brigid

O'Shaughnessy (Mary Astor) almost causes him to sink to her moral level, but he manages to rise above these impulses by finding a higher duty, and turns her over to the police instead. "When a man's partner is killed," he tells her, "he's supposed to do something about it. It doesn't make any difference what you thought about him. He was your partner and you're supposed to do something about it." The same is true of Henry Fleming in *Red Badge,* who, fearing that he's a coward, at first surrenders to that fear, then finally overcomes it through sheer force of will. Fred C. Dobbs on the other hand allows his greed and paranoia to get the best of him and is murdered by the Mexican bandit, Gold Hat (Alphonso Bedoya); while Toulouse-Lautrec succumbs to self-loathing over his dwarfish appearance and bitterly spurns the woman (Suzanne Flon) who loves him, thereby throwing away a chance for happiness.

Spade (Humphrey Bogart) threatens Brigid (Mary Astor) in The Maltese Falcon. *His amatory weakness for her almost causes him to sink to her moral level.*

The fact that not a few Huston protagonists are defeated by the dark clouds they carry with them has led to a critical misreading of Huston's work as basically pessimistic. Huston himself denies this. "I certainly don't know what the point of life is," he says, "but I don't indulge in depression. I think I see the world very clearly, though." Huston's films tend to bear him out—even so seemingly atypical a subject as *Annie* (1982), the director's only musical, which embraces Huston's statement as its basic theme. Interestingly, the latter part of his statement is also an apt description of the Huston style, which is a straightforward, eye-level approach to filmmaking that seldom goes in for obfuscation.

Huston likes to throw his heroes and heroines into adventures where they must act instinctively and with an almost reckless abandon—just to see how they'll come out. Invariably, those characters who lose their moral bearings or their lives do so because they give into self-deception or some other crippling inner malaise. Quite simply, they fail to come to terms with the stakes they're really playing

for. In *Sierra Madre*, for example, the issue at hand is not the gold, but rather the possibility of an aimless, wasted life spent in its pursuit. Dobbs's obsession with the gold leads to his death. His life *is* wasted. But his partners, Curtin (Tim Holt) and Old Howard (Walter Huston), come through the adventure winners. Though still broke, they have finally achieved something more important: a sense of purpose and direction. Howard returns to the Indian village where he is held in high esteem as a doctor, while Curtin sets off to make a life with the widow of Cody (Bruce Bennett), another gold hunter who'd been killed by Mexican bandits while trying to horn in on the trio's claim. This is scarcely the viewpoint of a total pessimist, and this positive outlook crops up in one Huston film after another.

In *The African Queen* (1953), drunken wastrel

Dobbs' (Humphrey Bogart) obsession with the gold leads to his death. Here, Curtin (Tim Holt) holds him back when he tries to strike old Howard (Walter Huston) with a rock. From Huston's The Treasure of the Sierra Madre.

Charlie Alnutt (Humphrey Bogart) and priggish spinster Rosie Sayer (Katherine Hepburn) are not really playing for the German gunship they've set out to sink, but rather for each other's love and respect—which they come to realize in the desperate moments following the apparent failure of their patriotic mission. Sentenced to be executed, they insist that the captain marry them. He does just as the *Queen* blows up and sinks the gunship after all—surely one of the happiest of all Huston endings. Conversely, in Huston's variation on *The African Queen*, the 1957 *Heaven Knows, Mr. Allison*, shipwrecked marine Robert Mitchum and stranded nun Deborah Kerr find out they are not playing for each other's love, nor even for their own survival against the Japanese, but for affirmation of their commitment to the respective paths they have chosen in life—the Marines in Allison's case, the Church in Sister Angela's. Through exposure to one another's strengths and weaknesses, they each come to that realization and achieve their mutual goal. If *Heaven Knows, Mr. Allison* can be said to end at all unhappily, it is because Huston denies our wish to

Drunken wastrel Charlie Allnutt (Humphrey Bogart) and priggish spinster Rosie Sayer (Katharine Hepburn) realize it's love, not patriotism, they're playing for. From Huston's The African Queen.

Danny (Sean Connery) in The Man Who Would Be King.
*Though Huston faults the weakness that defeats Danny, he does
not disdain Danny himself.*

have these two appealing people get together the way Charlie and Rosie do. But such an ending would have been false—as false as having Charlie and Rosie spurn each other at the end of *The African Queen*— and not at all consistent with the film's carefully developed theme. Though not much heralded as a major Huston work, *Heaven Knows, Mr. Allison* remains a personal favorite of the director himself.

Daniel Dravot (Sean Connery) in *The Man Who Would Be King* (1975) starts out knowing exactly what he's playing for: kingship of the benighted country of Kafiristan, which has been without a royal ruler since Alexander the Great departed many centuries before. Through guile, derring-do, and not a little luck, he becomes king. But as he and his partner, Peachy (Michael Caine), wait out the monsoon season so that they can make off with the royal riches, Danny falls victim to his own publicity and deceives himself into believing that he really is a king, and even a god. When

Huston the actor as degenerate land grabber Noah Cross in Roman Polanski's Chinatown. *He's seen here with Jack Nicholson as private eye Jake Gittes, a character who shares more than a little in common with Sam Spade.*

his subjects discover their god/king to be all too human after all, Danny is summarily executed for his blasphemy and Peachy is tortured and left to die.

Though Danny loses in the end due to his own weakness, we can't help but admire him. Facing death courageously, his only concern is that Peachy forgive him for developing a swelled head and blowing their successful scam. Though Huston faults the weakness that defeated Danny, he does not disdain Danny himself. Danny is not Fred C. Dobbs. There is a size to him. And the story of his unhappy fall is the stuff from which legends are made.

Captain Ahab (Gregory Peck) in *Moby Dick* (1956) is perhaps the most majestic example of a Huston character who is consumed by the dark clouds emanating from his own spirit. Like Dravot, Ahab has stature. There is even greatness in him. His charting of whale migrations and feeding grounds throughout all the oceans of the world is a scientific marvel. ''I've never seen the like!'' whispers his astonished first mate, Starbuck (Leo Genn), when Ahab shows it to him. Yet the chart's real purpose is to allow Ahab to track and kill the white whale that claimed his leg. His motivation is one of revenge—against a dumb brute that acted

only out of instinct.

To the megalomaniacal Ahab, however, Moby Dick has become something more than just a whale. "It is the face behind the mask I seek," he says. "The malignant *thing* that mauls and mutilates our race." Ahab knows the stakes he's playing for—his own soul. For to him, Moby Dick represents the deity, and his pursuit of it is a blasphemous challenge to God's power over mortal men. "I'd strike the sun if it insulted me!" he rages pridefully. By harpooning Moby Dick, he hopes to strike a fatal blow against God Himself.

Ahab's defeat resides in himself, but, like Dravot, there is a sense of grandeur about his fall. It is certainly most spectacular. Lashing himself to the whale's side, he strikes at it with venom until he drowns—a conclusion, it should be noted, that is not in Melville's book.

* * *

Captain Ahab (Gregory Peck) in Moby Dick *is, perhaps, the most majestic example of a Huston character who is consumed by the dark clouds emanating from his own spirit.*

What it takes to win and what it takes to lose. Huston knows his subject well. For throughout his life, he has experienced all the highs and lows of which a career in films is capable. He has earned and squandered fortunes. To make his films *his* way, he has been forced into many a pitched fight with unsympathetic studio heads and producers, not a few of whom bested him in the end by savaging one of his pet projects prior to its release—for example, *The Red Badge of Courage.* Some of his lesser films have received excellent notices and big box office returns, while more personal projects—like *Moby Dick*—received damning ones and little public acceptance, at least at the time of their original release.

Huston has been the subject of near deification as both man and artist, in James Agee's legendary 1950 profile of him in *Life* magazine, as well as pilloried, and parodied, in Peter Viertel's *White Hunter, Black Heart,* a scathing roman à clef about the shooting of *The African Queen.* Yet despite all this, he stands today not only at the top of his craft in terms of reputation, but at the peak of his form creatively, taking on new cinematic challenges each year with an almost unbroken stride—as witness his 1984 screen

adaptation of Malcolm Lowry's daunting novel, *Under the Volcano*.

There is also a bit of the ham in John Huston. This is not surprising in that theatre runs in his blood. His father, the celebrated stage and screen actor Walter Huston, took the younger Huston on the road with him in vaudeville, where the boy made his stage debut at the age of three. After he became a director, he made frequent cameo appearances in his own films à la Hitchcock, but never thought seriously about embarking on a second career *before* the cameras until 1963 when he accepted a major role in Otto Preminger's *The Cardinal* as a lark. He received an Academy Award nomination for his work, and there has been no looking back since. Today, John Huston is in as much demand as a character actor—and as a voice for TV commercials and documentaries—as he is as a director.

Despite having turned in such memorable portrayals as that of the degenerate land grabber Noah Cross in Roman Polanski's *Chinatown* (1974), Huston tends to deride his work as an actor. "I don't take that part of my life seriously," he says. "Each episode has been a lark—and they pay me to do it!"

Huston, of course, is equally modest about his body of work as a director, insisting that he is "only eclectic" and that he sees each picture he makes as being totally different from any other. "I'm a shallow soul, actually," he smiles, "who likes variety."

Huston may very well like variety—boredom, he says, is a feeling that terrifies him (a terror, incidentally, that he shares with many of the characters in his films)—but as has already been indicated, and as the following pages will continue to demonstrate, the films of John Huston are scarcely the work of a shallow soul.

The Screenwriting Years

JOHN MARCELLUS HUSTON, the only son of Walter and Rhea Gore Huston, was born in the small border town of Nevada, Missouri, on August 5, 1906. His Toronto-born father was an aspiring actor and vaudevillian whose career at the time seemed to be going nowhere. To pay the bills and keep food on the table, he was working as an electrical engineer, a job he would continue to pursue without enthusiasm over the next several years. His wife, a successful, former New York City news reporter, had meanwhile given up her own career to be with him and to take care of young John. The strain showed on both sides, and in 1909 the pair separated for good when Walter Huston met an aspiring dancer named Bayonne Whipple and teamed with her for another shot at the vaudeville circuit. Over the next few years, they toured the country as a song-and-dance team and were eventually married in 1913. Rhea Gore Huston returned to her newspaper career, eventually remarried as well, and settled in California. It was she who got custody of their son.

Throughout his formative years, John Huston continually shuttled back and forth between both of his parents, receiving his taste for the theatre from his father and his taste for the good life from his mother, an inveterate gambler and horse player who insisted on staying in only the best hotels while on assignment for her newspaper. It's safe to say that Huston probably developed his celebrated wanderlust from each of his parents during this time.

On occasion, Huston's mother would place the boy in a private school when she or her ex-husband couldn't afford to take him on the road with them. During one of these stays, the then twelve-year-old Huston fell ill and was diagnosed as suffering from an enlarged heart and kidney problems which threatened his life. Confined to bed, he spent much of his time reading and developed a thirst for books that has lasted to this day. (Huston says he still reads between three and four books a week.)

Much of what Huston read during this dire period in his life would have a significant impact on him and on the world in the years to come. Huston has always chosen to adapt most of his films from other sources—*The Barbarian and the Geisha* (1958), *The Misfits* (1961), *Freud* (1963), *The Life and Times of Judge Roy Bean* (1972). *Phobia* (1980) and *Victory*

19

Walter Huston and son John—circa 1930.

(1981) remain the few exceptions to this rule. Many of his best known films, he says, had their genesis when he read the original work as a sickly youth or as a young man. This may be why so many of his films—particularly the early ones—were drawn from detective or adventure novels; these are the genres that appeal most to young readers, particularly males. This is certainly true of *The Red Badge of Courage* (1951) and *The Man Who Would Be King* (1975), both of which Huston claims to have read twenty or thirty years before he actually came to film them. It may also be true of *Moby Dick* (1956) as well, though Huston brands anyone who claims to have read that difficult book as a youth to be a liar. Which is probably true. I know that in my case, I tried to read it around age twelve after seeing Huston's remarkable film version, but quickly gave up in frustration. Fifteen years later, I finally met

with success, however, and completed the book. Heresy of all heresies though, I *still* prefer the Huston film!

Huston no doubt acquired his interest in writing during this same period. Most bookworms do sooner or later take a stab at writing themselves. Huston, however, would not try his hand at it seriously for a number of years to come.

Equally significant about this time, however, is the oft-told tale about how the invalid Huston would sneak out of his room at night and go swimming in the icy river near the sanitarium where he was convalescing. Once in the water, he would be carried by the current to the edge of a steep waterfall, then plunge over. Night after night, he continued to sneak out and "ride the waterfall" until a suspicious sanitarium employee caught and reported

20

him. Re-diagnosed, he was pronounced healthy and thereafter rejoined the land of the living with a vengeance.

The tale is not apocryphal. Huston actually did it—not just to test his strength, which everyone was convinced was failing, but to test his courage by challenging the unfair hand fate had dealt him. "The first few times [I did it]," he has said, "it scared the living hell out of me. But I realized—instinctively, anyhow—it was exactly fear I had to get over." To this day, Huston is convinced that had he not recklessly tested himself in such a manner, he would have died in bed inside of a few months.

The significance of this incident to his later work is that it marked Huston's first brush with bad luck and that "dark fuming cloud" which he feels to be his, and all mankind's, greatest nemesis—a

Though Dashiell Hammett's The Maltese Falcon *had been filmed by Warner Bros. twice before, Huston felt the material had never been done justice. His version, a screen masterpiece, clearly rectified that situation.*

nemesis that might have finished him off for good. It would certainly have been easier for him to have accepted the doctors' diagnosis, languished in bed, and allowed his bad luck to run its inevitable course. But he didn't because, instinctively, he sensed in himself the ability to change that luck. As Rosie Sayer says in *The African Queen*, "Nature, Mr. Alnutt, is what we are put in this world to rise above." Which is precisely what Huston did. He not only challenged his own nature and its leanings toward fear, but nature itself, the waterfall; and he overcame both.

Evolving out of this incident is a portrait of the future Huston hero—and heroine, too—a portrait that would reach the screen full-blown beginning with *The Maltese Falcon* in 1941. It is a portrait that will reappear, acquiring various other nuances and shadings, in virtually all of the director's films to come. To the twelve-year-old Huston that confrontation with fate, as symbolized by the waterfall, must have seemed monumental indeed—and not at all dissimilar to Henry Fleming's brush with cowardice, or to Captain

Ahab's final moment of truth when he stared into the jaws of the white whale.

* * *

Several years after this incident, Huston left school permanently to pursue a boxing career in California. By the time he was eighteen, he had won a reported twenty-three out of twenty-five amateur fights on the circuit and earned for himself the title of Amateur Lightweight Boxing Champion of California. When he broke his nose in the ring, he left boxing for good, though he never stopped being a fan and returned to the sport in some of his earliest published short stories as well as in his vivid 1972 film *Fat City*. The film was set in Stockton, one of the small California towns Huston had actually fought in and featured a number of former Huston cronies from that period as extras.

While the younger Huston was still flailing

Many of Huston's best known (and favorite) films had their genesis when he read the original work as a sickly youth or as a young man. Moby Dick *is a prime example.*

about in search of an appropriate course to chart in life, the elder Huston's acting career had started taking off. Walter Huston had since left the vaudeville circuit for the Great White Way, achieving a notable success in the 1924 Broadway premiere of Eugene O'Neill's controversial play *Desire Under the Elms*. John rejoined his father in New York, and, exposed once more to the beguiling world of the theatre, decided to pursue an acting career himself. He also married for the first time.

Meeting with only limited success on the boards, and beset once more by wanderlust, Huston abandoned the stage in his early twenties to join the Mexican cavalry, a career move that also brought the curtain down on his marriage. For the next two years, Huston served as a lieutenant, headquartered in Mexico City. He whiled away his spare time drawing pictures of horses and even took his first stab at writing a play for puppets called *Frankie and Johnnie*. It was staged by his friend Sam Jaffe in New York in 1929 and published a year later in book form by Boni & Liveright. While in the cavalry, Huston also began writing short stories, the first of which, "Fool," was a semi-autobiographical opus set in a boxing milieu. The story came to the attention of editor H.L.

Mencken at *The American Mercury* magazine and was published in 1929.

Flushed with this success, Huston returned to the United States to pursue writing full-time, but didn't sell another story to Mencken until 1931. Titled, ''Figures of Fighting Men,'' it too had a boxing background. To help his son out during these lean years, Walter Huston, then in Hollywood, got the young man a day's work as an extra in a Paramount two-reeler called *Two Americans* (1929), an early talkie vignette in which Huston senior played the dual roles of Abraham Lincoln and Ulysses S. Grant. A year later the elder Huston played the part of the Great Emancipator once more in D.W. Griffith's talkie debut, *Abraham Lincoln* (1930).

Helen Chandler, Walter Huston and Kent Douglass (later Douglass Montgomery) in A House Divided, *the first film John Huston worked on as a writer.*

Still committed to a writing career, John Huston returned to Hollywood in 1930 to go to work for Samuel Goldwyn. But the relationship proved short-lived when Goldwyn failed to endorse any of Huston's projects. These included an adaptation of Wilkie Collins's Victorian detective novel *The Moonstone,* as well as a film version of Thomas Mann's *The Magic Mountain,* which Goldwyn vetoed as being ''too high-brow.''

Once again, Walter Huston intervened by asking his son to take a look at a script he was set to do for Carl Laemmle's growing Universal Pictures. Titled *A House Divided,* it was based on a tearjerker by Olive Edens called *Hearts and Hands,* which scenarists John B. Clymer and Dale Van Every had re-fashioned into a variation on Eugene O'Neill's *Desire Under the Elms,* one of Walter Huston's biggest Broadway successes. Once again, Huston was to play the cuckolded widower, a fisherman whose young mail-order bride (Helen Chandler) falls in love with his son (Kent

Douglass). The film was to be directed by William Wyler, here making the transition from two-reel "B" westerns to full length "A" features. The fledgling writer did a dialogue polish that pleased Wyler and went on to receive his first screen credit. He and Wyler worked together on Wyler's *Jezebel* (1938) and remained close friends until Wyler's death in 1981.

On the strength of his work on *A House Divided*, John Huston was put under contract at Universal, where he served as dialogue polisher on yet another of his father's starring vehicles, a western called *Law and Order* (1932) co-starring Harry Carey, as well as Robert Florey's *Murders in the Rue Morgue* (1932), starring Bela Lugosi. *Law and Order* was based on the novel *Saint Johnson* by W.R. Burnett, a writer much admired by Huston, who would later turn Burnett's tough crime novel, *The Asphalt Jungle*, into one of his most enduring films. An early version of the oft-told Wyatt Earp/Doc Holliday saga, *Law and Order* has since become a cult item deemed by many critics to be one of the tightest, toughest little westerns ever made. Tom Reed wrote the screenplay (with additional dialogue sup-

plied by John Huston) and it was directed by Edward L. Cahn, later known as "Fast Eddie" Cahn, whose directorial motto was, "If no one flubs his lines, it's a take!" Cahn's career would take a precipitous nosedive in the thirties and forties, but would rise again in the fifties with such potboiler items as *The Creature with the Atom Brain* (1955), *It! The Terror From Beyond Space* (1958) and a raft of exploitation programmers for American-International Pictures. He died in 1963.

Robert Florey had been set to direct *Frankenstein* (1932), Universal's big budget follow-up to its successful version of *Dracula* released the year before. It too was to star Bela Lugosi. Florey had already written the script and even shot some test footage, but then star director James Whale read the script and insisted that he film it instead. Universal gave in to its new fairhaired boy and Florey and Lugosi were out. *Murders in the Rue Morgue*, which again teamed Florey and Lugosi, was, perhaps, Universal's way of compensating them for the loss—although Lugosi didn't really want to do *Frankenstein* anyway, as the part of the monster didn't allow him any lines. In the new film, however, he was able to talk up a storm as Dr. Mirakle, a madman who seeks to mate a human woman with his pet gorilla. Florey adapted the film (loosely) from the story by Edgar Allen Poe. Tom Reed and Dale Van Every wrote the script. Huston was again brought in to supply additional dialogue, though his efforts went fairly to waste. "I tried to bring Poe's prose style into the

Huston wrote an early draft of Three Strangers *while working for Gaumont-British in London during the thirties. At one point, Alfred Hitchcock expressed interest in doing the film. It did not reach the screen, however, until 1946 with Jean Negulesco directing. Seen here: Sydney Greenstreet, Geraldine Fitzgerald and Peter Lorre.*

dialogue," he wrote in his autobiography, "but the director thought it sounded stilted, so he and his assistant rewrote scenes on the set. As a result, the picture was an odd mixture of nineteenth-century grammarian's prose and modern colloquialisms." Failing to get any other writing assignments in Hollywood, Huston then accepted an offer to write scripts for the London-based Gaumont-British film company and set sail for Europe.

* * *

Huston's employment with Gaumont-British lasted only a few months, when none of the projects he was working on managed to get a green light. They included a biography of British playwright Richard Brinsley Sheridan, a script about the founding of Oxford University, and an early draft of *Three Strangers*, which would eventually be filmed by Warner Brothers in 1946. *Three Strangers* is quintessential Huston, an ironic little fable about fortune, destiny and self-defeat in which three disparate individuals coincidentally share a winning sweepstakes ticket, but lose everything in the end due to their avarice, paranoia and other inner failings. Huston says that Alfred

Huston did a final dialogue polish on William Wyler's Jezebel, *starring Henry Fonda and Bette Davis.*

Hitchcock, whose career was then in its ascendancy at Gaumont, showed some interest in the project, but withdrew when studio head Michael Balcon rejected it.

Once again, Huston found himself down and out. To survive, he took to singing on street corners for handouts. Then he moved to Paris to study art and eke out a living painting sidewalk portraits of tourists. What money he earned, however, he soon lost trying to parlay into a fortune at the racetrack. Rather than turn to his successful father for help, however, he decided to take stock of himself. He scraped up enough money to return to the United States and set his life in some kind of order.

Through the efforts of his mother, he got a job with a New York newspaper where he worked, for a very brief time, as a reporter. Then he turned once more to the theatre, this time persevering long enough to get some lead roles, including the starring one in a WPA-funded Chicago run of *Abe Lincoln in Illinois*. He subsequently appeared as Lincoln again in another WPA-supported drama, *The Lonely Man*, written by aspiring playwright Howard Koch, with whom Huston later collaborated on the final screenplay of *Three Strangers*. After his stint with the WPA Theatre Project, Koch went to work writing radio plays for Orson Welles's celebrated *Mercury Theatre of the Air* on CBS (Welles's panic-spawning broadcast of *The War of the Worlds* was written by Koch), and shared an

Academy Award with Julius J. and Philip G. Epstein for the screenplay of the Warner Brothers classic, *Casablanca* (1943). Though blacklisted in the early fifties, Koch is today a successful producer.

Huston received a financial advance check from Warner Brothers to develop *Three Strangers* into a screenplay and returned to Hollywood for good, although *Three Strangers* would not actually see the light of a sound stage for almost another decade. Taking up with old friend William Wyler, he did a final polish on the script for Wyler's *Jezebel,* sharing his first bona fide screenplay credit with co-writers Clements Ripley and Abem Finkel. *Jezebel* also marked the beginning of Huston's long association with Warner Brothers production chief Hal B. Wallis, later to give Huston his first break as a director, and Wallis associate Henry Blanke, who proceeded to guide the young man's writing career at this point and later produced one of writer-director Huston's greatest films, *The Treasure of the Sierra Madre* (1948).

Huston's second script for Warner Brothers was *The Amazing Dr. Clitterhouse* (1938), directed by Anatole Litvak, who soon became another close Huston friend. Co-written by Huston and John Wexley, *Clitterhouse,* like *Jezebel,* also had its roots on the stage. It was based on a play by Barré Lyndon, which had starred Cedric Hardwicke as a psychiatrist who joins the underworld in order to get some inside dope on the workings of the criminal mind and eventually becomes a racketeer and murderer himself. Edward G. Robinson played the role in the film version, which also featured Claire Trevor and Humphrey Bogart. All three would later team with director Huston on *Key Largo* (1948), which he and writer Richard Brooks adapted from a play by Maxwell Anderson.

Though *The Amazing Dr. Clitterhouse* is not exclusively a Huston film, one can't help but notice how much the title character has in common with many future Huston protagonists. Clitterhouse starts out a winner (a respected doctor), but winds up a loser—a master criminal defeated by his own delusions of grandeur. Caught up in the milieu he is studying, he becomes addicted to crime, and, by surrendering to that weakness, loses all sense of morality and eventually even his life. His fatal flaw is that he lacks self-knowledge and never comes to grips with the stakes he's really playing for—his own soul.

While many Huston films can certainly be characterized as psychological dramas, few of them actually deal with the topic of psychiatry itself, a subject that seems to fascinate him. *Clitterhouse* is one of them, though it treats the subject only superficially—somewhat on the order of Huston's later *Phobia* (1980). While belonging to this same school, *Let There Be Light* (1946), his compelling World War II docu-mentary about shell-shocked soldiers, and *Freud,* his 1963 biopic about the father of psychoanalysis, remain more serious investigations, however,

Huston's next assignment for the studio was an original, *Juarez* (1939), which he co-wrote with Scotsman Aeneas MacKenzie, who provided much of the historical research, and German emigré Wolfgang Reinhardt, with whom he would again be associated on *Freud.* The plot centered around Napoleon III's (Claude Rains) attempt to annex Mexico around the time of our own Civil War by installing his politically naïve relative, Maximillian (Brian Aherne), as emperor. Bette Davis played the emperor's wife, Carlotta, while Paul Muni assumed the title role of the Mexican peasant who leads the revolt of his countrymen against the invading French. Again, self-deception and madness are at the core of the piece. Though initially just, Maximillian nevertheless comes to a bad end because he never comprehends the fact that he is but a pawn in a much larger game of power. He deceives himself into believing that the Mexican people want him as their emperor, eventually becomes a despot when the evidence shows otherwise, and is summarily executed when the *Juaristas* prevail. His wife meanwhile goes mad.

Huston considers his original draft of *Juarez* to be among the best things he's ever done. That draft, however, never reached the screen. When star Paul Muni complained to Warner Brothers executives that his character didn't have as many lines of dialogue as his nemesis, Maximillian, or even the mad Carlotta, Huston and his colleagues were instructed to transform the historically taciturn revolutionary into a garrulous spokesman for the cause of freedom everywhere. This alteration did not sink the picture alone, however. Brooklyn-born John Garfield, whose accent was clearly more New York than Mexico City, was fatally miscast as the fiery Mexican leader, Porfirio Diaz, and the film's staging can best be called heavy-handed. William Dieterle's expressionist direction is anything but subtle. For example, when Carlotta goes mad, a set of doors seems to open magically before her, and she runs headlong into the night, her long white gown flowing, until both she and it are swallowed by the oppressive darkness. Much of the rest of the film is like that as well. Though lavish and not without dramatic interest, *Juarez* is overall a rather leaden affair that simply never succeeds in springing to life.

Huston's next script for Warners, *Dr. Ehrlich's Magic Bullet* (1940), also directed by William Dieterle, turned out to be a very different matter, however. Co-authored by Huston, Heinz Herald and Norman Burnside (from a story by Burnside), it was based on the life of Dr. Paul Ehrlich (Edward G. Robinson), the nine-teenth-century German physician who shocked con-

Edward G. Robinson starts out a winner, but ends up a loser—a master criminal defeated by his own delusions of grandeur—in The Amazing Dr. Clitterhouse, *scripted by John Huston. Shown with Robinson: Claire Trevor and Humphrey Bogart, both of whom would go on to win Oscars under Huston's direction.*

temporary society and many of his own colleagues by openly discussing the disease syphilis and crusading for its cure—which he eventually found in a drug called salvarsan, the ''magic bullet'' of the title. A prestigious production in every way, the film was a critical and box office success that earned Huston his first Academy Award nomination, though he and his co-writers lost to Preston Sturges for *The Great McGinty* (1940).

One sees in the real-life character of Ehrlich a foreshadowing of such future real-life Huston protagonists as Toulouse-Lautrec, who also ran counter to society's morés by openly portraying Parisian street and cabaret life in his paintings, as well as Sigmund Freud (Montgomery Clift), whose contro-

versial advancement of the theory of child sexuality and the Oedipus complex so outraged his contemporaries that his career was almost finished. Freud's bitter denunciation by a contemptuous colleague, the influential Dr. Theodore Meynert (Eric Portman), is even reflected in Ehrlich's own on-going struggles with his equally scornful adversary, the influential Dr. Emil von Behring (Otto Kruger). It is worth noting that, professionally at least, all three of these courageous Huston protagonists not only prevailed but ultimately achieved the status of giants— thus giving lie to the critical consensus that Huston's work is inherently and completely pessimistic overall.

Huston followed up the success of *Dr. Ehrlich's Magic Bullet* with another prestigious Warner Brothers biopic, *Sergeant York* (1941), directed by Howard Hawks. Sharing screenplay credit with Harry Chandlee, Abem Finkel and Howard Koch, he earned his second Oscar nomination for best original screenplay. Ironically, he would be competing with

27

Huston considers his original draft of Juarez *to be the best script he's ever written. It never reached the screen, however, due to incessant tampering from star Paul Muni. Here Bette Davis as Empress Carlotta and Brian Aherne as Emperor Maximillian arrive in Mexico.*

himself in another category (best screenplay adaptation) for *The Maltese Falcon,* his directorial debut released that same year. *Sergeant York* lost to Herman Manckiewicz and Orson Welles for *Citizen Kane,* while *Falcon* lost to Sidney Buchman and Seton I. Miller for their adaptation of *Here Comes Mr. Jordan.*

In addition to marking Huston's debut as a writer-director, 1941 also saw the release of *High Sierra,* one of Huston's best and most personal non-directed efforts. Beautifully filmed by director Raoul Walsh, it was based on a novel by W.R. Burnett, a writer Huston had championed ever since working on the adaptation of Burnett's *Saint Johnson* for his father's 1932 western, *Law and Order. High Sierra* allowed him to actually work with Burnett, who took screenplay credit with him. Thematically, the two share a number of affinities—as would become even more obvious nine years later when Huston adapted and directed yet another Burnett novel, *The Asphalt Jungle.* The protagonist of *High Sierra,* ex-con ''Mad Dog'' Roy Earle (Humphrey Bogart), is, like thief Dix Handley (Sterling Hayden) in *Asphalt,* a premiere Huston self-deceiver who comes to a bad end chiefly through his own undoing. Earle is a bank robber who intends to use the cash from his latest heist to settle down with a handicapped young girl (Joan Leslie) he's become fixated on. By paying for the operation to repair her club foot, he believes she'll come to love him, too— even though the worlds they belong to, not to mention their ages, are dramatically opposed and obviously incompatible. When his bogus dream goes sour, he goes to hell fast. Blowing a last chance for happiness with the girl (Ida Lupino) who genuinely loves him, he winds up hiding in the mountains where he is shot down by police. Dix Handley's end is similar in that he deceives himself into believing that he can erase his past and settle down to a normal life by returning to his childhood roots after one big score—even though that score has gone irrevocably sour. Fatally wounded by one of his own cronies (there is no honor among these thieves), he makes it to his boyhood farm just in time to die. Earle and Handley carry a sense of doom about them like a backpack.

High Sierra and its Huston/Burnett companion piece, *The Asphalt Jungle,* remain two of Huston's most influential films if for no other reason than that their plots have either been stolen or remade several times since. Raoul Walsh himself reworked *Sierra* into a western, *Colorado Territory* (1949), starring Joel McCrea in the Bogart role, while Stuart Heisler returned the tale to its gangster milieu in *I Died a Thousand Times* (1955), starring Jack Palance. *The Asphalt Jungle*'s "big-caper-gone-wrong" motif has been borrowed from by directors as disparate as Stanley Kubrick (*The Killing,* 1956) and Jules Dassin (*Rififi,* 1954). The film has also been remade three times—as a western, *The Badlanders* (1958), directed by Delmar Daves (in which Anthony Caruso plays almost the same part that he did in *The Asphalt Jungle*); as a bit of foreign intrigue, Wolf Rilla's *Cairo* (1962); and as a blaxploitation thriller, *Cool Breeze* (1977), directed by Barry Pollack.

High Sierra also spelled the beginning of Huston's long and fruitful association with Humphrey Bogart. Bogart had played the supporting role of a gangster in the Huston-scripted *The Amazing Dr. Clitterhouse.* He got the role of "Mad Dog" Earle, his first important lead, when (to Huston's delight) Paul Muni declined the part, and then George Raft, who turned *High Sierra* down because he was sick of dying at the end of pictures. While *High Sierra* didn't make Bogart a star, his next film with Huston, *The Maltese Falcon,* did. Ironically, Bogart got that film by default too. Warner executives wanted George Raft to play Sam Spade, but Raft let the part slip to Bogart because he feared putting his career in the hands of an inexperienced, first-time director. With Huston's guidance, Bogart turned the role into a personal triumph and quickly eclipsed Raft as one of Warner Brothers' shining stars.

On the strength of Huston's recent no-strike-outs batting record as a screenwriter, his agent, Paul Kohner, negotiated a clause in their new Warner Brothers contract insisting that Huston be allowed to direct his next optioned screenplay. Huston had not forgotten the losing battle that had been waged with recalcitrant star Paul Muni over *Juarez,* and while he had little cause for complaint with the screen versions of his next three scripts, he felt that directing would give him greater creative control, as well as clout in the industry.

All the major studios had an unspoken policy of dusting off older properties to which they still owned the rights and reworking or remaking them into new films. Warner Brothers had made Dashiell Hammett's classic detective novel *The Maltese Falcon* twice before, though with little financial or critical success either time. It appeared first in 1931 under its original title, directed by Roy Del Ruth, then again as *Satan Met a Lady* (1936), starring Bette Davis. William Dieterle directed the latter version, which retained little of Hammett's novel; Huston mentor Henry Blanke produced. Huston felt the novel had not yet been faithfully translated to the screen—the Del Ruth version came close in terms of plot, but Ricardo Cortez's suave Spade lacked the moral uncertainty of Hammett's prototypical *noir* hero; Brigid (Bebe Daniels) and Gutman (Dudley Diggs) on the other hand were just plain bland. With the help of his secretary, Huston broke the book down into a scene-by-scene treatment that contained much of the novel's dialogue verbatim. Studio head Jack Warner got hold of the treatment, misinterpreted it as a final screenplay, enthusiastically endorsed it, and gave Huston the green light. The rest, as they say, is history.

Huston was well into his career as a writer-director, and only recently out of the army, when his long-evolving script for *Three Strangers* was finally filmed as a vehicle for Sydney Greenstreet and Peter Lorre, who had become a sort of unofficial team as a result of their memorable on-screen sparring in *The Maltese Falcon.* Jean Negulesco directed. That same year (1946), Huston put his boxing background to good use scripting *The Killers* with Anthony Veiller, a writer he'd met during the war. Veiller maintains that most of the script for this classic *film noir* was Huston's though he took no screen credit (Huston was under contract to Warner Brothers and *The Killers* was a Universal picture). Veiller, who received sole screen credit, went on to receive an Academy Award nomination that year for Best Original Screenplay—a misnomer considering the fact that *The Killers* was actually an enlargement of an Ernest Hemingway short story. Huston also worked with Veiller and Orson Welles on *The Stranger* (1946), the story of an escaped Nazi War criminal who hides out in a small Connecticut town. Producer S.P. Eagle

(Sam Spiegel), who would make *We Were Strangers* (1949) and *The African Queen* (1952) with Huston, had wanted Huston to direct the film, but, to secure Orson Welles's services as star, bowed to pressure from the actor that he be allowed to direct instead. This came as no crushing blow to Huston, however, as he was soon into preparing *The Treasure of the Sierra Madre.* He and Welles remained good friends, staunch admirers of each other's work, and occasional collaborators either as director or as actor until Welles's untimely death in 1985.

A HOUSE DIVIDED (1932)

A Universal Picture; Director: William Wyler; *Screenplay:* John B. Clymer and Dale Van Every with additional dialogue by John Huston; based on the novel *Hearts and Hands* by Olive Edens; *Running time:* 68 minutes; *Videocassette Source:* Not Available; *Cast: Seth Law* (Walter Huston), *Matt Law* (Kent Douglass), *Ruth Evans* (Helen Chandler), *Bess* (Vivian Oakland), *Woman* (Marjorie Main), *Minister* (Charles Middleton).

Gary Cooper as Sergeant York. *Huston was one of a team of writers on this film, directed by Howard Hawks.*

LAW AND ORDER (1932)

A Universal Picture; Director: Edward L. Cahn; *Screenplay:* Tom Reed, adaptation and dialogue by John Huston; based on the novel *Saint Johnson* by W.R. Burnett; *Running time:* 80 minutes; *Videocasette Source:* Not Available; *Cast: Frame Johnson* (Walter Huston), *Ed Brandt* (Harry Carey), *Deadwood* (Raymond Hatton), *Johnny Kinsman* (Andy Devine), *Lanky Smith* (Walter Brennan); *Poe Northrup* (Ralph Ince), *Walt Northrup* (Harry Woods), *Kurt Northrup* (Richard Alexander).

MURDERS IN THE RUE MORGUE (1932)

A Universal Picture: Director: Robert Florey; *Screenplay:* Tom Reed and Dale Van Every, adaptation by Robert Florey, additional dialogue by John Huston; based on the short story by Edgar Allan Poe; *Running time:* 62 minutes; *Videocassette Source:* Not Available; *Cast: Dr. Mirakle* (Bela Lugosi), *Camille L'Espanaye* (Sidney Fox), *Pierre Dupin* (Leon Waycoff), *Prefect of Police* (Brandon Hurst), *Janos the Black One* (Noble Johnson), *Monette* (Arlene Francis).

JEZEBEL (1938)

A Warner Bros. Picture; Producer: Henry Blanke; *Director:* William Wyler; *Screenplay:* Clements Ripley, Abem Finkel and John Huston; based on the play *Jezebel* by Owen Davis; *Running time:* 103 minutes; *Videocassette Source:* CBS/Fox Home Video; *Cast: Julie Morrison* (Bette Davis), *Preston Dillard* (Henry Fonda), *Buck Cantrell* (George Brent), *Amy Bradford Dillard* (Margaret Lindsay), *Aunt Belle Massey* (Fay Bainter), *Dr. Livingstone* (Donald Crisp).

THE AMAZING DR. CLITTERHOUSE (1938)

A Warner Bros. Picture; Producer: Anatole Litvak; *Director:* Anatole Litvak; *Screenplay:* John Huston and John Wexley; based on the play *The Amazing Dr. Clitterhouse* by Barré Lyndon; *Running time:* 87 minutes; *Videocassette Source:* Not Available; *Cast: Dr. Clitterhouse* (Edward G. Robinson), *Jo Keller* (Claire Trevor), *Rocks Valentine* (Humphrey Bogart), *Okay* (Allen Jenkins), *Inspector Lane* (Donald Crisp).

JUAREZ (1939)

A Warner Bros. Picture; Producer: Hal B. Wallis; *Director:* William Dieterle; *Screenplay:* John Huston, Aeneas MacKenzie, Wolfgang Reinhardt; based on *Maximillian and Carlotta* by Franz Werfel and *The Phantom Crown* by Bertita Harding; *Running time:* 132 minutes; *Videocassette Source:* Key Video; *Cast: Benito Juarez* (Paul Muni), *Empress Carlotta* (Bette Davis), *Emperor Maximillian von Hapsburg* (Brian Aherne), *Napoleon III* (Claude Rains), *Porfirio Diaz* (John Garfield), *Marechale Bazaine* (Donald Crisp), *Empress Eugenie* (Gale Sondergaard), *Colonel Miguel Lopez* (Gilbert Roland).

DR. ERHLICH'S MAGIC BULLET (1940)

A Warner Bros. Picture; Producer: Hal B. Wallis; *Director:* William Dieterle; *Screenplay:* John Huston, Heinz Herald and Norman Burnside; *Running time:* 103 minutes; *Videocassette Source:* Not Available; *Cast: Dr. Paul Ehrlich* (Edward G. Robinson), *Mrs. Ehrlich* (Ruth Gordon), *Dr. Emil von Behring* (Otto Kruger), *Minister Althoff* (Donald Crisp), *Franziska Speyer* (Maria Ouspenskaya), *Professor Hartmann* (Montagu Love), *Dr. Hans Wolfert* (Sig Rumann), *Mittelmeyer* (Donald Meek), *Dr. Robert Koch* (Albert Basserman), *Dr. Brockdorf* (Louis Calhern).

HIGH SIERRA (1941)

Warner Bros. Picture; Producer: Hal B. Wallis; *Director:* Raoul Walsh; *Screenplay:* John Huston and W.R. Burnett; based on the novel *High Sierra* by W.R. Burnett; *Running time:* 100 minutes; *Videocassette Source:* CBS/Fox Home Video; *Cast: Roy Earle* (Humphrey Bogart), *Marie* (Ida Lupino), *Velma* (Joan Leslie), *Babe* (Alan Curtis), *Red* (Arthur Kennedy), *Doc Banton* (Henry Hull), *Louis Mendoza* (Cornel Wilde).

SERGEANT YORK (1941)

A Warner Bros. Picture; Producer: Hal B. Wallis; *Director:* Howard Hawks; *Screenplay:* Harry Chandlee, Abem Finkel, John Huston and Howard Koch, based on a variety of sources; *Running time:* 134 minutes; *Videocassette Source:* CBS/Fox Home Video; *Cast: Alvin York* (Gary Cooper), *Pastor Pile* (Walter Brennan), *Gracie Williams* (Joan Leslie), *Pusher Ross* (George Tobias), *Ma York* (Margaret Wycherly), *George York* (Dickie Moore), *Rosie York* (June Lockhart), *Clem* (Howard Da Silva).

THE KILLERS (1946)

A Universal Picture; Producer: Mark Hellinger; *Director:* Robert Siodmak; *Screenplay:* Anthony Veiller and John Huston (uncredited); based on a short story by Ernest Hemingway; *Running time:* 105 minutes; *Videocassette Source:* Not Available; *Cast: Swede Lunn* (Burt Lancaster), *James Reardon* (Edmund O'Brien), *Kitty Collins* (Ava Gardner), *Jim Colfax* (Albert Dekker), *Sam Lubinsky* (Sam Levene), *The Killers* (Charles McGraw and William Conrad).

Huston's contibution to the script of The Killers *with Ava Gardner and Burt Lancaster was substantial, but he took no screen credit.*

Ida Lupino and Humphrey Bogart in High Sierra, *one of Huston's best and most personal non-directed scripts.*

THE STRANGER (1946)

An RKO Picture; Producer: S.P. Eagle (Sam Spiegel); *Director:* Orson Welles; *Screenplay:* Anthony Veiller, John Huston and Orson Welles (Huston and Welles went uncredited); based on a story by Victor Trivas and Decla Dunning; *Running time:* 95 minutes; *Videocassette Source:* Various public domain sources; *Cast: Franz Kindler* (Orson Welles), *Inspector Wilson* (Edward G. Robinson), *Mary Longstreet* (Loretta Young), *Judge Longstreet* (Philip Merivale), *Noah Longstreet* (Richard Long).

THREE STRANGERS (1946)

A Warner Bros. Picture; Producer: Wolfgang Reinhardt; *Director:* Jean Negulesco; *Screenplay:* John Huston and Howard Koch; based on a story by John Huston; *Running time:* 92 minutes; *Videocassette Source:* Not Available; *Cast: Crystal* (Geraldine Fitzgerald), *Arbutney* (Sydney Greenstreet), *Johnny West* (Peter Lorre), *Gabby* (Peter Whitney), *Prosecutor* (Arthur Shields), *Shackleford* (Alan Napier).

THE FILMS OF
JOHN HUSTON

*Spade (Humphrey Bogart) finds himself irresistibly—and
perhaps fatally—drawn to the deceptively vulnerable Brigid (Mary Astor).*

The Maltese Falcon (1941)

A WARNER BROTHERS PRODUCTION
B&W/100 minutes

CREDITS:

Director: John Huston; *Producer:* Hal B. Wallis; *Screenplay:* John Huston, based on the novel *The Maltese Falcon* by Dashiell Hammett; *Cinematographer:* Arthur Edeson; *Editor:* Thomas Richards; *Music:* Adolph Deutsch; *Art Director:* Robert Haas; *Videocassette source:* CBS/Fox Home Video.

CAST:

Sam Spade: Humphrey Bogart, *Brigid O'Shaughnessy:* Mary Astor; *Joel Cairo:* Peter Lorre; *Kaspar Gutman:* Sydney Greenstreet; *Effie Perine:* Lee Patrick; *Iva Archer:* Gladys George; *Lt. Dundy:* Barton MacLane; *Detective Polhaus:* Ward Bond; *Miles Archer:* Jerome Cowan; *Wilmer:* Elisha Cook, Jr.; *Frank Richman:* Murray Alper; *Bryan:* John Hamilton; *Luke:* James Burke; *Captain Jacobi:* Walter Huston (uncredited).

* * *

Detective Polhaus (Ward Bond) and Spade (Humphrey Bogart) discuss the weapon used to kill Spade's partner, Miles Archer.

Contemporary Reviews

"Mr. Huston might have been known at one time as the son of the celebrated actor, Walter Huston. He needs no parental identification after this job. He has followed the Hammett original with extraordinary faithfulness....The film moves through its various sequences with an electric tension. It is hard to say whether Huston the adapter or Huston the fledgling director is most responsible for this triumph. In any case, it is a knockout job of cinematic melodrama."—*The New York Herald Tribune*

First-time director John Huston shakes hands with father Walter on the set of The Maltese Falcon *as star Humphrey Bogart and cinematographer Arthur Edeson look on. The elder Huston made an uncredited cameo appearance in his son's debut film "for luck."*

"The Warners have been strangely bashful about their new mystery film, *The Maltese Falcon,* and about the young man, John Huston, whose first directorial job it is. Maybe they thought it best to bring both along under wraps, seeing as how the picture is a remake of an old Dashiell Hammett yarn done ten years ago, and Mr. Huston is a fledgling whose previous efforts have been devoted to writing scripts. And maybe—which is somehow more likely—they wanted to give everyone a nice surprise. For *The Maltese Falcon*...only turns out to be the best mystery thriller of the year, and young Huston gives promise of becoming one of the smartest directors in the field."—*The New York Times*

"*The Maltese Falcon* is frighteningly good evidence that the British (Alfred Hitchcock, Carol Reed, et al.) have no monopoly on the technique of making mystery films. A remake of Dashiell Hammett's hard-boiled

Spade (Humphrey Bogart) runs interference between Cairo (Peter Lorre) and Brigid (Mary Astor).

mystery, it is rich raw beef right off the U.S. range.''—*Time* magazine

* * *

The Maltese Falcon is a masterpiece, the *Citizen Kane* of detective movies, and the most probing character study in that genre the cinema has given us until *Chinatown* (1974), which, not coincidentally, bears a number of striking similarities to *Falcon* and even co-stars Huston himself.

The focus of *The Maltese Falcon* is on Sam Spade,

the prototypical Huston adventurer, a man whose greatest fear is boredom but whose real nemesis is himself. In Huston's *The Kremlin Letter* (1970), duplicitous spy Richard Boone describes his superconfident new assistant, Rone (Patrick O'Neal), this way: ''They say that heroes can't imagine their own deaths, and that's why they're heroes. But you go them one better. You imagine you're immune to violence.'' This is an equally apt description of Spade himself, who charges ahead with an almost reckless abandon, convinced that he's immune to the moral and physical dangers lurking in the shadows to claim him. But he isn't. In fact, he's drawn to them. Like Rone, whom Navy psychologists assess as having a death wish, spade finds danger irresistable.

When his partner, Miles Archer, is killed, we

Spade (Humphrey Bogart) and the bogus falcon, the "stuff that dreams are made of."

learn that Spade was having an affair with Archer's high-strung wife, Iva—surely a potentially explosive situation to create in a two-man office. When Spade finally gets hold of the prized falcon, an invaluable relic dating back to the 1500s, he—like Brigid, Gutman and Cairo—gets so caught up with the idea of possessing it that he absently grips his secretary's arm until she is forced to cry out, ''You're hurting me, Sam.'' And finally there is Brigid herself, Spade's very own Lilith—or, perhaps even more aptly, his Moby Dick. Even though he sees through her mask of innocence and vulnerability and pegs her for the liar she is (''Now you *are* dangerous,'' he says to her almost admiringly), he still allows himself to fall for her. Or, more precisely, it is because she is so dangerous that he just can't seem to help himself. Spade is no saint to begin with, but his infatuation with the amoral Brigid and pursuit of the black bird mark a turning point. His self-made pit finally yawns before him, and he is all too willing to jump in once and for all, but draws back just in time. The falcon and Brigid are both fake prizes and he turns them over to the police. Before they arrive, Brigid pleads with him to let her go, but even though he still loves her, he refuses. ''I won't because all of me wants to—regardless of the consequences,'' he confesses to her emotionally. And self-knowingly. At last.

Though the film's theme may be heady, Huston's treatment of it is not. His direction of *The Maltese Falcon* is fast-paced and remarkably assured for a beginner. As with *Citizen Kane*, one would never guess that this was the work of a newcomer. Strictly speaking, of course, it wasn't. Huston had directed live theatre before and had acted in both media. But it was his substantial gifts as a screenwriter that served him best here. *The Maltese Falcon* is extraordinarily faithful to Hammett's book, though, contrary to myth, not a literal transcription of it. Jack Warner may have bought Huston's quickie scene-by-scene breakdown, but that's not what Huston shot. He cut several characters and scenes from the book, eliminated Spade's affair with his secretary, Effie, as overkill, and fine-honed Hammett's dialogue until it fairly crackled from the mouths of Bogart, Astor, Greenstreet, and Lorre. And it was Huston, not Hammett, who gave Spade his famous exit line about the falcon. ''It's the stuff that dreams are made of,'' he tells detective Polhaus. Meaning that the falcon is not only an elusive prize, but an illusory one as well. Though the line doesn't recur in a Huston film, its thematic importance does, for ''the stuff that dreams are made of'' applies equally to the gold in *Sierra Madre*, the riches of Kafiristan in *The Man Who Would Be King*, the jewels in *The Asphalt Jungle,* and so on throughout practically Huston's entire filmography. In *The Maltese Falcon*, Huston, who admits a preference for drawing on sources other than himself for his primary material, found a novel whose themes meshed perfectly with his own interests.

Huston was also well served by a perfect cast. Humphrey Bogart etched a memorable portrait as Sam Spade, the definitive Huston hero, a flawed but brave adventurer in an amoral universe who ultimately refuses to let his flaws and self-deceptions get the best of him. Under Huston's direction, Bogart finally, and deservedly, achieved major star status. Mary Astor, who became a star opposite John Barrymore in the 1927 *Don Juan* while still in her teens, is simply ideal as the deceptively vulnerable Brigid, whose breathless earnestness masks the fact that she is a congenital liar who just can't seem to get the lies out of her mouth fast enough. Reportedly, Huston made her run around the set between takes in order to achieve that out-of-breath quality on camera. Sydney Greenstreet, a 61-year-old veteran of Broadway, where he was often typecast as a portly British butler, made his screen debut for Huston as the massive, greedy, and slyly homosexual Kaspar Gutman, who has spent seventeen years of his life in pursuit of the elusive black bird. He and Peter Lorre, as the more overtly homosexual Joel Cairo, made such perfect foils that they were frequently re-teamed throughout the forties as a sort of Laurel and Hardy of menace.

Elisha Cook, Jr., is equally effective as Wilmer Cook, the fat man's ''gunsel,'' an underworld slang term taken directly from Hammett that refers not to a gunman, but ''kept boy.'' Though Huston has often been accused of soft-pedaling the homosexual sub-theme that runs throughout Hammett's book, the film itself gives evidence to the contrary. Lorre's perfumed Cairo is fairly open about his sexual orientation. When Brigid teases him about it, he cattily denounces her for not being able to work her feminine wiles on everyone, and she tries to kick him. Gutman frequently expresses his ''fondness'' for Wilmer, whom he refers to as being ''like a son to him,'' though a son who can be easily replaced. And at his first meeting with Spade, he continually places his hand on the detective's knee as if trying to seduce him—which, of course, he is, in more ways than one.

Though unbilled, Walter Huston also offers a dramatic cameo as the ill-fated Captain Jacobi, who delivers the falcon to Spade's office shortly before expiring from several gunshot wounds. The elder Huston, who would receive his second Best Actor nomination this same year for his wily performance as the devil in William Dieterle's *All That Money Can Buy,* took the part, he said, ''for luck.''

Though the Academy of Motion Picture Arts

and Sciences recognized Huston's achievement by awarding *The Maltese Falcon* nominations in the Best Picture, Best Supporting Actor (Sydney Greenstreet), and Best Original Screenplay categories, the film failed to pick up a single Oscar. It remains, however, a classic, a great detective yarn, and the archetype for virtually all Huston films that followed.

Gunsel Wilmer Cook (Elisha Cook, Jr.) and Cairo (Peter Lorre) get their momentary revenge on Spade (Humphrey Bogart)—with the help of the fatman, Kaspar Gutman (Sydney Greenstreet).

In This Our Life (1942)

A WARNER BROTHERS PRODUCTION
B&W/97 minutes

CREDITS:

Director: John Huston; *Producer:* Hal B. Wallis; *Screenplay:* Howard Koch and John Huston (uncredited), based on the novel *In This Our Life* by Ellen Glasgow; *Cinematographer:* Ernest Haller; *Editor:* William Holmes; *Music:* Max Steiner; *Art Director:* Robert Haas; *Videocassette Source:* Not Available.

Bette Davis as Stanley Timberlake, who'd rather do anything *than keep still. And does.*

CAST:

Stanley Timberlake: Bette Davis; *Roy Timberlake:* Olivia de Havilland; *Craig Fleming:* George Brent; *Peter Kingsmill:* Dennis Morgan; *William Fitzroy:* Charles Coburn; *Asa Timberlake:* Frank Craven; *Lavinia Timberlake:* Billie Burke; *Minerva Clay:* Hattie McDaniel; *Betty Wilmouth:* Lee Patrick; *Passy Clay:* Ernest Anderson; *Bartender:* Walter Huston (uncredited).

* * *

Contemporary Reviews

"...neither a pleasant nor edifying film. It is, again, one of those Snow White and Rose Red sister yarns, in which the evil and mischievous sister, played by Miss Davis, of course, deserts her loving fiancé and runs off with her good sister's spouse.... She finally reaches rock bottom when she tries to escape a hit-run killing charge by brazenly alleging that the deed was done by a Negro boy. This last, as a matter of

fact, is the one exceptional component of the film—this brief but frank allusion to racial discrimination. And it is presented in a realistic manner, uncommon to Hollywood, by the definition of the Negro as an educated and comprehending character. Otherwise the story is pretty much of a downhill run, with Miss Davis going from bad to worse in her selfish pursuit of 'happiness' and the good people growing better and more beatified in marked contrast.''—*The New York Times*

''*In This Our Life* is billed as a cineversion of Ellen Glasgow's novel. Picture and book have only one thing in common: the title. The film's story is much more like *The Little Foxes*....The hard-working, competent cast is too high-powered for the picture.''—*Time* magazine

* * *

Stanley (Bette Davis) tauntingly provokes the weak-willed Peter (Dennis Morgan), ex-husband of her sister Roy, to anger.

The unexpected financial and critical success of *The Maltese Falcon* having established him as Warner Brothers' new boy wonder, Huston was given a top budget and top stars, including the studio's highest-paid actress, Bette Davis, to make his next film, *In This Our Life*. Based on a novel by Ellen Glasgow that had recently won the Pulitzer Prize, the project was viewed by the studio as its answer to *The Little Foxes*, Lillian Hellman's award-winning stage play about a self-destructive southern family which RKO and William Wyler had turned into one of 1941's most talked-about and successful films. Bette Davis starred in that film too—as megabitch Regina Giddens, a role originated on Broadway by Tallulah Bankhead. Howard Koch quickly wrote the screenplay for *In This Our Life* with an uncredited assist from Huston, who also put his sketching talents to work designing the film's sets.

Like *The Little Foxes*, *In This Our LIfe* is set in the modern-day south and deals with a well-to-do family that, putting it mildly, just doesn't get along. Davis plays Stanley, the bitchy older sister who steals the weak-willed husband (Dennis Morgan) of her placid younger sister, Roy (Olivia de Havilland), then drives

him to suicide. As if all this weren't enough, she maliciously attempts to lure back an old beau (George Brent), who has since fallen for Roy on the rebound. Rejected by him, she angrily takes off in her car and accidentally runs down a child, blaming the accident later on a local black man (Ernest Patterson), whom she accuses of having stolen her car on the night in question. The man subsequently stands trial but is found innocent when a bartender (Walter Huston) steps forward to testify that he saw Stanley driving her car that night from the roadhouse where he works. Unmasked, Stanley seeks solace and protection from her once lecherous though now dying uncle (Charles Coburn), but meets with no success. Attempting to flee from the police, she finally gets her just reward when she is killed in her car in a fiery crash.

As Stanley, Bette Davis fully indulges her penchant for chewing up the scenery, and Huston, perhaps because he was still a beginner and she, like

Stanley's old beau (George Brent) and sister Roy (Olivia De Havilland), both on the rebound, strike up a cigarette . . . and a relationship, much to Stanley's annoyance.

Paul Muni, was a star very much used to getting her own way, just lets her go. Which she does—right over the top. Her icy portrayals of quite similar characters in William Wyler's *Jezebel* (1938), *The Letter* (1940), and *The Little Foxes* (1941) remain models of subtlety by comparison.

She is not alone in her intense dramaturgy, however. The film itself, while perhaps not melodrama at its worst, is certainly melodrama at its most bombastic and contrived. Huston himself does not look back on the picture very fondly, finding only a few things to recommend about it—the most important of which was that it allowed him to present a dignified rather than stereotyped portrait of black Americans. This was rare in Hollywood films of the time and gives evidence of Huston's early alliance with such liberal causes as winning greater justice and respect for minorities, a topic that would emerge even more strongly in *Key Largo (1948)* and *The Unforgiven* (1960). With only one successful film behind him at the time, he also admits to having found the studio's offer of virtual carte blanche in terms of stars and budget to have been a heady experience.

Lecherous Uncle William (Charles Coburn) lavishes affection on his favorite niece, Stanley (Bette Davis).

The conniving Stanley (Bette Davis) is confronted by her suspicious old beau (George Brent) about the hit-and-run accident that has landed an innocent black man (Ernest Patterson) in jail.

All this being said, *In This Our Life* is not quite the anomaly in Huston's filmography that it appears. Stanley is clearly another variation of the Huston protagonist, though, in this case, one who self-destructs. Like Sam Spade before her, she is terrified of boredom. At one point in the film, she even admits, "I'd rather do *anything* than keep still." So, like Spade, she charges ahead recklessly, visits all sorts of bad luck upon herself, and then wonders how it happened. Stanley may know herself, but she doesn't understand herself. Her elusive goal is "happiness," which, to her, means total indulgence of her every whim, no matter how destructive those whims may be to others or to herself. Like Spade, her pit is self-made and it yawns before her. Unlike him, however, she finally jumps in feet first. In this respect, she resembles Brigid O'Shaughnessy, and Elizabeth Taylor's equally oblivious southern belle, Leonora Penderton, in Huston's *Reflections in a Golden Eye* (1967).

On the whole though, *In This Our Life* is not an example of Huston's best work. Nor was it the answer to *The Little Foxes* Warners had hoped for. Though a moderate box office success, it flopped badly with the critics and failed to pick up a single Oscar nomination. This time around, Walter Huston's unbilled cameo failed to bring his son "luck." Nor did those of most of the *Falcon* cast, who appear, along with the elder Huston, in the film's roadhouse scene.

Across the Pacific (1942)

A WARNER BROTHERS PRODUCTION
B&W/97 minutes

CREDITS:

Director: John Huston and Vincent Sherman (uncredited); *Producers:* Jerry Wald and Jack Saper; *Screenplay:* Richard Macaulay, based on the *Saturday Evening Post* serial "Aloha Means Goodbye" by Robert Carson; *Cinematographer:* Arthur Edeson; *Editor:* Frank Magee; *Music:* Adolph Deutsch; *Art Directors:* Robert Haas and Hugh Reticker; *Videocassette Source:* Not Available.

CAST:

Rick Leland: Humphrey Bogart; *Alberta Marlow:* Mary Astor; *Dr. Lorenz:* Sydney Greenstreet; *A.V. Smith:* Charles Halton; *Joe Totsuiko:* Victor Sen Yung; *Sugi:* Roland Got; *Sam Wing:* Lee Tung Foo.

* * *

Contemporary Reviews

"This time it is certain: Alfred Hitchcock, Carol Reed and all other directors who have hit the top flight with melodramas will have to make space for John Huston. For young Huston, who cracked out a scorching thriller in *The Maltese Falcon*, has done it again in *Across the Pacific*. Using the same trio of actors that spangled his previous film—Humphrey Bogart, Mary Astor, and Sydney Greenstreet—he has made a spy picture this time which tingles with fearful uncertainties and glints with the sheen of blue steel. Something new in the shock line has been added. Mr. Huston has definitely arrived.... The story literally hangs on characterization. And in a thriller, that's quite a trick.... Mr. Huston has given the Warners a delightfully fear-jerking picture. It's like having a knife at your ribs for an hour and a half."—*The New York Times*

* * *

After appearing in the background of Huston's last film just for luck, Humphrey Bogart, Mary Astor and Sydney Greenstreet returned once more to the foreground in *Across the Pacific,* a slight but entertaining melodrama that Warner Brothers and Huston hoped would prove as successful with audiences as *The Maltese Falcon.* It didn't, but was fairly popular and well received nonetheless.

Bogart plays Rick (a year later, he would play another Rick in what would become his most popular film, *Casablanca*), a cashiered American Army officer who tries to enlist in the Canadian armed forces only to be turned down because of his discredited reputation. Sailing back to New York aboard a Japanese freighter, he meets a vacationing shop girl, Alberta Marlow, with whom he falls in love, and a duplicitous Japanese sympathizer named Dr. Lorenz, whose life he later saves from an assassin's bullet.

Rick leaves New York for Panama, where he was once stationed, and Lorenz, a spy, offers the embittered ex-officer money for information about American military maneuvers in the Canal Zone, which he intends to hand over to his Japanese allies so that they can blow up the Panama Canal. Rick, who is actually a U.S. undercover agent on Lorenz's trail, agrees, and, once in Panama, is provided with the necessary details by his contact, whom Lorenz's henchmen kill shortly thereafter. Lorenz it seems has known of Rick's deception all along and has used

*Humphrey Bogart as undercover agent Rick Leland and
Mary Astor as possible spy Alberta Marlow in* Across the Pacific.

Rick (Humphrey Bogart), Alberta (Mary Astor) and their
mutual adversary, Dr. Lobrenz (Sydney Greenstreet), dine
with the captain and crew of the Japanese freighter Genoa
Maru, which is bound for New York, then Panama.

Rick's disarming of a Filipino assassin (Rudy Robles) later
puts him in Dr. Lorenz's good graces.

The trio arrives in Panama.

him to get what he needed. Held captive at Lorenz's base of operations—a plantation owned by Alberta's unwillingly involved father (Monte Blue)—Rick manages to break free and foil the plot by shooting the enemy plane down as it takes off. The defeated Lorenz decides to commit hara-kiri, but at the last moment discovers that his appreciation of Japanese culture and tradition doesn't extend that far and hands himself over to Rick instead.

Across the Pacific contains all the requisite Huston elements, but, unlike *The Maltese Falcon,* which it is clearly modelled after, these elements are not nearly so well drawn. Rick's interior motives for enduring disgrace to take on his dangerous secret mission are never

fully explored. At one point, his friend, Sam Wing, says of him, "All the time you like trouble." This assessment of Rick's character allies him to Sam Spade (and most other Huston protagonists), but it's as far as the director goes. Likewise, Lorenz revealingly speaks of boredom as "a condition of mine," but we never learn to what degree his treachery is motivated by that condition. If Huston hadn't so openly invited comparison with *The Maltese Falcon,* these criticisms would be minor—on its own, *Across the Pacific* is a fast-paced, witty and enjoyable romp—but over and over again Huston all but demands us to think of *The Maltese Falcon* while watching it, and by comparison the more lightweight *Pacific* inevitably suffers. The leads are the same. The characters they play are the same—though Astor's mysterious Alberta turns out to be a heroine rather

Rick's (Humphrey Bogart) suspicions of Alberta (Mary Astor) mount when she receives a mysterious message. The desk clerk is Keye Luke, better known to filmgoers as Charlie Chan's "number one son."

than a villainess. Even some of the dialogue is the same. Rick, for example, calls Alberta "Angel" and "Precious" just as Spade does Brigid. At another point, he even baits her with, "You're good, You're very, very good," when he feels he's being conned. Spade says the exact same thing to Brigid for the exact same reasons.

Across the Pacific is most memorable, perhaps, for a Huston legend that it has since given rise to, a legend perpetuated by Huston biographers William F. Nolan and Stuart Kaminsky, as well as by Huston himself, who substantiates it in his own autobiography. According to this legend, Huston, who prefers to shoot his films in continuity, received his orders to report for active duty just as he was reaching the film's grand

finale. Impishly, he rewrote the ending and shot it so that Rick was tied up and held captive by scores of Japanese. He then left the job of getting Rick out of this scrape to director Vincent Sherman—who purportedly solved the problem by having one of Rick's captors go improbably berserk and start shooting up the place, thus allowing Rick to struggle free of his bonds and escape during the fracas with the parting line, "I'm not easily trapped, you know!"

It's an amusing anecdote, but while Vincent Sherman did take over for Huston exactly as the legend says, the film itself contains no such scene. In the actual film, Rick is indeed captured, along with Alberta and her father, but he is not tied up and is guarded only by Joe Totsuiko, the Japanese "gunsel" (in yet another of the film's many *Falcon* references). Alberta tries to overcome Joe and he slaps her. This angers her father who gets up to intervene. When Joe turns to shoot him, Rick sees his chance, wrestles Joe to the floor, knocking him out, then flees to bring down the plane.

51

THE WORLD WAR II DOCUMENTARIES
Report from the Aleutians (1943)
San Pietro (1945)

FOR THE *WHY WE FIGHT* SERIES
Color/47 minutes

CREDITS:

Director: Captain John Huston; *Producer:* U.S. Signal Corps; *Screenplay:* Captain John Huston; *Cinematographers:* Lieutenants Ray Scott and Jules Buck; *Editor:* Colonel Frank Capra; *Music:* Dimitri Tiomkin; *Narrator:* Walter Huston; *Videocassette Source:* International Historic Films.

A U.S. ARMY PICTORIAL SERVICE PRODUCTION
Color/30 minutes

CREDITS:

Director: Major John Huston; *Screenplay:* Major John Huston; *Cinematographers:* Huston, Jules Buck, et al.; *Editor:* Lieutenant Jules Buck; *Music:* Dimitri Tiomkin; *Narrator:* John Huston; *Videocassette Source:* Western Film & Video and International Historic Films.

* * *

Huston and reporter Clete Roberts discuss the director's wartime experiences and documentaries on the KCET-TV special, John Huston: A War Remembered, *which aired nationally on PBS. (Mitzi Trumbo)*

Building a landing strip. From Huston's first wartime documentary, Report from the Aleutians.

A casualty of the Fifth Army's Italian campaign. From Huston's San Pietro.

The aftermath of war. From Huston's San Pietro.

Let There Be Light (1946)

NOT RELEASED
B&W/45 minutes

CREDITS:

Director: Major John Huston; *Producer:* U.S. War Department; *Screenplay:* Major John Huston and Charles Kaufman; *Cinematographer:* Stanley Cortez; *Editor:* John Huston; *Music:* Dimitri Tiomkin; *Narrator:* Walter Huston; *Videocassette Source:* Budget Video, Festival Films, International Historic Films.

* * *

Contemporary Reviews

"John Huston...has directed the film with the same regard for terseness that marked his Hollywood films. Here, in short, is one of the war's outstanding records of what our men are doing. It is furthermore an honest record. It tells as much of the story as can now be told, and that is a good deal more than most Americans yet know. It is imperative that *Report from the Aleutians* be seen by anyone intent on knowing something of the labor, the hazard, and the importance—both real and potential—of one long-forgotten theatre of war."—*The New York Times*

"...in every way as good a war film as I have seen; in some ways it is the best. It was made by six Signal Corps cameramen under the command of Major John Huston, who also designed the scenario and wrote and spoke the narration. Most of these men were veterans. That fact presumably helps to explain a number of things: how they all lived through the shooting of the film; how deep inside the fighting some of it was made; how well they evidently knew what to expect, how to shoot it, what it was good for, and its weight and meaning in the whole picture. But remarkable as the cameramen evidently were, it is fairly clear that the main credit for *San Pietro* goes to Major Huston."—*The Nation*

"*Let There Be Light,* John Huston's intelligent, noble, fiercely moving short film about combat neurosis and some of the more spectacular kinds of therapy, will probably never be seen by the civilian public for whose need, and on whose money, it was made. The War

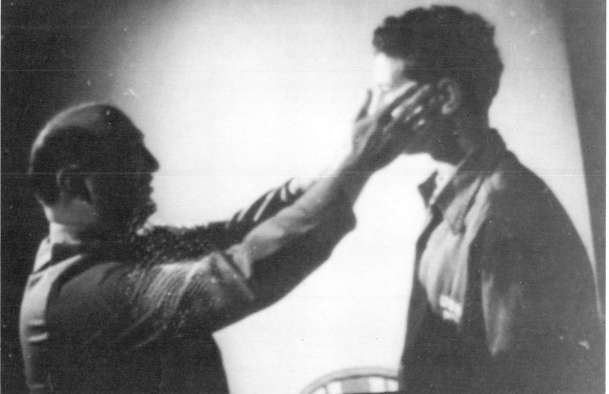

A shell-shocked soldier undergoes treatment via hypnosis in Huston's moving (and long unreleased) Let There Be Light.

Department has mumbled a number of reasons why it has been withheld; the glaring obvious reason has not been mentioned: that any sane human being who saw the film would join the armed services, if at all, with a straight face and a painfully maturing mind."—*The Nation*

* * *

Commissioned a lieutenant in the U.S. Army Signal Corps, John Huston was one of several Hollywood directors whose services were enlisted by the War Department to record the American fighting man's experiences in World War II for history and posterity. Others included John Ford, George Stevens, Anatole Litvak, William Wyler, and Frank Capra.

Huston's first assignment was to report to the Aleutians, a 1200-mile chain of islands running south-westward from Alaska, to record the building of a landing strip for B-24 Liberator bombers to embark on raids in the Pacific. He and his camera crew spent six months covering every facet of the strip's construction along with the hardships faced by all those stationed in this desolate theater of war. Subsequently, he and his crew went along on several bombing missions, enduring heavy flak, attacks by Japanese Zeros, and even crash landings. The compelling documentary he made of the experience, *Report from the Aleutians,* was completed in Hollywood and released to theaters in August, 1943. It was so well received that the *New York Times* listed it as one of the ten best films of the year—the only non-fiction film to make it on the *Time's* list.

As a result of this successful first effort, Huston was promoted to captain and sent to England to begin work on his next documentary about American participation in the Allied invasion of North Africa. Lack of bona fide American combat footage (it had been lost at sea) forced Huston and his crew into a situation that went decidedly against their grain. Returning to the U.S., they re-staged air battles over Orlando, Florida, and tank battles in the deserts of California. Though the film was completed, it was never released, "...which was a blessing," Huston says.

Huston spent the next several years in Europe covering the Italian campaign, which, for him, concluded in the little mountain town of San Pietro, where the Fifth Army launched a massive assault on the heavy German fortifications leading into Rome. The harrowing battle proved to be a turning point in the Allies' efforts to reclaim Italy. Casualties were heavy as the small town was all but destroyed. Huston's camera recorded every bloody detail from the foot soldier's point of view. When the film was completed and submitted to the War Department for approval, however, it was deemed "too strong" for home consumption and shorn of almost a half hour prior to its release. The missing footage has never been re-instated, and the film was not made available to the public until after V-E day. Several War Department brass, considering the film's potent images of modern warfare—even in the truncated version—powerful confirmation that war was indeed hell, didn't want *San Pietro* released at all. The feeling was that it would have a deleterious effect on future enlistments. This decision to permanently shelve the film was reversed, however, by General George C. Marshall, who, according to Huston, "...felt this picture should be seen by every American in training because it would prepare them for the shock of combat."

Promoted to Major, Huston moved on to his next and last war documentary, the moving *Let There Be Light,* a study of shell-shocked soldiers recuperating in a Long Island military hospital. After securing permission from the soldiers undergoing treatment to interview them about their wartime experiences and record their sometimes intense psychotherapy sessions, Huston shot hundreds of hours of film with his cameraman, Stanley Cortez. He still calls the experience of making the film, "...the most hopeful and optimistic and even joyous thing I ever had a hand in." When the War Department screened the film, however, it didn't quite agree and decided to shelve the film indefinitely. Thirty-five years later, largely through the lobbying efforts of Motion Picture Association of America President Jack Valenti, producer Ray Stark and a number of others, *Let There Be Light* finally received its first public showing at the Los Angeles County Museum, where it was heralded as "...a stunning work of art."

Many, including Huston, see these three wartime documentaries as a trilogy, which, ideally, should be experienced in sequence at a single sitting. There is a progression to them—beginning with preparations for war in *Report from the Aleutians,* to war itself in *San Pietro,* to the aftermath of war in *Let There Be Light.* In 1981, producer-director Jim Washburn of public television station KCET in Los Angeles combined the films, including the just released *Let There Be Light,* into a three-hour documentary titled *John Huston: A War Remembered,* hosted by Los Angeles newscaster Clete Roberts. In between each film, Roberts conversed with Huston about the director's trials and tribulations in making the films and his struggles to get them shown. Wrote the *Los Angeles Times* of the program, which aired nationally on PBS and is still shown in syndication, "All three [films] are spectacularly well photographed and edited." The *Daily News Tribune* added, "Approached as a trilogy, the documentaries weave a telling tapestry of wartime values and attitudes." About *Let There Be Light* specifically, critic Charles Champlin noted: "...if there is a reservation one has on seeing *Let There Be Light* in 1981, it is that it might have engendered too much optimism, have sounded too sweeping in its implicit assertion that the horrors of war could be erased from all the shattered personalities. But that is a concern born in large measure of different wars, Korea and Vietnam....It is, by any standards, an uncommonly subtle and dramatic motion picture, an affecting insight into the troubled silences after the battles and the parades."

* * *

The Treasure of the Sierra Madre (1948)

A WARNER BROTHERS PRODUCTION
B&W/124 minutes

CREDITS:

Director: John Huston; *Producer:* Henry Blanke; *Screenplay:* John Huston, based on the novel *The Treasure of the Sierra Madre* by B. Traven; *Cinematographer:* Ted McCord; *Editor:* Owen Marks; *Music:* Max Steiner; *Art Director:* John Hughes; *Videocassette Source:* Key Video.

CAST:

Fred C. Dobbs: Humphrey Bogart; *Howard:* Walter Huston; *Curtin:* Tim Holt; *Cody:* Bruce Bennett; *McCor-*mick: Barton MacLane; *Gold Hat:* Alfonso Bedoya; *El Presidente:* Arthur Soto Rangel; *El Jefe:* Manual Donde; *Pablo:* José Torvay; *Pancho:* Margarito Luna; *Boy Selling Lottery Ticket:* Bobby (Robert) Blake; *Man in White Suit:* John Huston (uncredited).

* * *

Contemporary Reviews

"*The Treasure of the Sierra Madre* is one of the best things Hollywood has done since it learned to talk; and the movie can take a place, without blushing, among the best ever made. The squeamish and the lovelorn may be wise to stay away, for it has no heroine and a few scenes are shatteringly brutal. But it is a magnificent and unconventional piece of screen entertainment."—*Time* magazine

"...John Huston, who wrote and directed it from a novel by B. Traven, has resolutely supplied the same sort of ruthless realism that was evident in his documentaries of war..."—*The New York Times*

* * *

Huston had read B. Traven's novel *The Treasure of the Sierra Madre* shortly after its American publication in the mid-thirties. After becoming a director, he persuaded Warners to buy it for him. It was his hope to launch into it after finishing *Across the Pacific,* but when Uncle Sam called, he was forced to put the project on hold. Having optioned the property, Warners considered assigning it to another director while Huston was away, but Henry Blanke, who was set to produce the picture, held out for his protégé, who began work on the screenplay almost immediately upon his return to Hollywood in 1946.

Like *The Maltese Falcon,* Huston's *Sierra Madre* is extremely faithful to the original source without being a literal transcription of it. In adapting the book, Huston again discarded certain elements while adding others so as to conform the work to his own particular vision and interests. The original novel, like most of socialist writer Traven's work, is an attack on capitalism, exploitation and greed. The film unquestionably retains these elements, but reduces the polemics in favor of characterization. While strengthening the irony of the story's conclusion (Huston deprives his survivors of any gold whereas in the book Curtin and Howard are left with two small bags), he also finishes on a thematically more positive note by having *both* Howard and Curtin find what Traven calls, "...the treasure which you think not worth taking trouble and pains to find, this alone is the real treasure you are

Tim Holt (back to camera), Humphrey Bogart, and Walter Huston on location with the director in Mexico for The Treasure of the Sierra Madre.

The down-and-out Dobbs (Humphrey Bogart) borrows yet another peso from the rich American in a white suit (John Huston in an uncredited cameo).

The three prospectors entertain dreams of gold in the Oso Negro Hotel. Though it's obvious in Howard's (Walter Huston) wise old eyes that he already seems to know what's coming.

Dobbs (Humphrey Bogart) brags about how he almost felled the Mexican bandit, Gold Hat (Alfonso Bedoya), following the attack on the train.

looking for all your life.'' In the novel, only Howard, who returns to the Indians who hold him in high esteem, finds this treasure. Curtin on the other hand, though certainly wiser for his experience, still seems fated to wander. Huston, however, has him set out to take care of Cody's widow and children, a change fully endorsed by Traven whose approval Huston sought upon finishing the screenplay.

To give the film a heightened sense of realism, Huston insisted on shooting as much of it as possible on location in Mexico, drawing many of his supporting players (including the memorable Alfonso Bedoya, who plays the cutthroat bandit, Gold Hat) from among the local populace. Humphrey Bogart and Walter Huston were the director's first and only choices for the respective roles of Dobbs and Old Howard. John Garfield was set to play Curtin but had to withdraw due to other commitments and the

role went to B-western star Tim Holt, whose own father, Jack, a star of silent and early sound westerns and action films, makes a brief one-line appearance at the beginning of the film as one of the many down-and-outers at the Oso Negro Hotel.

The younger Holt had hoped that his appearance in the Huston film (which was budgeted at $2,800,000) would get him out of his B-movie rut and catapult him into the big leagues. It didn't (though his performance in the film *is* first-rate) and he finished out his career as a radio time salesman in Oklahoma City. He made his last screen appearance as a revenue agent in *This Stuff'll Kill Ya!* (1971), a low-budget quickie directed by exploitation master Herschell Gordon Lewis. Future TV star Robert Blake (then known as Bobby Blake) also makes a brief appearance in *Sierra Madre* as the Mexican boy who sells Dobbs the winning lottery ticket that launches him on his fatal adventure.

While shooting in Mexico, Huston also got the opportunity to meet the novel's mysterious author, though he didn't know it at the time. The Chicago-

The three settle in for a year of hard work mining their strike.

born Traven (real name Traven Torsvan), who had spent some time in Germany during the twenties writing revolutionary pamphlets under the name Ret Marut before emigrating to Mexico, had a reputation for maintaining extreme privacy—to the extent that he didn't even allow photographs of himself to appear on the jackets of his books. Huston requested a meeting early on and Traven agreed, but at the last minute Traven sent an emissary instead— a little man named Hal Croves, who offered his services as a translator and accompanied Huston all through the shooting, then quietly disappeared. Huston still isn't positive, but it seems quite likely that Croves was actually the elusive Traven in disguise.

The film picks up the itinerant Dobbs in Tampico, sponging off a fellow American in a white suit (John Huston in an uncredited cameo). Later, another American, Pat McCormick, gives Dobbs a job working construction where he meets Curtin. McCormick tries to stiff the pair, however, when they return to Tampico, but Curtin and Dobbs manage to get their dough after they find McCormick and rough him up. Flush again, they hunt up an old prospector named Howard with the aim of going gold hunting, but their bankroll isn't enough to finance the expedition. Fate intervenes, however, when a lottery ticket Dobbs bought earlier turns out a winner and provides them with the needed funds. The trio sets off for the wilds by train, encountering bandits along the way. Once in the mountains, Howard locates a rich vein and the three settle in for a year of hard work mining their strike. Eventually, they grow suspicious of one another and take to dividing their goods and hiding them as they go along.

The continued solitude and hard work, not to mention the risk of bandits and claim jumpers, takes a toll on each of them, but especially Dobbs, who develops a case of paranoid psychosis and winds up shooting Curtin and leaving him for dead while

61

Dobbs (Humphrey Bogart) and his partners repel another attack by the Mexican bandit, Gold Hat (Alfonso Bedoya), who claims to be a Federale, but refuses to show any ''stinking badges.''

''I know you,'' Gold Hat (Alfonso Bedoya) says to Dobbs (Humphrey Bogart) at the waterhole, shortly before killing him with a machete.

Oscar night 1948. Sandwiched between the two winning Hustons is Claire Trevor, who received that year's Best Supporting Actress award for her performance in Key Largo, *also directed by John Huston.*

Howard is away at an Indian camp taking care of a sick boy.

Making off with all the gold and the burros, Dobbs runs into the same bandits that earlier attacked the train and their camp and is murdered. Uninterested in the gold, which they misperceive as sand, the bandits tear open the bags and dump them on the ground. In town, they try to sell the stolen burros, but their crime is discovered and they are arrested and executed. Howard and the wounded Curtin arrive just as a storm crops up and locate the torn bags only to find that the ferocious wind has already taken the gold dust back to the mountains from which it came. After howling with laughter at the joke fate has played on them, they say their goodbyes and head their separate ways, happy that they, unlike Dobbs, survived their adventure and have even found a purpose and a place to go.

With *The Treasure of the Sierra Madre*, John Huston completely fulfilled the extraordinary promise he had so clearly shown in *The Maltese Falcon*. Like *Falcon*, it remains not only one of Huston's best films but one of the all-time great movies the American cinema has given us. Contemporary critics lavished praise on it from one end of the country to the other, and at Academy Award time, the then 42-year-old Huston copped Oscars for best screenplay *and* direction. Perhaps even more satisfying to him, however, was the fact that the Academy also dubbed his father Best Supporting Actor for his peerless performance as Howard, the busted but wise old prospector, who, like Brigid O'Shaughnessy, speaks in a breathless rush—though in his case it's because he can't get the *truth* out of his mouth fast enough. Curiously though, Humphrey Bogart's equally memorable performance as Fred C. Dobbs, the typical Huston adventurer who this time caves in to his inadequacies and loses out,

was overlooked. The film was also nominated for Best Picture, but lost to Laurence Olivier's *Hamlet*.

Ironically (though perhaps not surprisingly), *Sierra Madre* was not a big box office success and took a number of years to recoup its nearly $3 million cost. Audiences perhaps found its subject matter (and Huston's treatment of it) too raw and rugged. It is as a number of critics pointed out a very brutal film—certainly for its time. Huston staged one scene after another with an eye for realism and authenticity. The barroom fight between Dobbs, Curtin and McCormick, for example, is no wild and woolly *Spoilers*-type battle, but a hard-won slugfest that leaves all parties maimed and exhausted. And while Dobbs's death at the hands of the machete-wielding Gold Hat does take place off camera, its impact is no less powerful and even ghoulish.

As *The Maltese Falcon* influenced most detective movies that followed in its wake, so has *The Treasure of the Sierra Madre* influenced most adventure movies. It has been borrowed from countless times since—even by Huston himself, who included a wry homage to it in his similarly-themed *The Man Who Would Be King* (1975)) by having a group of deadly tribesmen drool over Dravot's shiny boots in the same manner that the impoverished bandits covet Dobbs's shoes at the end of *Sierra Madre*. The late Sam Peckinpah, who admitted to being profoundly influenced by Huston (he even interviewed Huston for a national magazine, though the piece was never published) strongly echoed *Sierra Madre* in his equally powerful *The Wild Bunch* (1969). In addition to being set in a Mexican milieu and concluding on a similar (though bleaker) note of laughter in the face of disaster, the Peckinpah film also boasts a performance by Edmond O'Brien that is almost in a class with Walter Huston's as Howard—and is clearly meant as a salute to it. Peckinpah's subsequent attempt to make an outright *Sierra Madre* of his own—the preposterous *Bring Me the Head of Alfredo Garcia* (1974), which even includes a character named Fred C. Dobbs—emerged more travesty than triumph, however.

Key Largo (1948)

A WARNER BROTHERS PRODUCTION
B&W/101 minutes

CREDITS:

Director: John Huston; *Producer:* Jerry Wald; *Screenplay:* John Huston and Richard Brooks, based on the play *Key Largo* by Maxwell Anderson; *Cinematographer:* Karl Freund; *Editor:* Rudi Fehr; *Music:* Max Steiner; *Art Director:* Leo Kuter; *Videocassette Source:* CBS/Fox Home Video.

CAST:

Frank McCloud: Humphrey Bogart; *Nora Temple:* Lauren Bacall; *James Temple:* Lionel Barrymore; *Johnny Rocco:* Edward G. Robinson; *Gaye Dawn:* Claire Trevor; *Curly:* Thomas Gomez; *Toots Bass:* Harry Lewis; *Clyde Sawyer:* John Rodney; *Ziggy:* Marc Lawrence; *Ben Wade:* Monte Blue; *Angel Garcia:* Dan Seymour; *Johnny:* Jay Silverheels; *Tom:* Rodric Redwing.

* * *

Humphrey Bogart as Frank McCloud and Lauren Bacall as Nora Temple in Huston's Key Largo.

Boozy ex-singer Gaye Dawn (Claire Trevor) bums a cigarette from the sympathetic McCloud (Humphrey Bogart) as Nora (Lauren Bacall) watches.

The Temples (Lionel Barrymore and Lauren Bacall) and McCloud (Humphrey Bogart) are held at bay by the vicious thug, Johnny Rocco (Edward G. Robinson), and his off-camera gang.

The trapped McCloud (Humphrey Bogart) and Nora (Lauren Bacall) contemplate his next move, now that he has been slipped a gun by Rocco's moll, Gaye.

Contemporary Reviews:

"Even as a study of character under stress it is sometimes stagey and once or twice next door to hammy; and nearly all of it has the smell of the studio and of intelligent but elaborate compromised artifice. But it is exceedingly well acted, and as picture-making most of it is well worth watching as anything you will see this year. Huston manages kinds of vitality, insight, and continuance within each shot and from one shot to the next which are the most inventive and original, the most exciting and hard to analyze, in contemporary movies."—*The Nation*

"With remarkable filming and cutting, Mr. Huston has notably achieved a great deal of tension in some rather static scenes—and scenes, too, that give the bald appearance of having been written for the stage. Though largely confined to a few rooms, he keeps people on the move and has used an intrusive hurricane for some slam-bang melodramatic effects. He has also got stinging performances out of most of his cast—notably Mr. Robinson, who plays the last of the red-hot gangsters in top-notch style....But the script prepared by Mr. Huston and Richard Brooks is too full of words and highly cross-purposed implications to give the action full chance. Talk—endless talk—about courage and the way the world goes gums it up."—*The New York Times*

* * *

The Treasure of the Sierra Madre had yet to be released when Huston began his next project, a considerably revised and updated adaptation of Maxwell Anderson's pre-war stage play, *Key Largo*. The play, which was not a big success, starred Paul Muni as a disillusioned Spanish-American war deserter who comes back to the U.S. and finds courage and commitment at last when forced to take on a group of thugs. The film was to star Huston's screen alter-ego, Humphrey Bogart, in the Muni role, now a heroic, but equally disillusioned, World War II army major named Frank McCloud, who returns home to find that the values he fought for have seemingly become outmoded and that the lot of the returning vet is not an easy one. This latter theme, not found in the Anderson play, Huston and co-writer Richard Brooks borrowed from William Wyler's *The Best Years of Our Lives* (1946), one of Huston's favorite films.

McCloud lands in the Florida Keys to look up the Temples, the father and widow of an army pal, and there encounters a quartet of gangsters led by the flashy Johnny Rocco, a notorious deported crime king styled after Lucky Luciano. Rocco and his goons have commandeered the Temples' coastal hotel to prepare for a hop to Cuba once they've gotten cash from the sale of some counterfeit money. Together they wait out an impending hurricane. Rocco harasses the Temples and repeatedly threatens McCloud, who allows himself to be intimidated by the gun-wielding hood because he's no longer willing to take up another cause. "I had hopes once, but gave 'em up," he admits. "What were they?" Rocco sneers. "A world with no place for Johnny Rocco," McCloud replies, adding later, however, that, "One Rocco more or less ain't worth dyin' for." But when Rocco humiliates his alcoholic moll, Gaye, by promising her a drink if she'll sing, then withholding it due to her pathetic performance, McCloud exhibits his innate compassion by pouring her one himself. Rocco slaps him, but he still refuses to retaliate.

After the hurricane, during which the captain of Rocco's getaway yacht runs off, McCloud, a skilled sailor, is forced by Rocco to take them to Cuba. Slipped a gun by Gaye, whom Rocco has decided to leave behind, McCloud finally acts and, once at sea, whittles the gang down one by one until only Rocco is left. Luring the gangster out into the open, he shoots him and returns triumphantly to Key Largo.

As is fairly obvious, Huston and Brooks had transformed Anderson's play into a metaphor for World War II—with McCloud representing the Allies, Rocco and company the Nazis and the gathering storm of the hurricane the escalating likelihood of a clash betwen the two, a clash Rocco fears, as he knows it could spell his doom. Post-war social apathy had also left the way clear for the underworld to start making a renewed bid for power and influence. This bit of social commentary is distilled into the character of Rocco himself, a former mob bigshot who dreams of regaining his kingpin status—his "black bird." McCloud's self-deception is his belief that he no longer cares whether the Roccos of the world take over or not. But in the final analysis, he does care, does fight back, and defeats Rocco in the spirit of his dead war buddy. "George was a born hero," he tells the boy's father. "Couldn't imagine his own death, only dishonor." McCloud reflects Huston's own attitudes and echoes the director in other ways. Huston likewise returned from the war a major and also participated in the battle of San Pietro, a campaign to which McCloud makes a specific and dramatic reference.

Key Largo, like *In This Our Life* and *The Unforgiven*, also contains a sub-theme about racial injustice. Johnny and Tom, two Seminole Indian boys who are on the lam from the law, turn to Mr. Temple

Rocco (Edward G. Robinson) is lured out into the open at the exciting conclusion to Key Largo.

for guidance, as he's an old and trusted friend. Temple persuades them to give themselves up, but they turn against him and his advice when they and their families are refused sanctuary in the hotel during the hurricane and are almost swept away. They don't know that it was Rocco who'd ordered that they be left outside—Temple, in fact, didn't even know they were there. Rocco murders a cop, then pins the blame on the two Indians, who are both shot and killed by the sheriff while trying to flee. "Seems like we can't do anything but hurt these people even when we try to help them," Mr. Temple mourns later when he tells the distraught sheriff of his mistake.

Though the film is rife with heavy-handed discussions about the absolute villainy of fascist thugs like Rocco, the meaning of courage and the need to take a stand no matter what the odds, Huston's cast is outstanding and his direction never lets the pace or tension slacken. His handling of the hurricane's build-up is particularly effective. Even though these scenes were shot entirely in a studio, Karl Freund's atmospheric lighting effects convincingly suggest exactly the right look and feel of an approaching tropical storm.

Though *Key Largo* was a big box office success for Huston and also picked up an Oscar (for Claire Trevor as Best Supporting Acress), it marked the end of his long association with Warner Brothers, at least for a time. A dispute with studio head Jack Warner over the cutting of *Largo*, combined with Warner's persistent refusal to give Huston the go-ahead on a number of desired projects, prompted Huston to set out on his own as an independent writer-director. Which he has remained ever since.

We Were Strangers (1949)

A HORIZON PRODUCTION
Released through Columbia Pictures
B&W/106 minutes

CREDITS:

Director: John Huston; *Producer:* S.P. Eagle (Sam Spiegel); *Screenplay:* John Huston and Peter Viertel, based on the novel *Rough Sketch* by Robert Sylvester; *Cinematographer:* Russell Metty; *Editor:* Al Clark; *Music:* George Antheil; *Art Director:* Cary Odell; *Videocassette Source:* Not Available.

CAST:

Tony Fenner: John Garfield; *China Valdes:* Jennifer Jones; *Armando Ariete:* Pedro Armendariz; *Guillermo:* Gilbert Roland; *Miguel:* Wally Cassel; *Revolutionary Leader:* Ramon Novarro; *Clerk:* John Huston (uncredited).

* * *

Contemporary Reviews

"Beyond any question, the aspects of a devilishly original plot to bump off the whole administration of Cuba in one fell swoop are graphically screened. The back breaking physical labor and the terrible mental strain undergone by a group of dynamiters who tunnel beneath a burying-ground to plant a bomb are staggeringly pictorialized. The toil, the sweat, the cold anxiety—and the peculiarly ghoulish details—of such a mad endeavor are caught by Mr. Huston brilliantly. But this very concentration upon detail and upon the concrete mechanics of the plan has thrown the whole drama into the character of a passionless action film...instead of capturing a high tragedy on the level of *For Whom the Bell Tolls*, he

China (Jennifer Jones) keeps a lookout for her brother who's being trailed by the military police for his radical activities.

Director Huston relaxes between takes on the set of We Were Strangers, *his first independent production.*

70

[Huston] has wrapped up a morbid melodrama of an 'underground' plot gone sour.''—*The New York Times*

''As movie melodramas go, it is above average, but it is not Grade A Huston. Brightest spot in this murky yarn is the clear, vigorous, imaginative camerawork. There are beautiful shots of Havana's buildings rising like white frozen fountains at the end of receding alleys, and some brilliant bits on the revolution in full swing. Never for a moment a dull movie, *Strangers* is often too facile or too far away from strict artistic honesty. Coming from the man who made *Treasure of Sierra Madre*, it is a disappointment.''—*Time* magazine

''A shameful handbook of Marxian dialectics...and the heaviest dish of Red theory ever served to an audience outside the Soviet.''—*The Hollywood Reporter*

* * *

Tony (John Garfield) gets the idea for a bold assassination scheme when he and China (Jennifer Jones) visit a local cemetery.

Huston's first act as a maverick writer-director was to form a partnership with Sam Spiegel, an independent producer he'd met while working on *The Killers.* For their first film together, they chose *We Were Strangers,* the story of a group of revolutionaries struggling to free Cuba from dictatorship in 1933. The film was based on an incident drawn from an episodic novel, *Rough Sketch,* by Robert Sylvester, which Huston and writer Peter Viertel developed into a full-length screenplay. Huston and Spiegel pitched the idea to MGM, but a more lucrative financing and distribution deal was stuck with Columbia instead. MGM remained hooked on Huston, however, and signed him to make two pictures back-to-back for them as soon as *We Were Strangers* was completed.

The film opens with a quote from Thomas Jefferson: ''Resistance to tyrants is obedience to God.'' American Tony Fenner arrives in Cuba masquerading as a talent scout. His real purpose, however, is to finance and carry out an act of revolt against the Cuban dictatorship that will trigger a full-scale uprising by the people. Together with his Cuban contact (Novarro), a wise old customer whose rapid-fire patter is reminiscent of Walter Huston's in *Sierra Madre,* he links up with an odd-

Tony (John Garfield) and China (Jennifer Jones) try to play it cool when their conversation is interrupted by the suspicious police chief, Ariete (Pedro Armendariz).

The tunnelers give each other a progress report upstairs in China's kitchen.

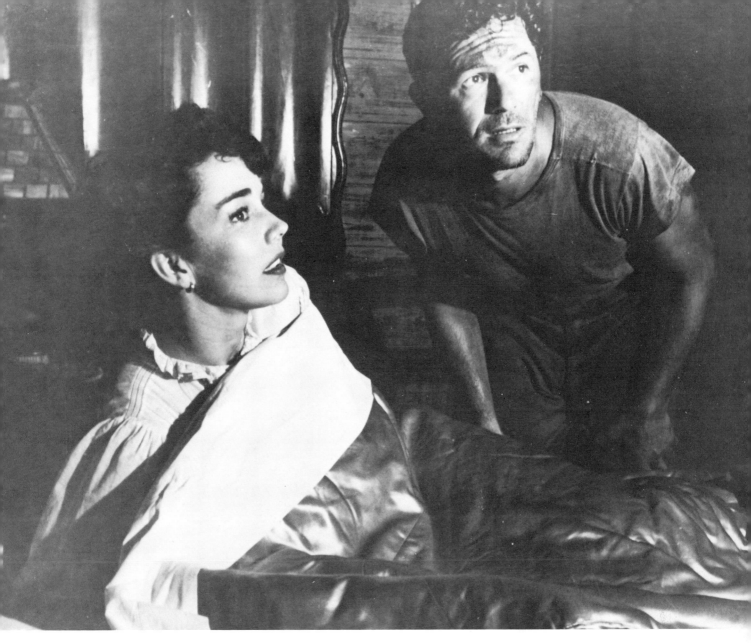

Revolutionaries turned lovers: Jennifer Jones as China Valdez and John Garfield as Tony Fenner in We Were Strangers.

mixed band of freedom fighters and works out a plan to assassinate the brutal dictator, his villainous chief of police, and other oppressive officials while they are attending the state funeral of an important senator whose murder has also been engineered by the rebels. Tunneling beneath the grave site from the cellar of a nearby house, they plan to detonate a powerful bomb while the funeral is in full sway. The plan goes awry, however, when the late senator's sisters opt at the last moment to bury their brother elsewhere. Fenner, the son of an exiled Cuban national, blows his chance for escape and is killed in a gun battle with police just as the streets of Cuba erupt in full-scale revolution. He thus achieves victory even in death.

The basic problem with *We Were Strangers* is that it falls apart as soon as Fenner's plan does. Up to that point, it is excitingly done. The intricate details of mapping out the plan, noiselessly excavating the tunnel, and contending with a guilt-ridden co-conspirator who falls ill and almost gives the scheme away in his delirium are expertly handled and quite tense. These sequences also serve as a warm-up for Huston's next film, *The Asphalt Jungle,* in which the director subjects a very different kind of caper to similarly microscopic treatment. Unlike *We Were Strangers,* however, *The Asphalt Jungle* actually becomes even more fascinating once the caper starts coming undone, the reason being that its failure is so closely tied to the characters' own weaknesses, a favorite Huston theme. Fenner and his cohorts have the rug pulled out from under them by pure chance, however, and once that happens there's little for them to do but pack up and go home. As this would have been a rather flat climax, Huston and Viertel proceeded to extend the story by having Fenner get killed in a contrived assault on the house. His reason for returning to the house (he has fallen for China, the Cuban girl who owns it, and refuses to flee the island without her) is pure romantic melodrama.

While the acting is uniformly solid throughout, Pedro Armendariz's slimy police chief, Ariete, stands out as the film's most memorable performance and character. The scene in which he visits China and tries to seduce her with an over-the-top display of machismo by eating and drinking like a pig, playing Russian roulette, and extolling his virtues as "a man of honor" until he passes out is a premier example of Huston's broad but sharp-edged approach to comedy. Even as he amuses us, Ariete repels us. Thirty-six years later, William Hickey's raspy, self-satisfied weazel, Don Prizzi, would generate a similar response in Huston's *Prizzi's Honor.*

Though it was a box office failure, *We Were Strangers* did stir up a certain amount of controversy due to Huston's casting of John Garfield, who was then being hounded by the House Un-American Activities Committee (HUAC) for his alleged communist sympathies. A few years later, Garfield died of a heart attack caused, some say, by the stress he'd undergone during this period of harrassment that had left his career in tatters. Several years before making the film, Huston and a number of other Hollywood luminaries, including Humphrey Bogart, had gone to Washington to protest HUAC's violation of First Amendment rights; their protest group was branded a communist front. Huston says of the experience: "It didn't do much good, but it gave us a secure feeling to be in there fighting for what we believed was right." This, of course, was one of the central themes of *We Were Strangers,* as well as Huston's earlier *Key Largo.* The cause stayed with Huston and in 1977 he narrated a documentary about the HUAC years called *Hollywood on Trial,* which aired nationally on PBS.

Huston's outspoken dislike of the communist witchhunters and all they stood for might have resulted in his being blacklisted too, but for some reason (luck perhaps), he and his career survived. *We Were Strangers* undeniably aggravated an already tense situation because of its espousal of outright rebellion in defense of freedom, an espousal some saw not as an attack on the methods of HUAC (which is what Huston intended), but as a subversive, Red-inspired suggestion to overthrow the U.S. government. Because of its poor box office performance—and other, unstated reasons, perhaps—Columbia quickly pulled the film from release.

The Asphalt Jungle (1950)

A METRO-GOLDWYN-MAYER PRODUCTION
B&W/112 minutes

CREDITS:

Director: John Huston; *Producer:* Arthur Hornblow, Jr.; *Screenplay:* John Huston and Ben Maddow, based on the novel *The Asphalt Jungle* by W.R. Burnett; *Cinematographer:* Harold Rosson; *Editor:* George Boemler; *Music:* Miklos Rozsa; *Art Director:* Cedric Gibbons; *Videocassette Source:* MGM/UA Home Video.

CAST:

Dix Handley: Sterling Hayden; *Alonzo D. Emmerich:* Louis Calhern; *Doll Conovan:* Jean Hagen; *Doc Riedenschneider:* Sam Jaffe; *Gus Minissi:* James Whitmore; *Cobby:* Marc Lawrence; *Hardy:* John McIntire; *Louis Ciavelli:* Anthony Caruso; *Maria Ciavelli:* Teresa Celli; *Angela Phinley:* Marilyn Monroe; *Dietrich:* Barry Kelley; *May Emmerich:* Dorothy Tree; *Bob Brannen:* Brad Dexter.

* * *

Contemporary Reviews

"*The Asphalt Jungle,* directed for MGM with a surface vivacity and tricky hucksterish flash that earlier Huston doesn't have, sums up a great deal about his work and adds a freakishness that isn't far from Camp. Almost all of his traits, the strange spastic feeling for time, lunging at what he feels is the heart of a scene and letting everything else go, the idea that authority is inherent in a few and totally absent in everyone else, a ticlike need for posh and elegance, are funneled into this film...."—*The Nation*

"A gangster picture of the old style—which packs as much wallop as almost anything of its kind since the days of *Scarface* or James Cagney's rendition of *Public Enemy.*"—*Newsweek*

"From the very first shot, in which the camera picks up a prowling thug, sliding along between buildings to avoid a police car in the gray and liquid dawn,

Huston with Sterling Hayden and Jean Hagen on the set of The Asphalt Jungle.

Doc (Sam Jaffe), back to camera, the criminal mastermind, spells out his plan to Cobby (Marc Lawrence), left, and the duplicitous lawyer, Emmerich (Louis Calhern).

Dix (Sterling Hayden) slugs a guard during the caper as Louis (Anthony Caruso) and Doc (Sam Jaffe) watch.

The cast of The Asphalt Jungle: *Louis Calhern, Sterling Hayden, Jean Hagen, and Sam Jaffe, examining the prize.*

there is a ruthless authority to this picture, the hardness and clarity of steel, and remarkably subtle suggestion that conveys a whole involvement of distorted personality and inveterate crime. Mr. Huston's *The Maltese Falcon*, which brought him to the fore as a sure and incisive director, had nothing in the way of toughness on this film.''—*The New York Times*

* * *

With the completion of *We Were Strangers*, Huston put his new partnership with producer Sam Spiegel on temporary hold and moved over to MGM to fulfill his contractual obligations for two successive films. The first of these was to be the epic *Quo Vadis?*, based on Henri Sienkiewicz's historical novel about Emperor Nero's persecution of the Christians and his burning of Rome. Huston was to both write and direct the film. Shooting in Italy halted indefinitely, however, when Gregory Peck, the film's star, developed a serious eye infection. Huston bowed out of the project and was replaced by Mervyn LeRoy, who, in turn, replaced Peck with Robert Taylor. The film opened to great

Doc (Sam Jaffe), Doll (Jean Hagen) and Dix (Sterling Hayden) look over the fruits of their successful heist shortly before everything begins to go sour.

success in 1951.

Casting about for a new MGM project for himself, Huston came upon *The Asphalt Jungle*, the latest crime novel by his longtime literary mentor, W.R. Burnett, two of whose works, *Saint Johnson* and *High Sierra*, Huston had successfully adapted for the screen already. As MGM already owned the film rights, Huston agreed to take on the project and was given a green light. He worked on the adaptation with screenwriter Ben Maddow, then submitted it to Burnett himself, who endorsed it with enthusiasm.

The Asphalt Jungle is essentially a reworking of elements already found in Burnett's earlier *High Sierra*. In both book and film, Doc Riedenschneider, a criminal mastermind recently released from prison, determines to make one last, big score, then retire to a quiet life of wealth and obscurity. He concocts a plan to steal a fortune in jewels and pitches it to a bookie named Cobby to secure the necessary financial backing. Cobbys' partner, of sorts, is a respected but larcenous lawyer named Emmerich, who has been living beyond his means to support a beautiful mistress. Emmerich, seeing a way out of his substantial debts, persuades Cobby to bankroll Doc's masterful plan, which is sure to make them all rich. In the meantime, he and his associate, Bannerman, scheme to steal the jewels for themselves once the heist is over.

The police nail Doc (Sam Jaffe).

The elaborately planned robbery goes off virtually without a hitch (though the safecracker, Louis Ciavelli, is killed), but once the thieves turn on each other, everything begins to go wrong. One by one, Cobby and various of Doc's henchmen are picked up by police and beaten into confessing details of the crime. When Emmerich and Bannerman attempt to confiscate the jewels for themselves, Dix Handley, one of Doc's closest allies, shoots Bannerman, but is fatally wounded in return. Emmerich commits suicide rather than face a public scandal. Dix and his girlfriend, Doll, escape to Dix's farm, but he expires almost as they arrive. Only the original mastermind behind the affair, Doc, is left to make off with the jewels, but even he sabotages himself in the end. Lingering too long at a local roadhouse to watch a nubile teenager dance, he is spotted by police and picked up with the jewels in his possession.

In *The Asphalt Jungle,* Huston corrected all the

problems that had so seriously marred his earlier—and quite similar—*We Were Strangers.* The film's lengthy, almost wordless robbery sequence set a new standard for suspense that has been copied, but seldom duplicated, by virtually every caper film made since. Beyond this, however, once the heist has been pulled off and the thieves begin to fall out, *The Asphalt Jungle,* unlike *We Were Strangers,* takes off even more, becoming more suspenseful and more intriguing as we watch and wait for the cast of characters to do themselves and each other in. This too set a new standard, which has been matched, in my view, only once—by Jules Dassin in his French thriller, *Rififfi,* which followed the Huston film four years later.

In addition to a tight script, tough direction—Huston's best since *Sierra Madre*—and Harold Rosson's stark and atmospheric photography (the film remains a classic *film noir*), *The Asphalt Jungle* benefits strongly from the fine ensemble work of its cast, which included Marilyn Monroe in her brief, but eye-popping, film debut as Emmerich's kittenish mistress. Sterling Hayden, who, like John Garfield, was also having troubles with HUAC around this time, registers solidly as the alcoholic Dix, the quintessential Huston loser, as does Jean Hagen as his luckless girlfriend, Doll. Sam Jaffe received an Oscar nomination for his performance as Doc, but lost to George Sanders in *All About Eve.* Huston received nominations for his screenplay and direction, but lost in both categories to *All About Eve* as well.

Though the film's bold and meticulous portrait of criminals and their "left-handed form of human endeavor" seemed to run counter to a number of tenets in the Motion Picture Production Code of the 1950s, Huston had little difficulty getting his script passed by Hollywood's self-censoring body, the Breen Office, except for one scene: Emmerich's suicide. As originally written by Huston and Ben Maddow, Emmerich calmly sits down and writes a note to his wife, then with equal calmness proceeds to blow his brains out. The Breen Office rejected the scene, however, because it implied that Emmerich was in full command of his faculties when he killed himself, a Code no-no. Huston countered that no one completely in his right mind opts for suicide, but his argument was rejected and he was forced to rewrite the scene. In the finished film, Emmerich attempts to write the note, but becomes increasingly agitated by what he is about to do and kills himself without completing it. "It turned out to be a better scene for the change," Huston said later. "But I wouldn't recommend trying to outfox the motion picture code as a way to achieve storytelling success."

The Red Badge of Courage (1951)

A METRO-GOLDWYN-MAYER PRODUCTION
B&W/69 minutes

CREDITS:

Director: John Huston; *Producer:* Gottfried Reinhardt; *Screenplay:* John Huston, based on the novel *The Red Badge of Courage* by Stephen Crane; *Cinematographer:* Harold Rosson; *Editor:* Ben Lewis; *Music:* Bronislau Kaper; *Art Director:* Cedric Gibbons; *Videocassette Source:* MGM/UA Home Video.

CAST:

Henry Fleming: Audie Murphy; *Tom Wilson:* Bill Mauldin; *Jim Conklin:* John Dierkes; *The Tattered Soldier:* Royal Dano; *Bill Porter:* Arthur Hunnicutt; *The General:* Tim Durant; *The Lieutenant:* Douglas Dick; *Thompson:* Robert Easton; *The Fat Soldier:* Andy Devine; *The Captain:* Smith Bellow; *Narrator:* James Whitmore.

*   *   *

Contemporary Reviews

"Scrupulously faithful to the novel, one of the best war films ever made...both the camera and the spoken commentary (taken word for word from the novel) are filled with human understanding."—*Time* magazine

"Mr. Huston, who made *San Pietro,* one of the great documentaries of World War II, can conceive a Civil War battle, and has done so magnificently in this film. Furthermore, he got the sense of soldiers in that long-ago day and war—their looks, their attitudes, their idioms—as suggested in the writings of the times...in most respects, Mr. Huston has put *The Red Badge of Courage* on the screen, and that means a major achievement that should command admiration for years and years."—*The New York Times*

*Huston demonstrates the proper way to brandish a rifle to his
"troops" on the set of* The Red Badge of Courage, *which
the director shot mostly on his California ranch.*

"Bids fair to become one of the classic American motion pictures."—*Newsweek*

* * *

While working for Huston on *The Unforgiven*, veteran actress Lillian Gish, whose career spans the history of the movies themselves, described her director as "...another D.W. Griffith." Undoubtedly, she was not just referring to whatever personality traits they shared in common, but to Huston's similarly dominating authority over his films and every facet of their production. Gish's description is apt in other ways, however, for had Huston been a contemporary of the great silent director, there is evidence in his work that he might have been a giant of the silent screen as well.

Huston's superb version of Stephen Crane's *The Red Badge of Courage* is a good case in point. Apart from the film's obvious similarity to Griffith's silent classic *The Birth of a Nation* in terms of subject matter, Huston's Civil War drama tells its story and reveals its characters' thoughts and feelings almost entirely in visual terms. The dialogue (most of it taken by Huston directly from Crane's text) is sparse and could effectively have been rendered via title cards, just as Griffith had done. In all respects, *The Red Badge of Courage* is essentially a silent film with sound. The irony then is that contemporary filmgoers, whose parents would have had little difficulty following the film, couldn't seem to fathom *Red Badge* at all. The film's initial previews, in fact, proved so negative (audiences deemed the film "too slow moving" and "in-

One can see the tension Fleming feels over the upcoming battle reflected in Audie Murphy's amazingly expressive eyes. In the background: cartoonist Bill Mauldin (center) and John Dierkes.

comprehensible") that MGM quickly pulled it, speeded up the action by eliminating certain "difficult" scenes, and added an intrusive and redundant narration to help explain all the nuances of what was going on. Though released to almost unanimously favorable reviews, the nearly $2 million film still failed to find an audience and disappeared from view soon after. Huston, who has often found himself in the unenviable position of making an initially unsuccessful film later recognized as being ahead of its time, had here made one that falls somewhere in between.

The actual proposal to bring *The Red Badge of Courage* to the screen was not Huston's, though he had read the book many years before and had always hoped to film it someday, but that of producer Gottfried Reinhardt, the brother of former and future Huston associate Wolfgang Reinhardt. Huston enthusiastically agreed to both write and direct the film and together they went to MGM production chief Dory Schary to secure his blessing and get the necessary go-ahead. Schary, a writer himself who had only recently become the studio's vice-president in charge of production, favored the project, but studio head L.B. Mayer, whose endorsement was also needed, did not.

Mayer hadn't liked Huston's previous film for MGM, *The Asphalt Jungle*, even though it had been a major critical and financial success for the studio. He felt that *Red Badge* was cut from the same cloth. "[It] has got no laughs, no songs, no entertainment value," he said of the project. "It will be ugly and not make money." On the latter count, he proved to be quite right.

The conflict over *Red Badge* quickly turned into an outright battle between the two studio chieftains. It was not the first, however. Mayer had vehemently opposed the making of two other Schary projects, *Battleground* (1949) and the as yet unreleased *Quo Vadis?* (1951) on the grounds that they too would lose money. *Battleground* had been a big success, however, and *Quo Vadis?* would prove an even bigger one. Convinced that *Red Badge* would be a success too, Schary took his case before Nicholas Schenck, president of Loew's, Inc., MGM's parent company. Schenck had already decided to go with Mayer's decision, but when Schary called in the marker he had earned with the unexpected success of *Battleground*, both Schenck and Mayer backed down and *Red Badge* got the green light. Not long after, Mayer, whose power at MGM had once been unassailable, was ousted by Schenck, thus ending the career of one of Hollywood's most legendary Rajahs. Schary, it should be noted, didn't last much longer. His career with MGM ended in 1957.

It's fairly obvious that even though *Red Badge*

The Union troops ford a river (actually California's Sacramento River) on their way to battle.

was set during the Civil War, Huston saw its theme of courage in the face of overwhelming fear as being equally pertinent to America's most recent war, indeed *all* wars. He therefore strived to give the film the look of one of his World War II documentaries. While clearly recalling the spectacular, smoke-filled battle scenes of Griffith's *Birth of a Nation* as well as cameraman Matthew Brady's historic studies of Civil War soldiers in repose and death, Huston's *Red Badge* also recalls the director's own *San Pietro*. It is a film that is told almost entirely from the foot soldier's point of view. And in a casting stoke of genius that ties the film even closer to World War II, Huston selected not some well-known Hollywood star to play the young soldier who must face and defeat his fear of cowardice and death to become a hero, but America's most decorated soldier of World War II, 26-year-old Audie Murphy, who had never acted a major role before. Huston figured that Murphy was someone who knew from personal experience exactly what Henry Fleming was going through and that the newcomer's inexperience before the camera would enhance rather than detract from his performance. Huston was right. Audie Murphy's debut performance as Henry Fleming is nothing short of

remarkable because it rings so solidly true. His subtly fearful eyes and every gesture of false bravado express Fleming's inner turmoil on the eve of his first battle perfectly. To understand what the director is saying in *Red Badge,* all one need do is study Murphy's amazingly expressive face, which Huston's camera explores constantly in the best tradition of the silent film.

Huston's cast of supporting actors, including another non-professional, World War II cartoonist Bill Mauldin, is no less impressive. Huston even took a small role himself, though his cameo was later cut from the film. Royal Dano's part as the Tattered Soldier was severely abridged and his dramatic death scene completely removed. Huston found this especially debilitating as he considered Dano's death scene one of the film's most powerful moments.

The lack of any big name stars in the cast was one of the main reasons why the studio felt *Red Badge* failed at the box office. It accused Huston of making an already uncommercial property even more uncommercial by doing so. Yet it is the very lack of recognizable faces in the cast of *Red Badge* that adds so much to its almost documentary feel. Having delivered his final cut of the film, Huston took off for Africa to begin work on *The African Queen*. Apart from occasional communiques with producer Gottfried Reinhardt, he took no active role in the studio's attempts to "rescue" the film.

One of Huston's scenes of battle from The Red Badge of Courage.

Fleming, having received his red badge of courage, waits nervously with his fellow troops to make the next assault.

Royal Dano as the Tattered Soldier shortly before his unexpected death, which was cut from the film.

In many ways, he knew after that first disastrous preview that the battle had been lost. "During the preview you could actually feel the audience stiffen against the film," he said, "...when it happened, I knew the picture had no future." Of the picture's anticipated failure, Nicholas Schenck subsequently remarked, "The next picture John Huston made [*The African Queen*]—and this time he was making it for his *own* company— he made a commercial picture, a tremendous hit." Ironically, although *The African Queen* was a great hit, Huston himself shared none of the profits, which, he says, all went to producer Sam Spiegel.

The late director George Stevens once said that a film's real merit can't honestly be calculated until it has been given the opportunity to stand the test of time. If so, John Huston got the last laugh, for even in its truncated form, *The Red Badge of Courage* now emerges as one of the most potent films of his career, a very personal and courageous experiment in "pure cinema" of which the director can well be proud.

The African Queen (1952)

A HORIZON-ROMULUS PRODUCTION
Released Through United Artists
Technicolor/105 minutes

CREDITS:

Director: John Huston; *Producer:* S.P. Eagle (Sam Spiegel); *Screenplay:* John Huston and James Agee, based on the novel *The African Queen* by C.S. Forester; *Cinematographer:* Jack Cardiff; *Editor:* Ralph Kemplen; *Music:* Allan Gray; *Art Director:* Wilfred Shingleton; *Videocassette Source:* CMS/Fox Home Video.

CAST:

Charlie Alnutt: Humphrey Bogart; *Rose Sayer:* Katharine Hepburn; *Samuel Sayer:* Robert Morley; *Ship Captain:* Peter Bull; *Member of Ship's Crew:* Theodore Bikel.

* * *

Trapped by the marshes, Charlie (Humphrey Bogart) must climb into the river and pull the Queen *to freedom.*

Contemporary Reviews

''*The African Queen* was shot entirely on location in the Belgian Congo, but the characters do almost nothing that couldn't have been done on one studio set with the aid of some library shots.''—*Commentary*

''Mr. Huston merits credit for putting this fantastic tale on a level of sly, polite kidding and generally keeping it there, while going about the happy business of engineering excitement and visual thrills.''—*The New York Times*

* * *

Having fulfilled his contractual obligations to MGM, Huston resumed his partnership with Sam Spiegel and Horizon Productions to make *The African Queen,* based on a 1935 novel by C.S. Forrester, author of the popular Horatio Hornblower sea adventures. Forrester's novel had been optioned twice before—by Columbia as a vehicle for Charles Laughton and Elsa Lanchester, and by Warner Bros. as a vehicle for Bette Davis and David Niven. The Laughton deal fell through when the actor set up his own production company, Mayflower Productions, with expatriate German producer Eric Pommer to make *The Beachcomber* (1938), a very similar story about the conflicts and growing love between a South Sea island bum (Laughton) and a prim missionary (Lanchester). The film was based on a story by Somerset Maugham called *Vessel of Wrath,*

Enemy bullets rain down on the Queen *as Charlie (Humphrey Bogart) and Rosie (Katharine Hepburn) pass a German fort overlooking the river.*

Their relationship starts to bloom as Rosie (Katharine Hepburn) sympathetically tends to Charlie's (Humphrey Bogart) wounded foot.

and, perhaps due to the popularity of Huston's *The African Queen,* remade once more as *The Beachcomber* in 1955, starring Robert Newton and Glynis Johns. The Davis/Niven deal fell through due to a falling out between Bette Davis and Huston mentor Henry Blanke, who was to produce the picture for Warners in 1938. Spiegel and Huston wrestled the rights away from Warners by arranging a co-production deal with British producers John and James Woolf, whose Romulus Productions would also be involved in the creation of Huston's next two projects, *Moulin Rouge* and *Beat the Devil..*

Huston had made two of his war documentaries in color, but *The African Queen* was to be his first theatrical film in color. Though the process was more costly than black and white, he insisted on color stock because the film was to be shot on location in Africa and he wanted cameraman Jack Cardiff to be able to

capture every brilliant hue of this lush tropical paradise. As it turned out, the Belgian Congo locales where the film was primarily shot proved to be predictably lush, but scarcely a paradise. Virtually everyone in the cast and crew fell ill from a variety of tropical diseases, ranging from malaria and dysentary to sun stroke. Katharine Hepburn became so ill that production had to be shut down for almost a week while she recuperated. Only Bogart and Huston remained unscathed, a feat Huston attributes to the medicinal benefits of consuming countless bottles of imported Scotch. Eventually, cast and crew were losing so much time due to illness that the unit was moved to the less hostile climate of Uganda, where, except for some interiors and additional footage shot on a London sound stage, *The African Queen* was completed. Six years later, Huston returned to Africa to make *The Roots of Heaven,* a film whose production was plagued by even more illness and hardship.

Huston chose novelist-film critic James Agee, who had interviewed him for *Life* magazine, to collaborate on the screenplay. All but the ending was written prior to Huston's departure for Africa. Agee

Charlie (Humphrey Bogart) and Rosie (Katharine Hepburn) arm the makeshift torpedo with which they hope to send the Louisa sky high.

Charlie (Humphrey Bogart) finds his body covered with
leeches when he climbs back on board. The leeches are real,
as is Bogart's shivery reaction to them.

was set to join him there to complete the remaining scenes but suffered a heart attack and was replaced by Peter Viertel, who had collaborated on the script of Huston's *We Were Strangers*. Agee and Huston had allegedly planned for Rosie and Charlie to die at the end of the film, their mission to blow up the German gunship *Louisa* a failure. This ending was a departure from Forrester's book and apparently turned into a major bone of contention between Huston and Viertel, who wrote of the experience in his 1953 novel *White Hunter, Black Heart*, a thinly disguised roman á clef about the making of *The African Queen* in which a hard-hearted Hollywood director named John Wilson (Huston), who is making a love story set in Africa, decides to cynically end his film with the lovers getting killed, an ending he sees as a bow to art over commerce. Huston on the other hand maintains that he and Agee grew so fond of the characters as they were writing the script that they decided not only to let them live but to successfully carry out their destruction

Their plans go afoul with the weather and the Queen *begins to sink.*

of the *Louisa* due to what could be interpreted as an act of Divine Intervention. Huston's films up to this point had gained a reputation for being cynical and down-beat—a reputation not justified by close scrutiny of the films themselves, as I think I've clearly demonstrated. Killing off Rosie and Charlie would certainly have been a cynical tactic, but, more importantly, it would have been a devious one, for as the film and characters evolve everything seems aimed in an entirely different direction. If Huston had entertained such an idea, he could scarcely have been all that serious about it, for if, as a writer, he excells at one thing it is plot con-struction, and killing off Rosie and Charlie would have made little dramatic sense.

The film's theme is not about carrying out a mission—this, as in virtually all of Huston's work, is merely a motif—but about overcoming weaknesses and the urge to self-destruct. The *Louisa* is not the prize Charlie and Rosie are after. The real prize is each other. Their mutual realization of this is carefully developed and dramatically hammered home when, captured by the Germans and sentenced to be hanged as spies, Charlie requests that the ship's captain marry them. ''What a time we've had, Rosie,'' Charlie con-

fesses shortly before they reach the limits of their endurance. "We'll never lack for stories to tell our grandchildren." Killing them even at this point would have been less of a bow to art than a concession to fuzzy thinking. And Huston's thinking has never struck me as fuzzy.

Humphrey Bogart and Katharine Hepburn were Huston's first and only choices for the roles of the mis-matched lovers, and their engaging performances were surely one reason why *The African Queen* proved to be such a big hit with audiences and critics of the time, and why it remains today one of Huston's most popular and oft-screened works. The coincidental pairing of these two winning "innocents in Eden" was surely a match made in casting heaven, as Huston himself admits.

To give credibility to the part of the repressed, spinsterish Rosie Sayer, who learns from her adventures aboard the *Queen* that there is freedom and exhilaration to be found in the physical aspects of life as well as the spiritual, Hepburn patterned her performance and even the timber of her voice after Eleanor Roosevelt. Bogart, whom Hollywood tended to typecast mainly as a tough guy, demonstrated equal, and heretofore unknown, comic talents as the scrungy, fearful, but thoroughly warm-hearted Charlie. Both were nominated for Oscars for their work, though it was Bogart who scored the prize, a victory Huston lays to a particularly skin-crawling scene in the film where Charlie, having towed the *Queen* through some especially murky water, climbs back on board to find his body all covered with leeches. Bogart's shivery on-screen reaction to the clinging bloodsuckers is potently real—as are the leeches, which Huston imported and placed on the actor's skin to give the scene an extra dimension of toughness and truth. After Bogart won that year's Best Actor nod, Huston told him, "It's like I said, kid. Real leeches pay off."

Huston was also nominated for his work as director though he lost to George Stevens for *A Place in the Sun*. He and James Agee were likewise nominated for best screenplay adaptation, but Michael Wilson and Harry Brown copped that prize for *A Place in the Sun* as well.

Like many Huston films, *The African Queen* has been imitated many times since—even by Huston himself, whose *Heaven Knows, Mr. Allison* (1957) is a basic reworking of the same formula though to a different purpose. Dapper Cary Grant took a shot at playing an atypical, Charlie Alnutt-type role opposite Leslie Caron as a straight-laced schoolteacher in *Father Goose* (1964), but the film, directed by Ralph Nelson, was little more than a meandering string of maudlin clichés. And Katharine Hepburn herself teamed with John Wayne for a sort of "African Queen Goes West"

comic adventure called *Rooster Cogburn* (1975), a sequel to Wayne's Oscar winning *True Grit* (1969). But lightning seldom strikes twice and the chemistry sparked by Hepburn and Bogart in Huston's *The African Queen* has yet to be duplicated.

Moulin Rouge (1953)

A ROMULUS PRODUCTION
Released through United Artists
Technicolor/123 minutes

CREDITS:

Director: John Huston; *Producer:* John Huston; *Screenplay:* Anthony Veiller and John Huston, based on the novel *Moulin Rouge* by Pierre La Mure; *Cinematographer:* Oswald Morris; *Editor:* Ralph Kemplen; *Music:* Georges Auric; *Art Directors:* Paul Sheriff and Marcel Vertes; *Videocassette Source:* Not Available.

CAST:

Toulouse-Lautrec: José Ferrer; *Marie Charlet:* Colette Marchand; *Myriamme Hayen:* Suzanne Flon; *Jane Avril:* Zsa Zsa Gabor; *La Goulue:* Katherine Kath; *Countess Toulouse-Lautrec:* Claude Nollier; *Count Toulouse-Lautrec:* José Ferrer; *Aicha:* Muriel Smith; *Patov:* George Lannes; *Chocolate:* Rupert John; *Aicha's Partner:* Tutte Lemkow; *Bar Owner:* Eric Pohlmann; *Bartender:* Francis De Wolff; *Valentin le Désossé:* Walter Crisham; *Madame Loubet:* Mary Clare; *Maurice Joyant:* Lee Montague; *Georges Seurat:* Christopher Lee; *Marne de la Voisier:* Peter Cushing.

* * *

Contemporary Reviews

"...bizarre and colorful....Huston hired *Life* photographer Eliot Elisofon as a color consultant who steered away from the usual unsubtle Technicolor lighting....Sometimes he used a rainbow of spotlights, like paints on an artist's palette, to tint every shadow and highlight...."—*Life* Magazine

"...beautifully patterned compositions conveying sentiments, moods and atmosphere...the eyes are

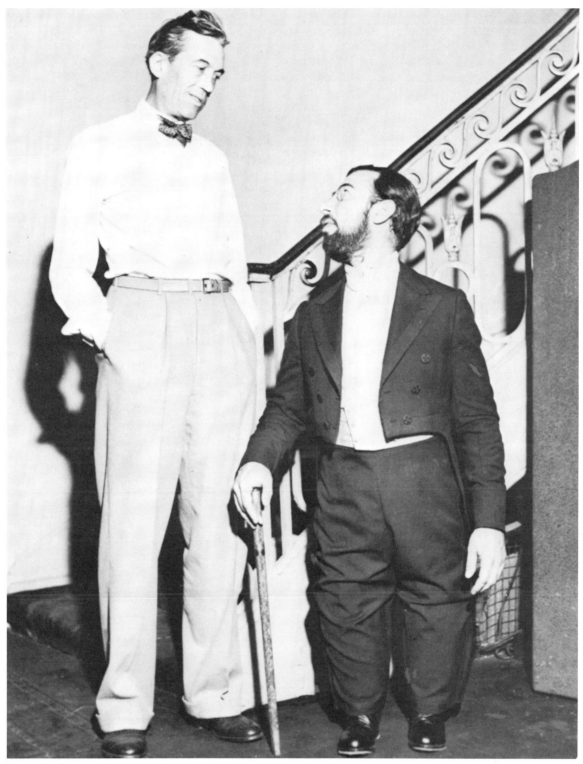

The lanky director with his 5' 10" star, José Ferrer, now transformed into the 4' 8'' Toulouse-Lautrec by means of special leg braces.

The Countess and Count Toulose-Lautrec (Claude Mollier and José Ferrer) present the bed-ridden Henri with bad tidings.

Myriamme Hayen (Suzanne Flon) offers Henri (José Ferrer) the key to her heart, as well as her apartment.

played upon with colors and forms and compositions in a pattern as calculated as a musical score…keyed, indeed, to the plot…."—*The New York Times*

"Pretty heavy going…reeks of sentimentalized invention….Yet it is irresistible in color."—*Newsweek*

* * *

A painter himself, Huston had long wanted to make a biopic about the life and work of an important artist. His own down-and-out years as a painter struggling to make ends meet on the streets of London and Paris often reminded him of the career of Henri de Toulouse-Lautrec, two of whose works he had purchased for his private collection. While completing *The African Queen* in London, he was fortuitously shown a copy of Pierre La Mure's *Moulin*

The despondent Henri (José Ferrer) demands another drink from bar owner Eric Pohlmann and bartender Francis De Wolff.

Rouge, a 1950 biographical novel about the life of the nineteenth-century artist, by producer James Woolf, who expressed an interest in turning the book into a film if the rights were available. Huston read the book and although he felt it to be a very romanticized account of Lautrec's life, its basic structure struck him as ideal for the kind of film he'd always had in mind. Not so much interested in the artist's life as in his work and the possibility of recreating some of Lautrec's most famous posters and paintings on the screen, he envisioned a scene in which Lautrec, dying in bed, sees not his life pass before him but a parade of the dancers and singers of the Moulin Rouge his work had celebrated. Ironically, this sequence would have echoes in Huston's own life when, lying in a hospital bed in 1981 suffering from advanced emphysema, he was visited by Michael Caine and Sean Connery, the two stars of his *The Man Who Would Be King* (1975), and he greeted them not as Mike and Sean, but as Peachy and Danny. "It was uncanny," Caine said of the experience. "He'd loved those damn characters so much, he'd lived with them in his head for so long."

The rights to La Mure's book turned out to be

owned by José Ferrer, the very actor Huston had selected to play the part of Lautrec. Ferrer had purchased the book with the aim of dramatizing it for the Broadway stage. Huston quickly convinced him that film was the more suitable medium and together with longtime friend and collaborator Anthony Veiller set about writing the screenplay. Though the Woolf brothers' Romulus Productions would bankroll the project, Huston decided to handle the producing chores himself.

Moulin Rouge also marked the beginning of Huston's long association with cinematographer Oswald Morris, with whom the director would make some of his best and most innovative films, including *Moby Dick* (1956). Early on he and Morris decided that in order to match the unusual look of Lautrec's paintings, the color photography of *Moulin Rouge* required special treatment. Together they devised a system of back-

Lautrec's concerned housekeeper and a friend try to awaken the besotted artist and help him up to bed.

lighting smoke-filled sets with colored filters in order to make the actors stand out from the background, as the figures do in Lautrec's work. They also employed the same colors the artist had used. Magazine photographer Eliot Elisofon was called in to act as a special consultant on this matter. Initial tests of the unusual color process prompted Technicolor to refuse to accept responsibility for the finished product, but the lab finally came around and eventually endorsed the look of the film as marvelous.

''*Moulin Rouge* broke every rule in the book,'' Morris told *Focus on Film* magazine in 1971. ''We colored the shadows and the filler lights for the various characters so that José Ferrer, who played Lautrec, always had a blue-green filter on his face and Colette Marchand, who played the part of the prostitute, a sort of purple-violet light which Lautrec had used in his paintings, while Suzanne Flon, who played a very honest, nice person, had a pink fill light. And with the colored smoke behind, this gave a most extraordinary effect. Half the time we didn't know where we were

going, but that was the gamble and we had a gambling director.'' Ironically, despite the fact that *Moulin Rouge* remains one of Huston's most breathtakingly photographed works, it failed to earn an Academy Award nomination that year for best color cinematography. It did, however, earn nominations for best picture, best actor (Ferrer), best direction, best art and set direction, as well as costume design. It only won in the last two categories.

For the 5' 10" Ferrer, the physical ordeal of playing the 4' 8" Lautrec proved quite painful. A special pair of leg braces with false shoes at the bottom was made into which the actor slipped his folded legs; this device enabled him to walk on his knees. After a half hour, however, the braces had to be removed and the actor's legs massaged to maintain proper circulation. Though Ferrer's performance was a tour-de-force that fully deserved its Oscar nomination, it does tend to strike only one or two notes of Lautrec's personality: anguish and bitterness. His legs stunted for life as the result of a childhood fall down the stairs of his parents' chateau, Lautrec remained angry and self-conscious over his dwarfish appearance to the end of his days. Huston and Ferrer present him as a supreme self-pitier except with regard to his work. He has a self-destructive affair with a prostitute, Marie Charlet, whom he allows to victimize him repeatedly, yet spurns the love of the elegant Myriamme Hayen on the grounds that her affection for him is only pity. Too late he realizes his mistake (Myriamme marries another) and proceeds to drink himself to death. When it comes to his work, however, Lautrec exudes self-confidence and inner strength, challenging his critics like a lion.

This is an important point, as *Moulin Rouge* has often been labelled one of Huston's most downbeat films. Yet this is hardly the case. Lautrec's greatness as an artist is what prompted Huston to make the film in the first place, for he saw in Lautrec's unwavering commitment to painting The Truth as the artist saw it a message of great courage. Whether Lautrec was, in fact, the lugubrious, alcoholic loser in his private life that the film presents him as is scarcely important, for Huston never intended to deal with Lautrec's sometimes scandalous personal life realistically, as the screen censors of the day wouldn't have permitted it. Somewhat in the manner of a Ken Russell biopic, he focussed instead on what he perceived to be the essential dichotomy of the man's character so that what emerged was yet another variation of the Huston hero, a man in self-conflict who loses one battle (with himself) while winning another (artistic greatness).

Huston's Lautrec is a man who defeats himself in his personal life—apart from his physical handicap, he brings on all his own bad luck—yet prevails as an artist because professionally he refuses to accept or even acknowledge defeat. Lautrec the man wears blinders whereas Lautrec the artist takes them off. As a result, Huston's tendency to let the vibrancy and honesty of Lautrec's art dominate the screen takes on added meaning. Rather than a necessity, this visual emphasis on the glory of Lautrec the painter becomes the film's central point. And the concluding death bed fantasy a significant coda.

Beat the Devil (1954)

A ROMULUS-SANTANA PRODUCTION
Released through United Artists
B&W/89 minutes

CREDITS:

Director: John Huston; *Producers:* John Huston and Humphrey Bogart; *Screenplay:* John Huston and Truman Capote, based on the novel *Beat the Devil* by James Helvick; *Cinematographer:* Oswald Morris; *Editor:* Ralph Kemplen; *Music:* Franco Mannino; *Art Director:* Wilfred Shingleton; *Videocassette Source:* RCA/Columbia Home Vidio.

CAST:

Billy Dannreuther: Humphrey Bogart; *Maria Dannreuther:* Gina Lollobrigida; *Gwendolyn Chelm:* Jennifer Jones; *Peterson:* Robert Morley; *O'Hara:* Peter Lorre; *Harry Chelm:* Edward Underdown; *Major Ross:* Ivor Barnard; *Ravello:* Marco Tulli.

* * *

Contemporary Reviews

''*Beat the Devil,* if it is any one thing at all, is as elaborate a shaggy-dog story as has ever been told. It was made up by author Truman Capote and director John Huston during the spring season last year at Ravello, on the Gulf of Sorrento, apparently by stirring Strega fumes slowly into a novel by James Helvick. Because Huston happened to have $1,000,000 and several talented actors at his disposal, everybody fell to and turned the bibble-babble into a movie....Surprisingly, *Beat the*

Devil turns out to be a sort of screwball classic."—*Time* magazine

"*Beat the Devil* is a John Huston film which tries hard to be a comic, frothy *Maltese Falcon,* and almost succeeds. The *Falcon* set a standard for criminal fantasy and excitement which the new film scarcely meets in comedy."—*Newsweek*

"...a pointedly roguish and conversational spoof, generally missing the book's bite, bounce and decidedly snug construction."—*The New York Times*

* * *

Dannreuther (Humphrey Bogart) finds himself irresistibly drawn to the wistful Gwendolyn (Jennifer Jones), who launches into every lie and flight of fancy with the phrase, "In point of fact."

Star and co-producer Humphrey Bogart called *Beat the Devil* "a mess," audiences were bewildered by it, and contemporary reviewers were evenly divided as to whether the film was a comic gem or a private joke that failed to come off. In any case, *Beat the Devil* was a resounding box office flop that all but disappeared from view until it was resurrected in the early sixties by college film societies for whom Bogart had become a sort of existential hero. Quickly heralded as a cult masterpiece, it sustains that reputation today.

Bogart's Santana Productions had purchased the property, a straight-faced but improbable thriller by James Helvick (the pseudonym of British journalist Claude Cockburn), at Huston's request. Helvick, a friend of Huston's, needed money at the time and the director believed he could turn the book into a film "somehow." As with Stanley Kubrick's *Dr. Strangelove*, however, Huston discovered

The Dannreuthers (Humphrey Bogart and Gina Lollobrigida) find their marriage a bit strained when he falls for Gwendolyn and she falls for Harry (Edward Underdown), right.

early on that the sobriety of the material lent itself more to spoofery than thrills, and, together with co-writer Truman Capote, set about revising the story with that aim in mind even as shooting began. "As it turned out," Capote said later, "I was rarely two or three days ahead of the shooting schedule with my scenes."

In transforming the material from drama to comedy, Huston went one step further and opted not only to spoof the thriller genre at large but his own contributions to that genre in particular. While these nuances apparently went over the heads of most audiences, critics quickly perceived and enjoyed the film's many comic references to Huston's

The Maltese Falcon. Jennifer Jones' breathless Gwendolyn, for example, is a blonde Brigid O'Shaughnessy, who launches into every fanciful lie with the tee-up phrase, "In point of fact." And Robert Morley's portly villain, Peterson, whom Bogart refers to as "Fatgut," is a comic amalgam of Sydney Greenstreet's fatman, Kaspar Gutman. But Huston's self-parody extended far beyond *Falcon,* for the film is shot through with amusing references not only to that film, but to *Across the Pacific, Key Largo, The Asphalt Jungle,* and even *The Treasure of the Sierra Madre*—except that in *Beat the Devil,* it is Bogart who is left laughing at the film's ironic conclusion.

Such as it exists, the plot centers on the efforts of four "desperate characters" (O'Hara, Peterson, Ravello, Major Ross) to buy some uranium-rich land in British-owned East Africa, aided by the once high-flying but now broke Dannreuther, who has

99

With two women in his life, no wonder Dannreuther (Humphrey Bogart) looks perplexed and worried. Of course, it could also be over the film's script, which Huston and writer Truman Capote were making up as they went along.

Gwendolyn (Jennifer Jones) launches into another flight of fancy in Huston's delightful comic caper, Beat the Devil.

the savvy and the government contacts needed to successfully pull off the scam. While waiting for a steamer to take them to Africa, the group encounters the Chelms, a mysterious British couple who appear to be wealthy landed gentry bound for Africa to visit their coffee plantation. Dannreuther falls for Chelm's capricious, over-imaginative wife, Gwendolyn, while his own wife, Maria, a voluptuous Anglophile, falls for Chelm himself.

Dannreuther's confederates, thinking the Chelms have money, try to enlist them in the scheme, but the stuffy Chelm refuses and threatens to turn them over to the authorities once they reach Africa. Midway in the journey, their broken down steamer malfunctions and starts to sink. All but the ship's crew and Chelm abandon ship and Chelm is subsequently thought to have drowned. Dannreuther and the others reach shore and are captured by Arabs, whose suspicious chieftain (Manuel Serano) arrests them all as spies. Peterson tries to convince him that they are innocent vacuum cleaner salesmen, but the Arab is no fool ("Hut to hut, I suppose?" he challenges sarcastically) and threatens to execute them. A fan of Rita Hayworth, however, who fancies himself the next Ali Kahn, the chieftain befriends the glib Dannreuther, who insists that he knows Rita and can introduce the two, and agrees to let them return to Italy. There, Gwendolyn receives a cable from her husband stating that he survived his

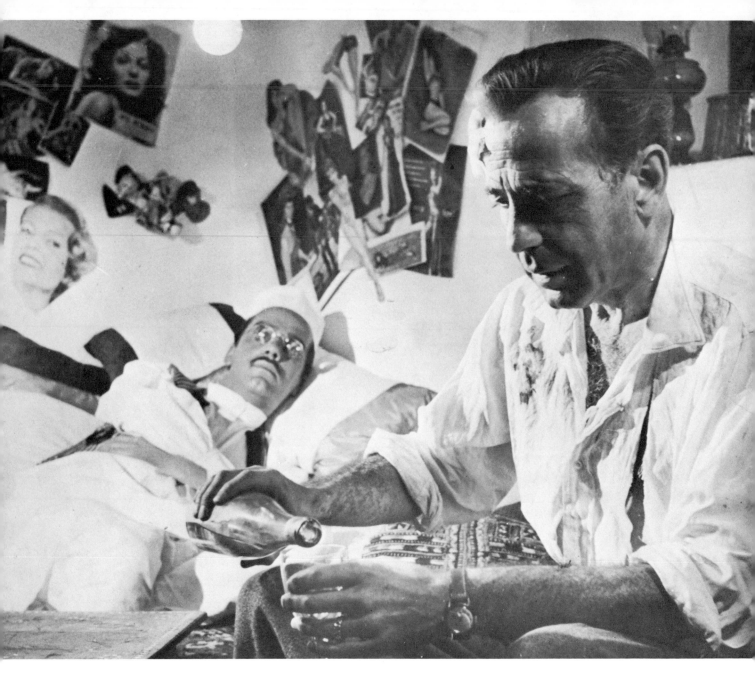

Dannreuther (Humphrey Bogart) turns the group's desperate situation around by pretending to know Rita Hayworth and assuring the smitten Arab chieftain (Manuel Serano) that he'll introduce him to her.

ordeal at sea, safely reached East Africa, bought the land himself and is now making a fortune in uranium. As Dannreuther reads the cable, he breaks out laughing at the irony of it all and announces, "This is *the end!*" Which it is. Fade to black.

Huston and Capote virtually made the film up as they went along, a fact that they even acknowledge on screen. As the steamer is sinking and Gwendolyn hysterically questions their chances of survival, Dannreuther amusingly replies, "I don't know if we will, but it's possible. *Anything's possible!*"

What might have emerged from this method of working as mere patchwork, however, emerged instead a delight, a Huston black comedy of deceit and bad manners whose devil-may-care style and cast of eccentric characters foreshadowed such later Huston films in a similar vein as *Sinful Davey* (1969), *The Life and Times of Judge Roy Bean* (1972), and, especially, *Prizzi's Honor* (1985), the only one of the four to achieve success at the box office (apparently audiences finally caught on to the joke).

In addition to his ideally cast comic leads, who obviously had a ball with their roles ("My name is O'Hara!" Lorre keeps insisting. "Julius O'Hara, from Chile, where many Germans are named O'Hara!"), Huston rounds out the film with an equally amusing and even more eccentric bunch of peripheral characters. These include the constantly drunk ship's captain who is given to screaming every order at the top of his lungs (we don't always see him, but we always hear him); the broadly fascist Major Ross; and the ship's unflappable purser (Mario Perroni), whose imperturbability in the face of every disaster at one point brings an unwitting smile to Bogart's lips that Huston caught on camera and decided to leave in. All this, plus Capote's very witty lines of dialogue—the film demands several viewings just to take them all in—add immeasurably to the fun. Ahead of its time in 1954, the experimental, offbeat, and frequently hilarious *Beat the Devil* may have been a creative gamble that the director originally lost, but has today resoundingly won.

Moby Dick (1956)

A MOULIN PICTURE
Released through Warner Brothers
Technicolor/116 minutes

CREDITS:

Director: John Huston: *Producers:* John Huston and Vaughan Dean; *Screenplay:* Ray Bradbury and John Huston, from the novel *Moby Dick* by Herman Melville; *Cinematographer:* Oswald Morris; *Editor:* Russell Lloyd; *Music:* Philip Sainton; *Art Director:* Ralph Brinton; *Videocassette Source:* CBS/Fox Home Video.

CAST:

Captain Ahab: Gregory Peck; *Ishmael:* Richard Basehart; *Father Mapple:* Orson Welles; *Starbuck:* Leo Genn; *Stubb:* Harry Andrews; *Flask:* Seamus Kelly; *Queequeg:* Friedrich Ledebur; *Manxman:* Bernard Miles; *Peleg:* Mervyn Johns; *Ship's Carpenter:* Noel Purcell; *Captain Boomer:* James Robertson Justic; *Elijah:* Rayal Dano; *Daggoo:* Edric Conner; *Tashtego:* Tom Clegg; *Bildad:* Philip Stainton; *Captain Gardner:* Francis De Wolff.

* * *

Contemporary Reviews

"Herman Melville's famous story of a man's dark obsession to kill a whale, told with tremendous range and rhetoric in his great novel, *Moby Dick,* has been put on the screen by John Huston in a rolling and thundering color film that is herewith devoutly recommended as one of the great motion pictures of our time. Space does not possibly permit us to cite all the things about this film that are brilliantly done or developed, from the strange, subdued color scheme employed to the uncommon faithfulness to details of whaling that are observed. This is the third time Melville's story has been put upon the screen. There is no need for another, because it cannot be done better, more beautifully, or excitingly again."—*The New York Times*

"Director John Huston set himself an enormous task: to bring to the screen the truth as well as the thrills that Herman Melville poured into his complex masterpiece. What emerges is a brilliant film both for Melville enthusiasts and for those who have tried to read the book and lost their way in the labyrinth of philosophical asides, historical reflections, cetology, and archaicisms."—*Time* magazine

"Peck's make-up for his role is expert, but the force needed for conviction is seldom present."—*Saturday Review*

* * *

Moby Dick was another long-cherished Huston project, and a very personal one. He'd first hoped to make it at Warner Bros. as a vehicle for his father after *The Treasure of the Sierra Madre.* Warners, which had made two earlier versions of the Melville saga — *The Sea Beast* (1926) and the early talkie *Moby Dick* (1930), both starring John Barrymore as Ahab—owned the remake rights, but prior Huston commitments and the unexpected death of his father cast the project into limbo.

After his move to Ireland in 1953, Huston reactivated the project. Coincidentally, his friend Orson Welles was also planning to bring his vision of the Melville tale to the screen at this same time. He bowed out, however, when he learned that Warners and Huston had the property tied up and instead adapted *Moby Dick* for the stage, starring himself as Ahab. The drama premiered in London in 1955; Welles later recorded a performance of the play for airing on American television, but the telefilm never debuted. In addition to Welles, the telefilm starred Patrick McGoohan, Kenneth Williams, John Plowright, and Christopher Lee.

Welles's ties to a big screen version of *Moby Dick* came full circle, however, when Huston signed him for

Director Huston helps Gregory Peck achieve the windblown look on location in Ireland for Moby Dick.

Father Mapple's (Orson Welles) sermon on God's beneficence contrasts mightily with Ahab's dark view of a malevolent Deity.

The Pequod's *chief harpooneers, Queequeg (Friedrich Ledebur), Tashtego (Tom Clegg) and Daggoo (Edric Conner), prepare for action.*

the small but important role of the New Bedford preacher, Father Mapple, which Welles brought off brilliantly in a single take.

Though Huston had worked on an adaptation of Melville's book some years before, he chose science-fiction writer Ray Bradbury to collaborate with him on a brand new screenplay, which he and Bradbury developed together at Huston's Irish estate. The film was to be photographed in England and Ireland with location footage shot at sea off the coast of Madeira. Second unit footage of Portuguese fishermen hunting whales in vulnerable longboats with hand-hurled harpoons was shot by assistant cameraman Freddie Francis under Huston's supervision to lend the film excitement and authenticity.

Typically, Huston chose to cast the film's supporting roles with unfamiliar faces—character actors, unknowns, and even amateurs. British actor Leo Genn, who'd played opposite Olivia de Havilland in the smash hit *The Snake Pit* (1948), was cast as the stalwart Quaker Starbuck, first mate of the doomed *Pequod*. Harry Andrews, another experienced British character actor, was selected for the part of Stubb, the hearty, practical-joking third mate, while Dublin drama critic Seamus Kelly, a non-professional, was cast as second mate Flask. For the role of the tattooed harpooneer, Queequeg, a former South Sea island cannibal, Huston iconoclastically chose another amateur, his close friend Count Friedrich Ledebur, an Austrian sportsman and playboy. Lord Kilbracken, another close Huston friend and screen novice, was initially selected to play Ishmael, the *Pequod's* sole survivor, but Huston later opted for the more experienced Richard Basehart instead.

Before agreeing to bankroll the multi-million dollar project, Warners insisted that a major star was needed for the key role of Captain Ahab, a role which some insiders say Huston really wanted to play himself. Gregory Peck, whose heroic screen image made him a seemingly odd choice, was approached by Huston, and the actor quickly agreed.

105

Convinced he is going to die, Queequeg (Friedrich Ledebur) instructs the ship's carpenter (Noel Purcell) to build him a coffin as Ishmael (Richard Basehart) looks on in consternation.

Though the film received mainly favorable reviews upon its release, and won some awards as well, Peck was almost universally singled out as a poor choice for the complex and demanding role of Ahab, which many critics felt was beyond the actor's range. To this day, Huston disagrees, insisting that Peck's stoicism and subtly revealed feelings of self-conflict and derangement were precisely right. I must admit that I quite agree. Like most Huston adaptations, *Moby Dick* was intended to be true to the spirit of its source but not a literal transcription of it. Peck's characterization of Ahab is a good case in point. Melville's fanatically self-assured, cunning and Godless hero seldom registers the nagging sense of inner conflict that is typical of the Huston hero, but Peck's Ahab does. He is truly a man who lives under a dark cloud emanating from his own spirit that succeeds in dragging him and his ship's crew to doom.

Huston frequently cites Peck's delivery of the "mild, mild day" speech near the conclusion of the film as an example of the actor's ability. "I can't imagine [the speech] being better spoken by any actor," he says. While I concur that Peck brings the speech off brilliantly, I think the earlier "chart scene" in Ahab's cabin is an even better example of the actor's versatility and deft handling of the role because of the complex and sometimes subtle range of mood swings to which the character is subjected. Awakened by Starbuck from a tormenting dream, Ahab switches from moroseness to obsessive fervor as he reveals his chart of whale migrations to another person for the first time. Starbuck is duly awed, but when he comes to realize the chart's real purpose, he upbraids the Captain for seeking nothing but revenge. At first the mate's words stir Ahab to anger, then cold resolve. "It will fetch me a great premium. *Here!*" Ahab responds chillingly as he taps his heart. In terms of staging, lighting and performance, this ranks as one of the most powerfully executed and memorable scenes in the entire movie. It is also a very key scene in which Peck remains the focal

Ahab (Gregory Peck) binds the crew to him and makes them swear an oath to hunt down and kill the white whale.

point throughout. Not only is his performance convincing, it's almost hypnotic.

As with *Moulin Rouge*— and, later, *Reflections in a Golden Eye*—Huston and cinematographer Oswald Morris sought to give the film a special look. "I wanted the final print to have the strength found in steel engravings of sailing ships," Huston said at the time. To do so, he and Morris reversed the approach they'd taken with *Moulin Rouge* by attempting to desaturate rather than enrich the film's colors. "It was a period film and modern colors gave it a veneer, a gloss, which was completely bogus," Morris explains. "You could not believe these whaling men were really suffering in those boats because the colors were too lush and glossy. So we evolved a system of desaturation…but we found that it desaturated the blacks and it became wishywashy and anemic and not masculine—and it was a very masculine picture—so to reinforce the black we added a grey image [black and white] onto the desaturated colors and that brought the contrast back without bringing in the colors." The effect of this new technique on the big screen was quite striking, though

not nearly so discernible today on the 16mm prints now circulating on television. Complemented by Philip Sainton's primarily brass and woodwind score, the film fully achieved the hard-edge look and feel of an engraving that the director had sought. History repeated itself come Oscar time, however, when the Academy's nominating committee once again chose to ignore Morris (and Huston) for his ingenuity.

Requiring equal ingenuity were the film's many elaborate special effects. Huston's expensive, electronically controlled Great White Whale was a 92-foot long rubber model that weighed several tons. Three of the leviathans were built just in case one of them got lost at sea during one of the many storms Huston and his crew had to shoot through. As it turned out, one of them did break loose and drifted all the way to the coast of Holland. For in-studio tank shots, twenty additional electronic mini-Mobys were built that could variously breach, crunch whaling boats as well as bleed and roll dead out when harpooned. These sequences were also shot by assistant cameraman Freddie Francis. Several individual sections of the giant whale were also built for specific close-up sequences such as the finale where Ahab lashes himself to the side of the beast and is drowned—a fate that almost befell

Starbuck (Leo Genn) attempts to cut the sails before the ship capsizes in the storm, but Ahab (Gregory Peck) threatens to run him through if he does.

Ahab (Gregory Peck) goes to his death lashed to the side of Moby Dick.

Gregory Peck as well when the submerged section refused to come back up for almost a minute due to a technical malfunction. The matching of the effects shots with the actual whaling footage shot on location is brought off with great skill. As is the final confrontation where Moby Dick lays waste to the Pequod and her crew. The scene is surely one of the best action sequences Huston has ever staged.

Though it was a box office success, *Moby Dick* remains one of Huston's most underrated films. The New York Film Critics and National Board of Review did vote Huston the year's best director, but at the 1956 Academy Awards the film failed to earn a single nomination. Huston, however, has always rated the film one of his best, which indeed it is. Yet he also confesses certain reservations about it. "Translating a work of this scope into a screenplay was a staggering proposition," he writes in his autobiography. "Looking back now, I wonder if it is possible to do justice to *Moby Dick* on film." Huston's remarks, though honest, are also too humble, for it is doubtful that anyone will ever come closer to achieving that aim than he has here. *Moby Dick,* is not only a whale of an adventure movie, but a film of character and ideas that stirs the mind as well as the eye.

Heaven Knows, Mr. Allison (1957)

A 20th CENTURY-FOX PRODUCTION
DeLuxe Color/107 minutes

CREDITS:

Director: John Huston; *Producers:* Buddy Adler and Eugene Frenke; *Screenplay:* John Lee Mahin and John Huston, based on the novel *Heaven Knows, Mr. Allison* by Charles Shaw; *Cinematographer:* Oswald Morris; *Editor:* Russell Lloyd; *Music:* Georges Auric; *Art Director:* Stephen Grimes; *Videocassette Source:* Not Available.

CAST:

Mr. Allison: Robert Mitchum; *Sister Angela:* Deborah Kerr

* * *

Contemporary Reviews

"That frequent and often popular story of a pious woman and an impious man cast together in circumstances that test the righteousness and fiber of each is tackled again by John Huston (he tackled it last in *The African Queen*)....And once more, as with that previous picture, Mr. Huston comes up with a film that is stirring and entertaining."—*The New York Times*

"Cinemascope and censorship effectively destroyed its chances for distinction. The film is nonetheless good entertainment, technically competent, and perceptive in the characterizations of Mitchum and Deborah Kerr."—*Films and Filming*

* * *

The screen rights to *Heaven Knows, Mr. Allison*, Charles Shaw's two character novel about the relationship between a U.S. marine and a nun stranded on a Pacific island held by the Japanese during World War II, were first offered to director William Wyler. Adapting the novel to the screeen proved a sticky situation, however, for in Shaw's book the marine and the nun gradually fall in love, a conclusion Wyler knew would never pass muster with the Catholic Church's film censoring body, The Legion of Decency. To avoid a confrontation with the Church, whose denunciation of the film would almost certainly hinder its chances of success at the box office, Wyler and his writers altered the ending of the story by revealing that the nun was not a nun at all, but a woman who has disguised herself as one for protection against the Japanese. Though Wyler's script did receive the Church's endorsement, the director moved on to another project, and the property languished on 20th Century-Fox's shelf for five years until John Huston was approached with the idea of making the film instead.

Huston considered the solution Wyler and his writers had come up with to be a bogus one, however, and insisted not only that Sister Angela turn out to be a real nun, but that she remain true to her calling by rejecting the marine in favor of her higher commitment to God. He saw in the project a variation on *The African Queen*, where two basically incompatible people had come together under unusual and trying circumstances, drawn strength and courage from one another, and eventually fallen in love. In the new film, however, the two characters would not fall in love, but rather draw from each other the courage to overcome despair and self-doubt and pursue their separate destinies with renewed strength and conviction. "These people are too incompatible," Huston told Jack Vizzard, the Motion Picture Production Code advisor assigned to oversee the film's shooting. "Had

Stranded on a Japanese-held island, Allison (Robert Mitchum) finds a cross in the ruins of a bombed out mission.

Sister Angela (Deborah Kerr) and Allison (Robert Mitchum) set up housekeeping (of sorts) in the cave where they're hiding out from the Japanese.

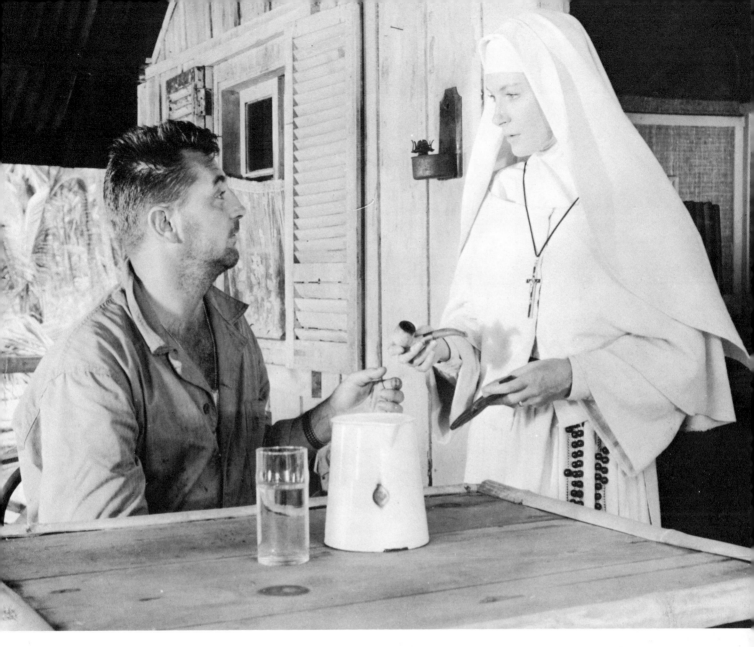

Sister Angela (Deborah Kerr) presents Allison (Robert Mitchum) with a gift.

they met in the normal course of life, there would have been nothing in common between them. It is unsuitable to imagine them coming together, even in these exceptional circumstances."

Huston's decision created a fundamental problem, however, by returning the project to square one with the Legion of Decency, whose influence over Roman Catholic filmgoers had grown considerably over the years. The Legion had recently made headlines by condemning Elia Kazan's controversial *Baby Doll* (1956) as immoral. The film had been denounced from pulpits coast to coast, and Roman Catholics had rejected it in droves. Huston did not want this situation to be repeated with *Heaven Knows, Mr. Allison,* a story

he viewed not as an opportunity for exploitation, but as a testament to faith and inner strength. The marine and the nun are wedded to different courses in life, a bond that each would see as being stronger than the one they hold for each other. That was the point Huston wanted the film to make and he was not to be dissuaded. Still, before the two characters could come to their separate realizations, there had to be conflict between them, otherwise there would be no film. In reviewing the script Huston and John Lee Mahin had prepared, Monsignor Devlin of the Legion of Decency assessed this conflict as "oozing with sex," however, and requested, indeed insisted, on substantial revisions, a situation that rankled Huston, who did not cotton to interference from non-studio sources and saw in it shades of a new kind of McCarthyism that wasn't just political in tone, but religious as well. "That's not right,

111

Sister Angela (Deborah Kerr) accompanies Allison on a sea-going search for food. He has just been pulled overboard by a huge tortoise.

Sister Angela (Deborah Kerr) and Allison (Robert Mitchum) hear the sound of enemy planes overhead.

not in a democratic society," he told Jack Vizzard on location in Tobago. Nevertheless, he bent over backwards to avoid a confrontation with the monsignor by making minor changes in the script even as the film was being shot.

The irony of all this was that Huston and Monsignor Devlin were basically on the same side. The director was not out to titillate his audience but to uplift it with an entertaining and believable yarn about two likable people from very different walks of life who are thrown together by war and help each other to survive. From the very beginning, Huston's attitude toward Sister Angela was inviolate, and quite romantic. According to Jack Vizzard, the director felt that, "...she had given her heart to her Beloved, and it was once and for all as far as he [Huston] was concerned." Huston saw nothing censorable in his approach to the material and was invariably surprised, as well as infuriated, when Monsignor Devlin did. One such instance involved a scene where a Japanese plane makes a reconnaissance pass over the island, and Allison, fearing that Sister Angela will be spotted and strafed, makes a sudden dive for her, covering her with his body. The Monsignor rejected this implication of bodily contact, however, and Huston was compelled to alter the scene by having the fast-thinking Allison cover her with palm fronds instead.

Despite these seemingly endless arguments over nuances, shooting of *Heaven Knows, Mr. Allison* proceeded fairly smoothly— for a Huston film, that is. And in the end all parties agreed that the film had been made with great sensitivity. The Catholic Church even went so far as to endorse it with its highest audience rating, an A-1 classification. Deborah Kerr was nominated for an Academy Award for her performance as Sister Angela, but she lost to Joanne Woodward in *The Three Faces of Eve* (1957). John Huston and John Lee Mahin were likewise nominated for their screenplay, but they too lost—to Pierre Boulle for *The Bridge on the River Kwai*.

Heaven Knows, Mr. Allison also went on to become one of Huston's biggest moneymakers, proving almost as popular with filmgoers all over the world as *The African Queen* had been. Huston too ranks it high on his list. "*Allison* is seldom referred to," he says. "But I think it was one of the best things I ever made."

* * *

The Barbarian and the Geisha (1958)

A 20th CENTURY-FOX PRODUCTION
DeLuxe Color/105 minutes

CREDITS:

Director: John Huston; *Producer:* Eugene Frenke; *Screenplay:* Charles Grayson; *Cinematographer:* Charles G. Clarke; *Editor:* Stuart Gilmore; *Music:* Hugo Friedhofer; *Art Directors:* Lyle Wheeler, Jack Martin Smith and Walter M. Scott; *Videocassette Source:* Not Available.

CAST:

Townsend Harris: John Wayne; *Okichi:* Eiko Ando; *Henry Heusken:* Sam Jaffe; *Tamuro:* So Yamamamura; *Captain:* Norman Thomson; *Lieutenant Fisher:* James Robbins; *Prime Minister:* Morika; *Daimyo:* Kodaya Ichikawa; *The Shogun:* Hiroshi Yamato; *Harusha:* Tokujiro Iketaniuichi; *Lord Hotta:* Fuju Kasai; *Chamberlain:* Takeshi Kumagai.

* * *

Contemporary Reviews

"...if you can go to it without expecting anything of what a Huston picture once was, you can see some exquisite color photography of Japan. There are sequences in it that are as lovely as any color film I have seen since the Japanese *Gate of Hell* and for the same reason: the scenery and the clothes are beautiful. But what a reason for commending a Huston film!"— *The New Republic*

"...an hour-and-three-quarter film in color that is just about as lovely to look at as any we have ever seen."—*The New York Times*

"This is an unusually beautiful film, directed with spirit and remarkable taste by John Huston, absolutely undaunted by his uninspiring plot material."—*Saturday Review*

John Wayne as the ''barbarian'' of the title, Townsend Harris, American diplomat and adventurer.

Sam Jaffe, as Harris' sidekick (and translator), Henry Heusken, experiences some local color.

Eiko Ando as the Geisha, who has been sent to spy on Harris, but falls in love with him instead.

Unlike many directors of the current generation, John Huston has seldom been inspired to make a film because of another film. His influences remain primarily literary, which is why so many of his films are adaptations. There are exceptions to this, of course. *Moulin Rouge* grew out of his love of the paintings of Toulouse-Lautrec and his desire to recreate them in another medium. The book the film was based on, indeed the story of Lautrec himself, was almost secondary. Likewise, *The Barbarian and the Geisha* appealed to the painter in him as well. Struck by the dazzling visual qualities of the colorful Japanese film *Gate of Hell* (1954), he decided to have a go at making a pictorially beautiful, Japanese-located film himself. Again, the story to be told was almost secondary. For it he chose an obscure but important incident in American history, the negotiating and signing of the first

Japanese-American trade treaty in 1855, a treaty that irrevocably opened the feudal doors of Japan to the influences of the West.

The man who negotiated the treaty was Townsend Harris, an adventurous but rather stolid American diplomat about whom little was known. The film's screenplay by Charles Grayson was therefore largely fiction, though the film's original title, *The Townsend Harris Story*, suggested otherwise. In the film, Harris, accompanied by his translator, Henry Heusken, arrives in Japan and boldly requests a meeting with the Shogun to arrange a treaty between their two countries. Suspicious of all foreigners, not just Americans, the Shogun denies the request and forces Harris to cool his heels for a time. Meanwhile, the Shogun arranges for a beautiful Geisha to move in with Harris and spy on him. Ultimately, she is forced to take part in an assassination plot against the diplomat, but by this time she has fallen in love with him and so commits suicide rather than harm her lover. The treaty

Harris (John Wayne) orders a Japanese village burned to the ground to halt the spread of plague.

is eventually signed, but not before Harris has incurred the wrath of his suspicious Japanese benefactors by burning one of their villages to the ground in order to stop the spread of cholera.

The Barbarian and the Geisha boasted another of director Huston's iconoclastic casting choices. Though the film is not devoid of action, it is mainly about Harris's experiences as a stranger in a strange land as he waits in frustration for his audience with the Shogun. For the role of the stalled hero, Huston selected action star John Wayne. There were other reasons for the choice, of course, not the least of them being symbolic. "I want to send Duke's gigantic form into this exotic world that was the Japanese empire in the 1800s," Huston told the press. "Imagine!—this massive figure, with his bluff innocence and naîveté,

with his rough edges, moving among these minute people. Who better to symbolize the big, awkward United States of 100 years ago?" Though certainly inspired (Wayne is visually perfect and quite effective in the atypical role), the choice proved to be a disastrous mistake in terms of audience response. Seeing Wayne's name in the credits, filmgoers expected the film to be full of thundering excitement, which *The Barbarian and the Geisha* is definitely not. For this and other reasons, perhaps, the film was not a box office success.

Huston's selection of John Wayne proved ill-advised in other ways, for even as shooting began it quickly became obvious that the director and his star didn't see eye-to-eye. Wayne, who was used to the "shoot it and print it" styles of directors like John Ford, John Farrow, and others, felt Huston's pace was too slow and his attention to visual details, which Wayne considered irrelevant, to be almost an obsession. He later termed Huston's directorial repu-

116

Harris (John Wayne) finally gets his audience with the Shogun.

tation "overrated." For his part, Huston simply admits that between him and the late star there was just "...no great meeting of souls."

Though *The Townsend Harris Story* could scarcely be considered a title guaranteed to ensure a box office draw, *The Barbarian and the Geisha*, which Fox renamed the film midway through shooting, was felt by Huston to be too exploitative and downright horrible. He still feels that way. Frankly, it does sound more like the title of a Samuel Fuller film (*House of Bamboo, the Crimson Kimono*) than a John Huston one. But the sudden name change was not the only thing that rankled. After Huston had delivered his director's cut, the studio (at Wayne's insistence, Huston maintains) re-edited the film, eliminating some scenes while adding and re-shooting others, until the film no longer resembled the one Huston had made. "When I finally saw it, I was aghast," Huston says. For awhile, he even considered a lawsuit to have his name removed from the film's credits, but gave up the idea out of deference

to the film's co-producer, Buddy Adler, who was critically ill at the time.

It would be interesting to view Huston's original cut of the film (if it exists), for even in its present form, *The Barbarian and the Geisha* is not nearly so bad as Huston and most critics allege. Though certainly problematic, it does rank as one of the director's top five most stunningly photographed works, which, in terms of visual beauty, rivals the Japanese *Gate of Hell* that inspired it. As this was the main goal Huston had set for himself and his cameraman, Charles Clarke, in the first place, their achievement can hardly be considered a failure.

Once again, though, the Academy of Motion Picture Arts and Sciences chose to ignore the colorful fruits of yet another Huston pictorial experiment. Not only did *The Barbarian and the Geisha* fail to win the 1958 Oscar for Best Cinematography, it wasn't even nominated.

117

The Roots of Heaven (1958)

A 20th CENTURY-FOX PRODUCTION
DeLuxe Color/131 minutes

CREDITS:

Director: John Huston; *Producer:* Darryl F. Zanuck; *Screenplay:* Romain Gary and Patrick Leigh-Fermor, based on the novel *The Roots of Heaven* by Romain Gary; *Cinematographer:* Oswald Morris; *Editor:* Russell Lloyd; *Music:* Malcolm Arnold; *Art Director:* Stephen Grimes; *Videocassette Source:* Not Available.

CAST:

Forsythe: Errol Flynn; *Morel:* Trevor Howard; *Minna:* Juliette Greco; *Abe Fields:* Eddie Albert; *Cy Sedgewick:* Orson Welles; *Saint Denis:* Paul Lukas; *Orsini:* Herbert Lom; *Habib:* Gregoire Aslan; *Peter Qvist:* Friedrich Ledebur; *Waitari:* Edric Conner.

* * *

Contemporary Reviews

''The primary count against Huston is that he consented to direct this clumsy, overlong script. Its

Juliette Greco as the concentration camp survivor who joins Morel's (Trevor Howard) quest because it has awakened her spirit . . . with Friedrich Ledebur as the Dutch naturalist, Peter Qvist, who joins Morel for ecological reasons.

The mercenary Forsythe (Errol Flynn) listens as Morel (Trevor Howard) simmers down an African soldier.

major errors of flatulence and muddy, mechanical switches of motivation are accompanied by numerous small flaws, such as the line 'I don't know why I'm telling you all this' and three arbitrarily inserted disrobings of Juliette Greco. The Huston who did *Sierra Madre* would have lighted his cigar with this script."—*The New Republic*

"Maybe some sort of allegory was intended to run through this film. Maybe the elephant lover was meant to be a modern Messiah, followed by feeble disciples and a Mary Magdalene. If so, the symbols are flimsy and the ideas are never firmed. There is no real dramatic implication, except that the elephant's jig is up."—*The New York Times*

* * *

To complete his three picture contract with 20th Century-Fox, Huston chose for his next film author-diplomat (and future film director) Romain Gary's prize-winning environmentalist novel *The Roots of Heaven*, the story of an enigmatic Frenchman's quest to stop the wholesale slaughter of African elephants by greedy ivory hunters. The Frenchman's idealistic mission, and frequent use of force to carry it off, soon attracts the attention of the world press, plus

119

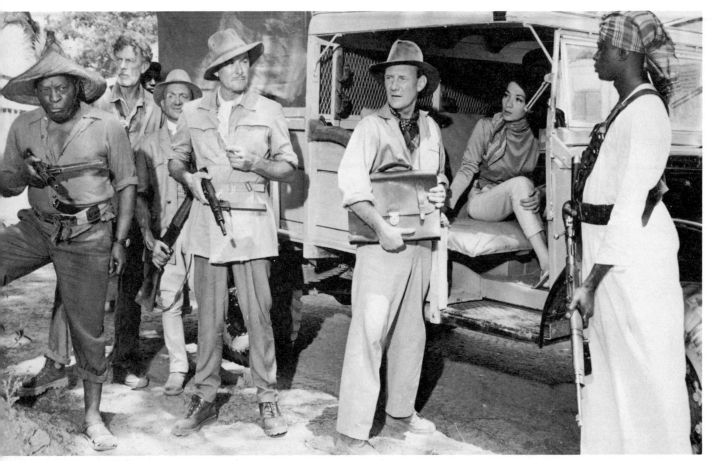

Morel and his followers stand ready for trouble.

an entourage of mercenaries, naturalists, and numerous other hangers-on and lost souls. The novel was exciting material and the prospect of shooting it on location in Africa excited Huston, whose last African adventure, *The African Queen,* had been a big critical and commercial hit for him.

When the director inquired about screen rights, however, he found they'd been purchased by producer Darryl F. Zanuck and that novelist Gary was already hard at work adapting his book into a screenplay. Zanuck considered Huston's enthusiasm for the project quite fortuitous, however, and quickly signed him to direct. With an assist from Irish novelist (and first time screenwriter) Patrick Leigh-Fermor, Huston then set about revising Gary's script. Gary later insisted that only one line from his original draft was left intact and went on to denounce the film as a travesty of his book. Huston himself admits that the script of *The Roots of Heaven* left a lot to be desired. "The script wasn't what it could have been," he says. "It called for a profound approach. As it turned out, it was a kind of adventure picture—which it shouldn't have been."

Whatever faults may have existed in the screenplay prior to shooting, they eventually proved the least of the director's problems, for once cast and crew arrived on location in French Equatorial Africa, the oppressive climate, disease, accidents, and sundry other difficulties encountered there soon lay waste to the entire production. Because the heat rose to 135° in the daytime and never fell below 100° at night, Huston was forced to shoot in the morning and quit before noon; this slowed progress on the film considerably. Co-star Eddie Albert suffered sunstroke and was out of commission—and out of his mind, some say—for almost three weeks, while female lead Juliette Greco developed a rare blood disease that almost killed her. One crew member who refused to take his malaria tablets did die. According to Zanuck biographer Mel Gussow, 160 members of the cast and crew reported 624 sick calls during the on-location shoot. Eventually, things got so bad that pages of the script were dropped simply to speed up production so that everyone could get the hell home. "It was the most difficult location in the history of motion pictures," Zanuck told Gussow and insisted that that more than any other reason

Forsythe (Errol Flynn) and Minna (Juliette Greco) make friends with the natives.

accounted for the film's failure to jell or exert any emotional pull.

Zanuck may have been right, but the rigors of shooting in Africa do not account for all the film's shortcomings, the largest of which, for me, is the total miscasting of Trevor Howard as the cynical but idealistic Morel, the messianic elephant savior. Originally, William Holden had been sought for the role, but he had to bow out due to another commitment. Holden would have been ideal, for even at his most hard-edged and cynical—as in Billy Wilder's *Sunset*

Boulevard (1950) and *Stalag 17* (1953)—he was a very winning actor whose screen persona always invited an audience's empathy. This is a characteristic that even the most negative and self-destructive of Huston heroes—such as Fred C. Dobbs in *Sierra Madre*— share in common, which is why they capture our interest and involvement and remain so memorable. Trevor Howard, admittedly a fine actor, does not exude such qualities on screen. He tends toward the abrasive, which is ruinous for Morel, a character the audience is supposed to like, if not exactly understand. In my view, Howard's irascible, abrasive and finally inscrutable Morel comes across not as a hero, but as a thoroughly obnoxious man.

121

The Unforgiven (1960)

A HECHT-HILL-AND LANCASTER PRODUCTION
Released through United Artists
Technicolor/125 minutes

CREDITS:

Director: John Huston; *Producer:* James Hill; *Screenplay:* Ben Maddow, based on the novel *The Unforgiven* by Alan LeMay; *Cinematographer:* Franz Planer; *Editor:* Russell Lloyd; *Music:* Dimitri Tiomkin; *Art Director:* Stephen Grimes; *Videocassette Source:* Not Available.

Mrs. Zachary (Lillian Gish) hides the truth from Rachel (Audrey Hepburn) that she's an Indian orphan.

CAST:

Ben Zachary: Burt Lancaster; *Rachel:* Audrey Hepburn; *Matilda Zachary:* Lillian Gish; *Johnny Portugal:* John Saxon; *Zeb Rawlins:* Charles Bickford; *Charlie Rawlins:* Albert Salmi; *Cash:* Audie Murphy; *Abe Kelsey:* Joseph Wiseman; *Andy Zachary:* Doug McClure.

* * *

Contemporary Reviews

"It has become almost a ghoulish task to comment on a new John Huston picture. The latest is called *The Unforgiven,* is set in the Texas Panhandle in 1971, and is, in a word, ludicrous. The direction shows a now-pathetic flash or two of the old Huston quality, but for the most part it is feeble and disconcerted. That Huston could not get a good performance out of Lancaster cannot be held against him, but he has achieved what no other director has done: he has got a bad performance out of lovely, miscast Audrey Hepburn."—*The New Republic*

"The scenery is great, the horses vigorous. Those who expect to see a settlement of the racial question will not be satisfied."—*The New York Times*

* * *

Following the completion of his three picture deal with 20th Century-Fox, Huston signed a contract with United Artists to direct a series of films, only two of which, *The Unforgiven* (1960) and *The Misfits* (1961), got made for UA. The third project, *Freud* (1963), was transferred to Universal, while the fourth, an epic recounting of Cortez's conquest of Mexico, was scrapped altogether due to its prohibitive cost.

Huston calls *The Unforgiven* the one film of his that he actively dislikes because the picture he wanted to make—a story about racial prejudice on the frontier—clashed with co-writer Ben Maddow and pro-

Ben (Burt Lancaster) faces down the Kiowas, who have come to collect their long-lost sister.

ducer James Hill's concept of a larger-than-life standard western. "This difference of intention did not become an issue until we were very close to shooting time," he writes in his autobiography, "and quite mistakenly I agreed to stick it out, thus violating my own conviction that a picture-maker should undertake nothing but what he believes in—regardless. From that moment, the entire picture turned sour. Everything went to hell. It was as if some celestial vengeance had been loosed upon me for infidelity to my principles."

The "celestial vengeance" Huston speaks of involved recurring bad weather, co-star Audie Murphy's near drowning while on an off-hours hunting trip, and an on camera accident in which Audrey Hepburn fell from her horse and broke her back. Her convalescence took three weeks. All this combined sent production costs soaring in excess of $5 million, making it his most expensive film to date. The cost went unrecouped, however, as the film was not a box office success. Contrary to Huston's expectations, though, the film did get some good reviews, particularly in the hinterlands, where westerns of any kind have always been greeted warmly.

Ben (Burt Lancaster) prepares for the upcoming assault by the Kiowas, who are determined to return Rachel to their tribe.

Huston terms the film "inflated and bombastic," and it is that. Essentially a small film with only a few settings and characters, it boasts a musical score by Dimitri Tiomkin that ranks among his loudest and most overpowering, a score more befitting a vast western epic like *Giant* (1956) or *The Big Country*. And to the key part of Ben Zachary, the justifiably troubled Huston protagonist who must come to terms with his sexual and racial feelings toward his Indian sister (Hepburn) while staving off the bigotry of his neighbors, enmity within his family, and, finally, a series of attacks by Kiowas who have come to reclaim the girl, Burt Lancaster brings far too much strength and grit. He seems to have stepped out of one of his earlier films—*The Kentuckian* (1955), perhaps, or *The Crimson Pirate* (1952).

The plot of the film is essentially a reversal of John Ford's *The Searchers* (1956), which was also based on a novel by Alan LeMay and contains a similar subtext of racial intolerance. In the Ford film, a young white girl (Natalie Wood) is brought up by Comanches after they've massacred her family. The majority of the film centers on the decade-long search of her Indian-hating uncle (John Wayne) to find her and bring her back. When he does, he has to fight the urge to kill her because by then she has virtually become an Indian herself. In the Huston film, it is a Kiowa girl, Rachel, who is adopted by a white family, the Zacharys, who have taken part in a revenge raid on her village. Years later, the Kiowas, having learned of the girl's whereabouts from an enemy of the Zacharys, a vindictive ex-Civil War vet named Abe Kelsey (Joseph Wiseman), seek to reclaim her. When one of their own is killed by the thwarted Indians, the Zacharys' neighbors accept Kelsey's accusations about the girl and turn on their

124

Ben (Burt Lancaster) takes aim at one of the approaching Indians as the others in the cabin watch nervously. From left to right: Doug McClure, Audrey Hepburn, Audie Murphy, and Lillian Gish.

former friends. Even Rachel's half-brother, the Indian-hating Cash (Audie Murphy), refuses to live any longer with "a red hide nigger in the house" and lights out. The Kiowas return and the remaining Zacharys are forced to defend themselves during a night-long seige that climaxes when the guilt-ridden Cash returns to help out and Rachel winds up shooting her very own brother (Carlos Rivas), the leader of the Kiowa band.

Mixed in with all this *Sturm and Drang* is a Eugene O'Neill-like undercurrent of sexual tension between Rachel and her older brother, Ben, who are in love with each other, but, for reasons that aren't totally logical, suppress that love until the truth comes out that she's an Indian. The fact is that even though neither of them is aware of her racial heritage until Kelsey shows up to spread the truth about it, they have always known that they weren't really brother and sister. Ben's late father claimed that she was a white orphan he'd found and brought home, a half-lie that even his mother re-affirmed. Why then should the revelation that she's an Indian orphan foster an acknowledgment of their feelings toward each other? They could justifiably have stopped suppressing them long ago.

This is not the only plot contrivance that fails to hold water. Another is Cash's confirmed ability to "smell an Injun a mile away." Why then has he never sensed the truth about Rachel? Apparently his nose just works selectively, according to the dictates of the script. Finally, there is the Indian attack on the Zachary home itself. As one contemporary critic aptly noted: "A fully-armed war party of real

Andy (Doug McClure) and Ben (Burt Lancaster) confer.

Kiowas would have swept over that sod house in short order, killing everyone in it...[and] Audie Murphy's one-man rescue had all the believability of a single marine winning the battle of Tarawa.''

Despite its major flaws, *The Unforgiven* is compellingly directed. The scenes of Kelsey appearing then disappearing like some ragged ghost from *The Red Badge of Courage*, shouting his message of "I am the sword of vengeance...whereby the wrong shall be righted and the truth be told" from the sand-swept hilltops, are striking indeed. At one point, the messianic Kelsey even proclaims his "wise blood," a haunting phrase that would become both theme and title of another Huston film almost twenty years later. And while the final Indian assault does lack credibility (unless you believe Indians are suicidal), it is excitingly staged, particularly the denouement where the Kiowas drive a herd of cattle onto the roof of the Zacharys' sod hut, which is built into the side of a hill, and the roof starts to collapse. To fend the steers off, Ben gives them a hot foot by setting the roof on fire, then, after they've gone, has to dowse the flames with buckets of water. Virtually this entire scene is shot from inside the hut itself, creating a very potent sense of claustrophobia and real panic. It's good stuff. But it's not enough to save the film overall.

The Misfits (1961)

A SEVEN ARTS PICTURE
Released through United Artists
B&W/124 minutes

CREDITS:

Director: John Huston; *Producer:* Frank Taylor; *Screenplay:* Arthur Miller; *Cinematographer:* Russell Metty; *Editor:* George Tomasini; *Music:* Alex North; *Art Directors:* William Newberry and Stephen Grimes; *Videocassette Source:* CBS/Fox Home Video.

CAST:

Gay Langland: Clark Gable; *Roslyn Taber:* Marilyn Monroe; *Perce Howland:* Montgomery Clift; *Guido Dellini:* Eli Wallach; *Mr. Taber:* Kevin McCarthy; *Isabelle:* Thelma Ritter.

* * *

Huston and scriptwriter Arthur Miller.

Contemporary Reviews

"John Huston's direction is his best in years, well knit and hard, at times even recalling *The Treasure of Sierra Madre.* Too bad that his camera occasionally peers lubriciously down the girl's bodice or elsewhere to remind us that Roslyn is really Marilyn Monroe."— *The New Republic*

"Miss Monroe, on screen, is again the dumb blonde trying to act interpretively and introspectively. But the wonderful intuition of her earlier career is gone; and the cerebral method has now taken over. You can see the wheels working behind those wide eyes and furrowed brow. Mr. Gable in his last picture, was, as always, an old pro—wonderfully expert—as the ex-pilot, Wallach is splendid, and so is Clift as the rodeo rider. John Huston directed with great power, sensitivity, pictorial excitement—and, I have been told, much patience."—*Cue* magazine

"It has a vitality so rich that I dare say it can scarcely be taken in at one viewing. It gives that sense of warm, almost fleshly contact with reality that one never experiences except where a film has grown out of somebody's response to life."—*The New York Herald Tribune*

Marilyn Monroe as the love-starved but symbolically life giving Roslyn.

"Mr. Huston's direction is dynamic, inventive and colorful. But the picture just doesn't come off."—*The New York Times*

* * *

Superstar American playwright Arthur Miller (*All My Sons, Death of a Salesman*) drew the inspiration for *The Misfits,* his first original screenplay, from a short story he'd written some years before. The story was about a group of modern-day cowboys, who, accompanied by a troubled divorcee, set out to capture a string of wild mustangs in order to sell them to a dog food manufacturer. In the end, they come to view the misfit animals as symbols of themselves and decide to let them go.

Miller expanded the story into a full-length screenplay for his then wife, Marilyn Monroe, who was looking for a strong vehicle in which to demon-strate her abilities as a straight dramatic actress. John Huston was approached to direct by producer Frank Taylor, and, after reading the script, quickly agreed, for the theme of the film had much in common with his own past work. All the characters in *The Misfits* are reckless, easily bored types whose lives seem plagued by ill luck. Typically, the source of this bad luck rests not in their stars but in themselves, a truth they are forced to confront when they trek into the hills to capture a herd of wild mustangs that one of the group, a cowboy pilot named Guido, has reported seeing from the air. As in the short story, the mustangs are to be sold to a dog food manufacturer, a situation that the divorcee, Roslyn (whom Guido describes as having the "gift of life"), protests against violently. In dealing with Roslyn and the mustangs, the cowboys are forced to take stock of themselves and at the conclusion all but Guido, who prefers to continue deceiving himself, opt to set the animals free again.

Though this material proved ideally suited to Huston's sensibilities, shooting of *The Misfits* did not proceed smoothly. Creative and personal conflicts quickly arose on all fronts. The marriage between Marilyn Monroe and Arthur Miller, which was on

Roslyn (Marilyn Monroe) and Gay (Clark Gable) pick up Perce (Montgomery Clift), a busted rodeo rider, along the roadside.

Roslyn (Marilyn Monroe) wows the cowboys with an energetic display of paddle ball and body movement. Others in the scene: Clark Gable, James Barton, Thelma Ritter, Eli Wallach, and Montgomery Clift.

Perce (Montgomery Clift) and Roslyn (Marilyn Monroe) discover they're soulmates.

Guido (Eli Wallach), Perce (Montgomery Clift) and Gay (Clark Gable) capture a wild mustang.

rocky ground even before shooting began, quickly deteriorated once everyone arrived on location. As the filming wore on, the actress's legendary pill-popping increased to such a degree that she finally collapsed and production was stalled for two weeks while she recuperated in a hospital. Huston endured the internal strife with great patience and in the end turned out a film that surely ranks as one of his best-directed efforts—though not, in my view, one of his most distinguished.

The basic problem with *The Misfits* is that its script is a bit too heavily laden with *weltschmerz*. And the dialogue at times is almost howlingly pretentious. When Guido confesses to the recently divorced Roslyn that he never took the time to teach his late wife how to dance, she introspectively responds, "We're all dying, aren't we? The husbands and the wives. Without teaching each other what we know." The remark is typical, not just of her, but of others in the film as well, for unlike the troubled protagonists in many of Huston's other films, the characters in *The Misfits* tend to wear their inner conflicts on their sleeves. After awhile, the effect of their endless soul-searching becomes numbing. One tends to want to call them the "screw ups" rather than the "misfits."

The miracle of the film, though, apart from Huston's sure-fire staging of virtually every scene, is that despite the script's tendency towards pretentious and at times unbelievable dialogue, the performances are all quite good. The behind-the-scenes

conflicts do not show on the screen and there is a very real sense of camaraderie between all the characters that is quite pleasing and effective. Eli Wallach, who received the least notoriety during the making of the film, is a particular standout as the manipulative Guido, who pretends to be one type of person when, in fact, he is quite another. Monroe is occasionally erratic but on the whole quite remarkable. As the love-starved but symbolically life-giving Roslyn, who brings the group together and eventually falls for the aging cowpoke, Gay, she is at times almost luminous. As Perce, the rodeo rider who has been kicked in the head one too many times, Montgomery Clift is especially endearing, particularly in his scenes with Monroe.

Clark Gable has a tougher time with Gay, however. A drunk scene where he imagines that his children have come to see him and he falls off a truck trying to spot them in a crowd is fraught with hamminess. At other times, however, when forced to mouth lines to Roslyn such as, "It's almost an honor just to be sitting here beside you," Gable rises heroically to the challenge (and quite a challenge it is!) and delivers them with remarkable sensitivity and conviction.

Though Gable considered his performance in *The Misfits* to be the best of his career—and apart from his flawless Rhett Butler in *Gone With the Wind* (1939) it probably is—he never lived to see the completed film. Three days after the film wrapped, he died at age

Huston instructs Eli Wallach on the fine points of capturing a mustang.

59 of a heart attack. Some still maintain that Gable's unexpected coronary resulted from the strain of doing his own stuntwork during the film's climactic mustanging scenes. Huston denies this, however, claiming that although Gable insisted on doing many of his own stunts for the required close-ups, the real rough-and-tumble action was carried out in long shot by Gable's double, a professional stuntman. Close examination of these scenes, where Gay is literally tossed about by the wild mustang he is trying to recapture, confirms what Huston says. The actor is not Clark Gable.

Freud (1962)

A.K.A. *Freud: The Secret Passion*

A UNIVERSAL PICTURE
B&W/120 minutes

CREDITS:

Director: John Huston; *Producer:* Wolfgang Reinhardt;
Screenplay: Wolfgang Reinhardt and Charles Kaufman;
Cinematographer: Douglas Slocombe; *Editor:* Ralph
Kemplen; *Music:* Jerry Goldsmith; *Art Director:* Stephen B. Grimes; *Videocassette Source:* Not Available.

*Director Huston confers with stars Susannah York, Larry
Parks, and Montgomery Clift on the set of* Freud.

CAST:

Sigmund Freud: Montgomery Clift; *Cecily Koertner:* Susannah York; *Joseph Breuer:* Larry Parks; *Martha Freud:*
Susan Kohner; *Frau Koertner:* Eileen Herlie; *Professor
Charcot:* Fernand Ledoux; *Carl von Schlosser:* David
McCallum; *Freud's Mother:* Rosalie Crutchley; *Freud's
Father:* David Kossof; *Dr. Meynert:* Eric Portman.

*   *   *

Contemporary Reviews

"A bold and momentous quest for knowledge in the
realm of psychology—the quest of Sigmund Freud to
bare the secrets of the subconscious mind—is rendered as daring and dramatic as the probing of a
dark, mysterious crime....It is an excellent, tasteful
picture that amateur wig-pickers should especially
enjoy."—*The New York Times*

Freud (Montgomery Clift) puts the troubled Carl von Schlosser (David McCallum) under hypnosis. Their session provides Freud with his first clue to the existence of child sexuality and the Oedipus Complex.

Martha Freud (Susan Kohner) convinces her doubting husband (Montgomery Clift) that he should continue with his controversial studies when she reads him a letter he once wrote about pursuing the truth, whatever the cost.

Through various intense sessions with Cecily (Susannah York), whose mind is a maze of repression and self-deception, Freud confirms his theory of child sexuality.

"...a period piece in every sense of the word...looks and sounds exactly like a belated addition to the Warner waxworks of the late thirties...although there is one rather good, sustained passage in which Susannah York is twice taken through the details of her father's death until she's forced to admit that he died, not in a hospital, but in a brothel."—*Films and Filming*

"...a taut, intellectual thriller...directed with dominating intelligence."—*Time* magazine

* * *

The rigors of shooting *The Roots of Heaven* in Africa and dealing with Marilyn Monroe's neuroses on the set of *The Misfits* were nothing compared to what Huston faced in bringing his long-cherished project of *Freud* to the screen. Apart from the legendary difficulties he encountered with star Montgomery Clift, who was suffering from a variety of mental and physical disabilities during shooting, there were massive script problems beforehand as well as distribution headaches afterward. In retrospect, Huston admits that the experience of making *Freud* was one he would never willingly repeat. The wonder is that *Freud* got

made at all—usually such constant disharmony spells the kiss of death for a film. The greater marvel, however, is that the film turned out to be one of the director's best, a major achievement that seems to get even better with each passing year, boasting a central performance by Clift that is nothing short of magnificent.

As with many Huston projects, the director got the idea to make his biopic of the father of psychoanalysis many years before he got the opportunity. While working on *Dr. Ehrlich's Magic Bullet* (1940) together, he and Wolfgang Reinhardt, the film's associate producer and an expert on Freud, first discussed the possibility, but subsequently dismissed it in light of the censorship problems they felt the project would be unable to overcome. Huston's real-life encounter with psychoneurotic disorders and the use of hypnotherapy while making his wartime documentary *Let There Be Light* (1946) increased his fascination with the subject, however, and reinforced his commitment to someday make a film about Freud and his work. That idea popped up once more in 1955 when Charles Kaufman, who had scripted *Let There Be Light* with Huston, broached the subject again. Again it was declared unfeasible.

In 1959, however, while visiting Huston at his Ireland estate, St. Clerans, Wolfgang Reinhardt discussed the possibility once more and he and Huston decided the time was now right. Huston commissioned existentialist playwright Jean Paul Sartre to develop a screenplay, but Sartre's script turned out to be an unwieldy 1600 to 2000 page tome that would have taken years to shoot and almost a full day to screen—something no audience or distributor in the world would sit still for. Huston then turned for help to Charles Kaufman, who took a crack at altering and paring the Sartre script down. Kaufman succeeded, but the result, says Huston, too much resembled a sentimentalized biopic in the old Warner Brothers tradition, a treatment he and Reinhardt wanted to avoid. Ironically, even though Huston and Reinhardt reworked the script to erase these elements, their film would still be accused by many critics of being a throwback to their old Warner Brothers days.

Even as shooting commenced, Reinhardt and Huston continued to hone the script. This quickly proved to be the least of the director's problems, however. Montgomery Clift, with whom Huston

Freud (Montgomery Clift) has his first session with Cecily (Susannah York), who has been suffering a variety of hysterical symptoms ever since the death of her father.

had gotten along famously while making *The Misfits*, was but three years away from his premature death (at age 45) when he began *Freud*. An alcohol and drug abuser ever since the near fatal 1956 car crash that had left much of his face paralyzed, Clift also suffered from a number of other debilitating conditions, including a tendency towards memory loss which severely affected his ability to deal with the lengthy scientific dialogues he had to deliver in *Freud*. To compensate for this, Huston took to placing cue cards all around the set so that Clift could read from them. Soon, though, Clift developed a cataract problem that hampered his ability to read the cards; in fact, he thought he was going blind.

Today, Huston bristles at accusations that he mistreated Clift in any way during the making of *Freud*. Yet there is no question but that Clift's incessant problems, both real and imagined, drove the director to distraction. He insists that he drove Clift solely to get a performance out of him. Yet Clift's difficulties were not just emotional. They were very real. In fact, during the film's third and final dream sequence when Huston's camera offers a rare tight close-up of the actor's face,

one can clearly see the cataracts clouding over Clift's eyes. Still, Huston had his own problems as well. *Freud* was not only a very important project for him, but millions of dollars were at stake. The net result of all this once the film was finished was a series of lawsuits and counter lawsuits between Clift, Huston, the film's distributor, and other parties for a whole host of grievances.

And *still* the director's problems were not over. Prior to *Freud*'s release, Universal insisted that Huston cut the film to just over two hours, eliminating several significant though not key scenes. When it was discovered that audiences were staying away in droves, Universal cut the film still more and re-titled it *Freud: The Secret Passion* as a come on. The ploy failed to work. Though *Freud* netted a number of good reviews and turned up on several "ten best" lists, it flopped badly at the box office. Huston still doesn't know why, though my own theory is that the film should never have been

Cecily (Susannah York) remains uncured at the end, but her doctor has helped her focus on the root cause of her psychological conflict.

broadly released. It was simply not a mass market item and had it not been released as such it might have caught on slowly—which, over the years, is precisely what has happened. *Freud* still has its detractors, to be sure, but many critics, including myself, now rank it among Huston's finest efforts.

Huston's *Freud* is not so much a biopic of a man as of an idea. Set between the years 1885 and 1890, it chronicles the various steps and mis-steps that led to Freud's development of his controversial theory of infantile sexuality and the Oedipus Complex. Here, truth is the elusive goal that is being pursued, a goal once again that can only be achieved when the protagonist has come to terms with himself. The theme of the film, as it is in virtually all of Huston's work, is "Know Thyself." Like Sam Spade, Freud is surrounded by people in pursuit of the same elusive goal. It is denied them, however, because, unlike him, they opt to continuing deceiving themselves and, in fact, denounce Freud's findings in the end as completely false.

Freud links up with a sympathetic colleague, Dr. Joseph Breuer, who hands over a number of his more hysterical cases to the young doctor with the

aim of jointly publishing their findings. An early encounter with a neurotic young man named Von Schlosser, who assaulted his military man father with a knife and is about to be committed to an asylum, provides Freud with an important first clue. Under hypnosis, Von Schlosser caresses the nude torso of a mannequin while denouncing his father for having repeatedly "raped" his mother. Freud shrinks from the implications of the boy's revelation and gives psychology up for a year. But Von Schlosser's reappearance in a symbolic dream, pointing the way to The Truth, prompts Freud to press on and develop his theory that hysterical neuroses are sexual in origin.

Breuer disagrees and poses an acid test, the case of a young girl named Cecily who has been suffering a variety of hysterical symptoms ever since the death of her father. Freud takes the case on and through various intense sessions with Cecily, whose mind is a maze of repression and self-deception, is led to re-examine his earlier theory and finally conclude that Cecily's disorder is the result of guilt she still carries for having had sexual feelings towards her father as a child. Freud confirms this when he discovers similar neurotic symptoms in himself. At his father's funeral, he psychologically bars himself from the cemetery by collapsing outside its gates. As with Cecily, he traces the cause back to his childhood, re-experiencing the jealousy he felt whenever his father took his mother from him. He presents his conclusions about infantile sexuality to his medical colleagues, but is greeted as a scandalmonger and pariah. Later, however, he returns to the cemetery where his father is buried and is at last able to enter freely and without guilt.

Contemporary critics were quite astute in pointing out that *Freud* is essentially a detective story with Freud himself, the typically reckless and restless Huston adventurer, the detective assigned to the case— a sort of psychoanalytic Sam Spade. Layer by layer, he strips away the mystery until the guilty party is finally unmasked.

Remarkably, the additional trimming to which the film was subjected prior to and after release draws us into the mystery all the more. Some critics disagree, however. Huston biographer Stuart Kaminsky argues that some of the cuts render certain details of the plot a muddle. I disagree. Kaminsky cites as an example an early scene where Freud, embarking to Paris to study with Professor Charcot, is presented with his father's watch as a parting gift at the train station. As the train lurches, Freud drops the watch on board and it shatters in extreme close-up. As this incident is never recalled and its symbolic meaning never directly explained due to apparent

cuts, Kaminsky suggests the scene lacks clarity. In light of Freud's subsequent neurotic breakdown and discovery of his own unresolved Oedipus Complex, however, it makes perfect sense. Symbolically hinting at Freud's repressed feelings of hostility toward his father, it provides us and him with an early clue to the overall mystery, a clue whose full import is not realized until the mystery becomes clear and starts to unravel.

Critic James Agee noted of Huston's work: "Most movies are made in the evident assumption that the audience is passive and wants to remain passive; every effort is made to do all the work—the seeing, the explaining, the understanding, even the feeling.... [Huston's] pictures continually open the eye and require it to work vigorously." *Freud* is certainly an example of this. Its very succinctness, imposed or otherwise (and not all of it was imposed), compels us to work along with Freud, sifting clues, making associations and drawing conclusions together with him.

The compactness of its storytelling does not invite our involvement alone, however. Douglas Slocombe's moody black and white photography and Jerry Goldsmith's equally moody score contribute mightily as well. As does Montgomery Clift's remarkably empathetic performance as Freud.

The List of Adrian Messenger (1963)

A UNIVERSAL PICTURE
B&W/98 minutes

CREDITS:

Director: John Huston; *Producer:* Edward Lewis; *Screenplay:* Anthony Veiller, based on the novel *The List of Adrian Messenger* by Philip MacDonald; *Cinematographers:* Joseph McDonald and Ted Scaif; *Editor:* Terry Morse; *Music:* Jerry Goldsmith; *Art Directors:*

Stephen B. Grimes and George Webb; *Videocassette Source:* MCA Home Video.

CAST:

George Bruttenholm: Kirk Douglas; *Anthony Gethryn:* George C. Scott; *Lady Jocelyn Bruttenholm:* Dana Wynter; *Marquis of Gleneyre:* Clive Brook; *Sir Wilfred Lucas:* Herbert Marshall; *Mrs. Karoudjian:* Gladys Cooper; *Raoul LeBorg:* Jacques Roux; *Adrian Messenger:* John Merivale; *Derek Bruttenholm:* Tony Huston; *Lord Acton:* John Huston; *Guest Stars:* Tony Curtis, Burt Lancaster, Frank Sinatra, Robert Mitchum.

* * *

Contemporary Reviews

"In *The List of Adrian Messenger,* John Huston pulls a stunt that helps neither his reputation nor his plainly mediocre film. He has some well-known Hollywood

Raoul (Jacques Roux) voices his suspicions to Lady Jocelyn (Dana Wynter) over a friendly card game with Gethryn (George C. Scott) and the Marquis of Gleneyre (Clive Brook).

actors got up in disguises appear as assorted small characters in the picture without identifying them. Then, when the drama is over, he has them pull off their rubber masks and show themselves, with winks and simpers, as though they were clever, indeed. They aren't. Nor is this picture. How Mr. Huston got mixed up with this deception...is hard to understand."—*The New York Times*

"The program of murders by which the charming villain hopes to get a marquisate is merely a framework for John Huston's clever work. Huston has had a good time, and he lets his audiences in on it."—*Newsweek*

"The viewer keeps hoping that *Messenger* is another of Director John Huston's deadpan spoofs, like *Beat the Devil;* but it turns out to be only a tribute to the art of Makeup Man Bud Westmore."—*Time* magazine

* * *

It is quite understandable considering the abundance of difficulties Huston faced in bringing

Gethryn (George C. Scott) probes the clues left behind in the dead Messenger's list.

George Bruttenholm (Kirk Douglas) prepares for the foxhunt he's sure will net him another victim.

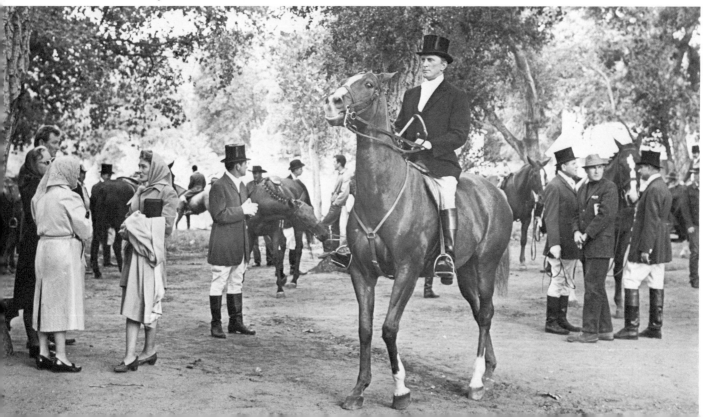

The foxhunters observe the real villain of the piece receive his just reward.

Freud to the screen that he should want to relax a bit with his next project. And he did just that. *The List of Adrian Messenger* was essentially a working vacation for Huston. Shot mainly on location in England and Ireland, his home at the time, it was completed quickly and effortlessly—though, at a $3 million price tag, a bit expensively—earning mainly good reviews and solid box office. The film climaxed with a fox hunt that Huston turned into a labor of love. The sequence took twelve days to shoot and allowed Huston to have, as he says, "...a marvelous time." As one critic noted of the sequence: "Huston comes within striking distance of doing for fox hunting what Hemingway did for the bullfight....His direction is firm, sharp and atmospheric in giving us a panoply of a hunt in full cry."

Alas, the bulk of the film is not quite so engaging, though it does boast a charming and "veddy British" atmosphere as well as one of Jerry Goldsmith's best scores. In keeping with the Huston method, *The List of Adrian Messenger* is less of a mystery, or whodunit, than a psychological cat and mouse game that keeps us asking, "Will he get away with it?" Kirk Douglas plays the centerpiece Huston adventurer, George Bruttenholm, a Canadian actor and master of disguise who almost succeeds in murdering his way into inheriting a British title and fabulous estate until he pushes his luck too far. Scotland Yard detective Anthony Gethryn catches onto his scheme when a list of Bruttenholm's eleven previous victims (all witnesses to a wartime act of treason by Bruttenholm that would jeopardize his inheritance if the scandal ever came out) that comes into his possession via a man named LeBorg, the survivor of a plane crash engineered by Bruttenholm to claim another passenger, Adrian Messenger. Only the aging Marquis of Gleneyre and his twelve-year-old nephew, Derek, now stand in Bruttenholm's way. As the charming mass murderer makes plans to do away with the boy, Gethryn and LeBorg lay a trap to smoke him out by using Gethryn himself as bait. After they let him know that Gethryn is on to him, Bruttenholm impulsively arranges for Gethryn to suffer a fatal accident with a piece of farm equipment during a fox hunt in which everyone has agreed to take part. But at the last moment, the tables are turned and the unmasked

Huston with son Tony on the set. They both played credited parts in the film.

Bruttenholm, while attempting to escape on young Derek's horse, is killed when he falls and is speared on the machinery instead.

As Gethryn, the archetypal British gumshoe, George C. Scott looks the part, but performs rather colorlessly. His dogged sleuth is simply no match, in style anyway, for Douglas's flamboyant villain. Scott's vain attempts at wrestling with a bogus British accent, which he absently wanders in and out of, also hampers his performance. *The List of Adrian Messenger* just isn't one of this gifted actor's shining moments. But Scott is not the only problem with the film. Cleverly scripted by longtime Huston collaborator Anthony Veiller, *Messenger* could have stood nicely on its own as a genial and engaging old-style detective yarn, requiring no extra gimmicks to ensure our interest. But Huston provided one anyway that ultimately proves very disconcerting. He has us keep an eye out for top stars Burt Lancaster, Tony Curtis, Robert Mitchum and Frank Sinatra, all heavily disguised, in bit parts, then, at the conclusion of the film, has them peel off their make-up and reveal themselves in a special curtain call.

There is a two-fold problem with this gimmick. First, it constantly competes for our attention with the actual story. But more importantly, Bud Westmore's make-ups for these gentlemen are unconvincing. Mitchum, an early victim of Bruttenholm's, is easy to spot because Westmore's make-up barely conceals his very recognizable features. Lancaster, Curtis, and Sinatra on the other hand are not so readily identifiable as themselves, but the make-ups they wear stand out because they look so obviously fake. The wigs, nose putty and other appliances Westmore supplies them with aren't even remotely realistic-looking or convincing. Though we don't know which of the actors these characters are, they *look* so made-up, especially when standing next to someone who isn't made up, that they stand out like sore thumbs. With all deference to Mr. Westmore's skills as a make-up artist, he's simply no Dick Smith, who just might have been able to pull this gimmick off for Huston.

For two-thirds of its running time, *The List of Adrian Messenger* is a leisurely and diverting entertainment, but, like George Bruttenholm, the director ultimately pushed his luck too far.

Ava Gardner as the bawdy Maxine, whom Huston turns into the means of Shannon's salvation rather than his destruction.

The Night of the Iguana (1964)

A SEVEN ARTS PICTURE
Released through Metro-Goldwyn-Mayer
B&W/118 minutes

CREDITS:

Director: John Huston; *Producers:* Ray Stark and John Huston; *Screenplay:* John Huston and Anthony Veiller, based on the play *The Night of the Iguana* by Tennessee Williams; *Cinematographer:* Gabriel Figueroa; *Editor:* Ralph Kemplen; *Music:* Benjamin Frankel; *Art Director:* Stephen Grimes; *Videocassette source:* MGM/UA Home Video.

CAST:

Reverend T. Lawrence Shannon: Richard Burton; *Maxine Faulk:* Ava Gardner; *Hanna Jelkes:* Deborah Kerr; *Charlotte Goodall:* Sue Lyon; *Hank Prosner:* James Ward; *Judith Fellowes:* Grayson Hall; *Nonno:* Cyril Delevanti; *Miss Peebles:* Mary Boylan; *Miss Dexter:* Gladys Hill; *Miss Throxton:* Billie Matticks; *Barkeeper:* Emilio Fernandez; *Pepe:* Fidelmar Duran; *Pedro:* Robert Leyra.

* * *

Contemporary Reviews

"A picture that excites the senses, persuades the mind, and even occasionally speaks to the spirit—one of the best movies ever made from a Tennessee Williams play."—*Time* magazine

"It has difficulty in communicating precisely what it is that is so barren and poignant about the people it brings to a tourist hotel run by a sensual American woman on the coast of Mexico....Who are these dislocated wanderers? From what Freudian cell have they been sprung, and why are they so aggressive in punching their loneliness home to the world? These are the basic revelations that are not communicated by the film."—*The New York Times*

"*The Night of the Iguana* is that fine rarity, an improvement on the play. Everything good has been retained and refined. Huston understands the heat and the rain forest and the sea as a kind of moral crucible."—*Newsweek*

* * *

The Night of the Iguana is yet another John Huston film whose upbeat reworking of the source material it's based on contradicts all those critics who still see Huston as a pessimist ruled by a philosophy of failure. The film is quintessential John Huston and a comparison between it and the 1961 Tennessee Williams play it came from is instructive.

Both play and film focus on the trials and

The guilt-ridden and anguished Shannon (Richard Burton) denounces his flock at the beginning of Night of the Iguana.

Shannon (Richard Burton) arrives at Maxine's (Ava Gardner) Puerto Vallarta resort, where she's accompanied everywhere by two native boys.

Shannon (Richard Burton) is in danger of being seduced by Charlotte (Sue Lyon).

tribulations of a down-on-his-luck man of the cloth, the Reverend T. Lawrence Shannon, who has been defrocked for dallying with an underage parishioner. Shannon winds up south of the border, conducting bus tours of the breathtaking, Edenesque Mexican countryside for tourists. In the play, he lands at an out-of-the-way Acapulco resort hotel with a busload of Nazi vacationers and there becomes the object of conflict between two very different women, the bawdier, and more vindictive of whom destroys him at the play's conclusion.

The play's theme is fairly heavy going, but Williams brings to it a light touch and some very witty dialogue. Huston's film lightens that touch even more, retains much of the play's dialogue, but eliminates the Nazis (who become a busload of American women of various ages), and transposes the locale to an isolated resort hotel in Puerto Vallarta on the Mexican coast. The film also alters the story's outcome, as well as the character of the bawdy Maxine, who becomes the means of Shannon's salvation rather than his destruction.

Williams wholeheartedly disapproved of Huston's new ending, which was not in keeping with the late playwright's quite different and primarily

Shannon (Richard Burton) orders the tempting Charlotte (Sue Lyon) out of his room.

defeatist world view. But this was Williams's play as filtered through the eyes of John Huston, and, as such, conforms more to the director's very dissimilar point of view, which is succinctly expressed in the film's prologue when Shannon, torn by inner conflict, opines to his Sunday flock that, ''He that hath no rule over his own spirit is like a city that is broken down and without walls.'' For Huston's Shannon, the film thereafter becomes a sort of spiritual adventure (not unlike Huston's future *Under the Volcano*) in which the once idealistic but now broken protagonist struggles to regain control over himself and reclaim his ideals. By resolving to settle down at the end with the open and generous Maxine rather than continue to drift aimlessly, ruled by happenstance and self-deception, Shannon finally triumphs over his own weaknesses and achieves that goal. Obviously, this is not Williams Territory we are in, but Hustonland.

The Reverend T. Lawrence Shannon is very much a Huston hero in the mold of Sam Spade, who also chooses to overcome, rather than be overcome by, himself. Like Spade also, Shannon's ultimate contest is between reality and illusion— ''The stuff that dreams are made of.'' Shannon is descended from a long line of churchmen, but unlike them is not suited to the rigors of the cloth. He keeps insisting not that he has been defrocked, but that he was wrongly locked out of his church. In the end, he compels himself to see the truth and is all the better

for it. Likewise, his initial inclination to move on with the whimsical Hanna, who lives in her own fantasy world, and seeming obliviousness to the more concrete and realistic alternative presented by the down-to-earth Maxine, also reflects his tendency to keep deluding himself. Quite movingly, it is Hanna, herself a broken woman (she refers to her unstated inner conflict as "the blue devil"), who points Shannon in the right direction.

The Night of the Iguana also shares a number of things in common with Huston's earlier *The Misfits,* not the least of them being the reconstructed character of Maxine, who, in Huston's hands, becomes an extension of the earlier film's symbolically life-giving Roslyn. There is also much of the wide-eyed and innocent

Roslyn in Deborah Kerr's vulnerable Hanna. Similar too is the key device of the iguana, which, like the mustangs in *The Misfits,* is captured and tied up and fated to be eaten. The iguana's predicament also serves as a metaphor for Shannon, who, at one point, is also tied up, for his own safety, after he tries to commit suicide out of drunken despair. Williams used this metaphor to a much different purpose, however, for in the play Shannon is figuratively devoured by the monstrous Maxine. In the film, Shannon is released by Hanna, and he, in turn, releases the iguana— just as Gay and Perce do the mustangs in *The Misfits. The Night of the Iguana* lacks the heavy-handed and often pretentious dialogue of *The Misfits,* and, as a result, is not only the more entertaining film, but packs a greater punch.

The Night of the Iguana is also a consistently witty and very amusing film in which the frequently ill-used (and all too often unselective) Richard Burton gives

Shannon (Richard Burton) and Hanna (Deborah Kerr) assist an aged tourist as Maxine (Ava Gardner) looks on.

Maxine (Ava Gardner) has a heart-to-heart with the despondent Shannon (Richard Burton) who has been tied up to prevent another suicide attempt.

one of his best screen performances. It is certainly his most skillfully comic. The scene (written by Tennessee Williams expressly for the film) in which Shannon drunkenly walks on broken shards of glass in order to overcome his desire to bed down the luscious, but underage, Sue Lyon is expertly handled by the actor—harrowing, funny, and expressive of Shannon's troubled character all at the same time. Burton was nominated as best actor that year, but for his more solemn and stagey performance as *Becket*, not as Shannon, which, to me, was the more difficult and

demanding role of the two. He nevertheless lost anyway to Rex Harrison for *My Fair Lady*.

Deborah Kerr is equally good as the ephemeral Hanna, as is Ava Gardner, though she does tend to go over the top a bit as Maxine. Only Grayson Hall, as the repressed lesbian in charge of the nymphet Lyon, earned *The Night of the Iguana* an Oscar nomination for acting honors, however, though she too lost—to Lila Kedrova for *Zorba the Greek*. Though nominated, cinematographer Gabriel Figueroa (who would again work with Huston on *Under the Volcano*) lost as well—to *Zorba's* Walter Lassally. Neither Huston nor scenarist Anthony Veiller received nominations for their work. Nevertheless, *The Night of the Iguana* remains their most effective collaboration, as well as one of Huston's best and most personal films.

148

The Bible (1966)

A DINO DE LAURENTIIS PRODUCTION
Released through 20th Century-Fox
Technicolor/ 174 minutes

CREDITS:

Director: John Huston; *Producer:* Dino De Laurentiis;
Screenplay: Christopher Fry with dialogue by Mario
Soldati; *Cinematographer:* Guiseppe Rotunno; *Editor:*
Alberto Galliti; *Music:* Toshiro Mayuzumi; *Art Director:*
Stephen Grimes; *Videocassette source:* RCA/Columbia
Home Video.

*Adam (Michael Parks) and Eve (Ulla Bergryd) partake of the
forbidden fruit in John Huston's epic production of* The
Bible.

CAST:

Adam: Michael Parks; *Eve:* Ulla Bergryd; *Cain:* Richard
Harris; *Abel:* Franco Nero; *Nimrod:* Stephen Boyd;
Noah: John Huston; *Abraham:* George C. Scott; *Sarah:*
Ava Gardner; *Lot:* Gabriele Ferzetti; *Lot's Wife:* Elea-
nora Rossi Drago; *Noah's Wife:* Pupella Maggio; *Three
Angels:* Peter O'Toole.

* * *

Contemporary Reviews

''Extravagant production, extraordinary special
effects, stunning projection on the wide screen...the
scenes of the formation of the earth...the great, dark
city of Sodom is a triumph of the scene-designer's
craft.''—*The New York Times*

''What partly saves *The Bible* from the pathos, awe,
elephantiasis and sameness which seem automatically

Noah (John Huston), playing his pipe, leads the animals to the Ark, two by two.

to strike any film costing more than $10,000,000 is really John Huston playing Noah. The director portrays the Ark-building patriarch with the humility and naïveté of a Giotto fresco of St. Francis and gives the 174-minute 70mm Color de luxe Dino De Laurentiis production its only moment of grace.''—*Cinema*

''Huston's triumph is that despite the insanity of the attempt and the grandiosity of the project, the technology doesn't dominate the material: when you respond to the beauty of such scenes in *The Bible* as the dispersal of the animals after the landing of the Ark, it is not merely the beauty of photography but the beauty of conception.''—*The New Yorker*

*   *   *

It was while Huston was on location in Mexico shooting *The Night of the Iguana* that producer Dino De Laurentiis approached him with the idea of participating in the Italian movie mogul's planned, multi-million dollar production of *The Bible*. De Laurentiis' grandiose scheme was to outdo Cecil B. DeMille by filming all the works of the Bible, beginning with the Book of Genesis, at an estimated cost of $90,000,000, which would make the film the most colossal and expensive religious epic to date. He wanted Huston to supervise the entire production, which would consist of different directors—Orson Welles, Federico Fellini, Robert Bresson and Luchino Visconti—shooting individual sections of the film. Opera star Maria Callas had already been approached to make her film debut as Sarah, the Mother of the Jews, and Sir Laurence Olivier had been enlisted as the voice of God, the narrator of the film.

Impressed by the producer's chutzpah, Huston agreed to take on the challenge, but was not at all surprised when the producer's ambitious plans later began to fall apart. First one director bowed out, then another. Then Callas and Olivier went their separate ways as well. Eventually, De Laurentiis was forced to scale down the project to include only the first half of the Book of Genesis. The new budget was $15,000,000 and Huston alone would serve as director of the script by Christopher Fry, who had also written *Barabbas* (1962). Ava Gardner, George C. Scott, Stephen Boyd, Richard Harris and Peter O'Toole

Noah (John Huston—or, rather, his stuntman) atop the massive Ark.

were set to star, along with Huston himself, who had given himself the plum role of Noah, the builder of the Ark. At De Laurentiis' urging, Huston also agreed to narrate the film.

It was basically Huston's suggestion that the new script be pared down to cover only those events in Genesis leading up to the story of Abraham, whom Huston saw as the first figure in the Bible of whose existence there was historical proof. "The picture should describe man's emergence from the mists of mythology into the light of history," he said. His approach was similar to that of *Freud*, which was also about the casting of light on previously misty and uncharted territory—that of the unconscious mind. And he narrated that film as well.

Huston films as varied as *Moby Dick, The Roots of Heaven*, and, most recently, *The Night of the Iguana* had also possessed religious overtones. Huston admits that *Moby Dick*, both as a book and as a movie, was "a great blasphemy" that challenged God's seeming inhumanity to man. In *The Night of the Iguana*, the Reverend Shannon expresses a quite opposite point of view by

questioning man's seeming inhumanity to God: his spoiling of the Eden-like planet God gave him and the violence he has done to its creatures. This is a concern fully shared by the zealous Morel in *The Roots of Heaven*, and as a theme pops up once again in *Under the Volcano*. Under the circumstances, it is not surprising that *The Bible*, considering its title and its subject matter, is often viewed not just as an expansion on Huston's previous religious-themed films but as some kind of ultimate statement on religion itself. The director disagrees with this assessment, however. "I look at the Bible as a collection of myths and legends," he says. "Not from a religious standpoint at all."

The film begins, naturally enough, with the Creation, then moves on to tell the stories of Adam and Eve, Cain and Abel, Noah's Ark, the Tower of Babel, and, finally, the tale of Abraham, whose devotion God tests by demanding that he sacrifice his only son. It also includes the sordid saga of Sodom and Gomorrah, which Huston destroys in a fiery explosion that looks like an atom bomb blast— an image that director Robert Aldrich had used earlier in his DeMille-like Biblical epic, *Sodom and Gomorrah* (1963).

Huston hired celebrated photographer Ernest

151

Noah (John Huston) and his children hear the voice of God (Huston also) as they ready the Ark for the oncoming deluge.

Panic grips the people as the Tower of Babel is destroyed and their language confounded.

Haas to canvass the world and shoot footage of erupting volcanos, storms at sea, and other natural phenomena for the opening Creation sequence. Italian artists Manzu, Corrado Cagli, Marco Chiari and a battery of other artists and sculptors were employed by the director to design the film's imaginative and sometimes massive sets—such as the huge 200' by 60' Ark—as well as its costumes. The result was a Huston film whose visual beauty outshined anything the director had done previously—not to mention the films of DeMille—but which, it must also be admitted, unfolded at a snail's pace. The film comes most comically alive during the Noah's Ark sequence and most dramatically alive during the concluding passage dealing with Abraham.

Upon the film's release, reviewers tended to take favorable notice of the film's impressive visuals and the delightful Noah's Ark sequence, but dismiss the film overall as somewhat of a bore. The Harvard *Lampoon* was perhaps the most unkind, listing the film as one of the year's ten worst and denouncing Huston's Noah as the year's worst performance by an actor in a supporting role. The *Lampoon* also went on to bestow the film with a special award honoring "...the one lone cow in *The Bible* who supplied an estimated nine hundred seventy-four gallons of milk to all the animals on the Ark for forty days and forty nights." The Academy of Motion Picture Arts and Sciences was equally uncharitable; it chose to ignore the film all together.

Nevertheless, *The Bible* was a big hit with audiences and remains the most financially successful film of Huston's career.

Casino Royale (1967)

A COLUMBIA PICTURE
Technicolor/130 minutes

CREDITS:

Directors: John Huston, Ken Hughes, Val Guest, Robert Parrish, and Joseph McGrath; *Producers:* Charles K. Feldman and Jerry Bresler; *Screenplay:* Wolf Mankowitz, John Law and Michael Sayers, based (loosely) on the novel *Casino Royale* by Ian Fleming; *Cinematographer:* Jack Hildyard; *Editor:* Bill Lenny; *Music:*

Burt Bacharach; *Art Directors:* John Howell, Ivor Beddoes and Lionel Couch; *Videocassette source:* Not Available.

CAST:

Evelyn Tremble: Peter Sellers; *Vesper Lynd:* Ursula Andress; *Sir James Bond:* David Niven; *Le Chiffre:* Orson Welles; *Mata Bond:* Joanna Pettit; *Jimmy Bond:* Woody Allen; *Agent Mimi:* Deborah Kerr; *Ransom:* William Holden; *The Detainer:* Daliah Lavi; *Le Grand:* Charles Boyer; *McTarry:* John Huston; *Smernov:* Kurt Kasznar; *French Legionnaire:* Jean-Paul Belmondo; *Moneypenny:* Barbara Bouchet; *Miss Goodthighs:* Jacqueline Bisset.

* * *

Contemporary Reviews

"*Casino Royale* escalates the humor of gadgetry beyond human capacity to cope. It has no story, because the characters have no fixed strengths....Part of *Casino Royale* was directed by John Huston (who also does a garnet cameo in Scotch-Irish accent I still don't believe), and one reflects that this same Huston has a lot to answer for concerning these farce-thrillers."—*Esquire*

"It's the sort of reckless, disconnected nonsense that could be telescoped or stopped at any point. If it were stopped at the end of an hour and 40 minutes instead of at the end of two hours and ten minutes, it might be a terminally satisfying entertainment instead of the wearying one it is."—*The New York Times*

* * *

As with *Freud,* the long and difficult task of bringing *The Bible* to the screen prompted Huston to relax with his next project, *Casino Royale,* a lighthearted romp which, like *The List of Adrian Messenger,* allowed the director to unpack his bags and shoot virtually on his St. Clerans doorstep. While the end-result of such a relaxing switch may have been mixed in the case of *Messenger,* it clearly was not in the case of *Casino Royale,* which remains the worst film (or semi-film) of Huston's career. It is so bad, in fact, that the director fails even to mention it in his autobiography.

To be fair, of course, *Casino Royale* is not wholly a Huston film. He was only one of five directors who contributed to it. That being said, however, one must quickly add that his segment, the film's opening half hour, doesn't stand apart from the rest either. Overall, *Casino Royale* is an unfunny shambles of a film, and Huston's portion of it is no less so.

The film rights to *Casino Royale,* the first of Ian Fleming's popular James Bond novels, had been pur-

John Huston as McTarry, better known as ''M,'' James Bond's boss in Casino Royale.

Agents McTarry (Huston), Ransom (William Holden), Le Grand (Charles Boyer) and Smernov (Kurt Kasznar) visit Bond (David Niven) at his country home in an effort to coax him out of retirement.

Ex-enemy agent Mimi (Deborah Kerr), wife of the late ''M,'' assists the back-to-work Bond (David Niven) with one of the film's less elaborate gadgets.

chased some years before by director Gregory Ratoff, who subsequently sold them to producer (and former talent agent) Charles K. Feldman. Originally, Feldman sought to bring the book to the screen as a straight Bond thriller starring Sean Connery. Failing to wrestle Connery's services away from producers Albert R. Broccoli and Harry Saltzman, however, he decided to spoof the Bond phenomenon instead. Though three writers are officially credited for their work on the script, at least twice as many actually took part in its development, including producer Feldman, co-star Woody Allen, and co-director Huston. The patchwork result bore almost no relationship to the Fleming novel on which it was "based." In the book, 007 is sent to topple a Russian agent and fabulously wealthy casino owner known as Le Chiffre, a task he accomplishes with a combination of derring-do and skill in a protracted game of baccarat against his evil adversary.

Little of this but the names of the characters turned up in the film, however.

As the film opens, M (Huston) and three intelligence agents representing the various super-powers arrive at Bond's estate to try and coax him out of retirement. The ostensible reason for this, according to M and his compatriots, is that es-pionage has become an impure business in this last half of the twentieth century (a foreshadowing of *The Kremlin Letter?*) and needs Bond back. Initially Bond refuses, but when his estate is blown up by enemy agents and M and the others are killed, he dons his double 0 spurs once more. He visits M's widow (Deborah Kerr), an enemy agent herself who tries to kill him. But when he displays his Bondian manliness to her, she has a change of heart and in a woefully unfunny in-joke reference to Kerr's appearance in Huston's *Heaven Knows, Mr. Allison* (1957) decides to become a nun. A mindless car chase in which Bond is pursued by a remote-controlled milk truck through Ireland's narrow country roads mercifully concludes Huston's segment of the film.

Reflections in a Golden Eye (1967)

A WARNER BROTHERS-SEVEN ARTS PRODUCTION
Technicolor/108 minutes

CREDITS:

Director: John Huston; *Producer:* Ray Stark; *Screenplay:* Chapman Mortimer and Gladys Hill, based on the novel *Reflections in a Golden Eye* by Carson McCullers; *Cinematographers:* Aldo Tonti and Oswald Morris (uncredited); *Editor:* Russell Lloyd; *Music:* Toshiro Mayuzumi; *Production designer:* Stephen Grimes; *Videocassette source:* Warner Home Video.

The secret lovers (Brian Keith and Elizabeth Taylor) out for a ride.

CAST:

Leonora Penderton: Elizabeth Taylor; *Major Weldon Penderton:* Marlon Brando; *Lt. Col. Morris Langdon:* Brian Keith; *Alison Langdon:* Julie Harris; *Private Williams:* Robert Forster; *Anacleto:* Zorro David.

* * *

Contemporary Reviews

''Mean, moody and rather magnificent tale of strange desires and bizarre fancies on an army post in the Deep South. Huston's best job of direction in some time and very striking, even in its simplified color version.''—*Sight and Sound*

''Huston overdirects *Reflections* for the sake of a mass audience in which he has little confidence. His film lacks the special stillness of the novel. There is too much expressionistic foliage on the screen and too much declamatory thunder on the sound track.''—*Village Voice*

''Hell hath no homicidal fury like a homosexual scorned. This is the commonplace conclusion that is abruptly and melodramatically reached after a detailed and devastating study of officer life on an

Huston on the set with Elizabeth Taylor.

The wantonly sensual Leonora (Elizabeth Taylor) is observed
with barely concealed disgust by her husband, the
homosexual Major Penderton (Marlon Brando).

American army base. The shame of it is that this conclusion is so anti-climactic and banal, because so much in the picture seems to be leading—certainly prepares us to expect—much more.''—*The New York Times*

*   *   *

Reflections in a Golden Eye, Carson McCullers' brooding psychological detective story about the mixing of a group of neurotics on a Deep South army base and the murder that results, was yet another of those elusive and virtually unfilmable books that Huston looked upon as a challenge. It is the kind of interior work that few directors would see as having much cinematic potential—and absolutely none at the box office. For this reason, it was decided early on that the cast had to consist of the biggest names in Hollywood, names that would ensure a box office draw.

Elizabeth Taylor, having confounded the critics with her atypical, Oscar-winning performance as Martha, the boozy, venomous slattern in *Who's Afraid of Virginia Woolf* (1966), saw in *Reflections* an opportunity to repeat that triumph. Indeed, *Reflections* and *Virginia* are very similar in both mood and theme. Taylor's selfish and abusive Leonora Penderton, an

Leonora (Elizabeth Taylor) and Lieutenant Colonel Langdon (Brian Keith) play cards, as well as footsy, as Penderton (Marlon Brando) sits apart from them, isolated by his own ''love life.''

army brat whose officer husband is a repressed homosexual whom she despises, is a virtual stand-in for Martha. Of course, in her inability to deal with boredom and total obliviousness to the wants and needs of others, she also resembles Stanley Timberlake, the ''unlucky'' heroine of Huston's *In This Our Life,* as well as many other Huston characters.

For the role of her tormented husband, a ramrod major who must face the fact that he is more Oscar Wilde than George S. Patton, Taylor wanted her close friend, Montgomery Clift. Despite the rough sledding they'd had on *Freud,* Huston and Clift each agreed. Clift, however, died of a coronary prior to shooting and his role went to Marlon Brando, who had originally been considered for the part played by Brian Keith, Taylor's equally neurotic paramour in the film.

The setting of the film is a peacetime fort in the south where, according to a title card, ''…a few years ago there was a murder committed.'' We do not know who the murderer or victim is until the end, after which the same title card reappears. Like *Let There Be Light* and *Freud,* the film thus becomes a kind of intellectual thriller inviting us to guess along with it as the characters slowly reveal themselves and the unconscious motives that drive them. As with *Freud,* sex is at the bottom of it all.

Leonora is a wantonly sensual creature for whom horseback riding is a primary form of sensual excitement. Her empathy and fondness for her stallion, Firebird, is greater than it is for people, whom

Penderton (Marlon Brando) readies the drunken Leonora (Elizabeth Taylor) for bed, though he will not share it with her.

she considers toys. She gloats in humiliating her husband Weldon, a prissy career officer who is no longer able to make love to her because he's coming out of the closet at last and has taken to pursuing an enlisted man named Williams, a shy and strange young soldier whose buddies tease him about his virginity and apparent hands-off attitude toward women. Williams, a horse fetishist also, has meanwhile fallen for Leonora, into whose bedroom he creeps each night to watch her sleep and fondle her underwear. Leonora's lover, Lt. Col. Langdon, is a man who is caught up in his own macho image. He can't tolerate his wife's Filipino houseboy, Anacleto, because the boy is so effeminate and fairly clings to his wife's side. At one point Langdon remarks to Weldon that, ''If Anacleto was in the Army, it would have made a man of him.'' Weldon, self-knowingly, fails to agree.

Langdon's invalid wife is no less neurotic, having recently cut off her nipples with a pair of garden shears following the death of their baby. Discovering her husband's affair with Leonora, she threatens to divorce him, but he commits her to a sanitarium instead, rather than face a blow to his masculine and professional pride. Anacleto vanishes when Mrs. Langdon suffers a fatal heart attack,

Penderton (Marlon Brando) shoots Private Williams in his wife's bedroom.

leaving Langdon alone to brood that, "...there's only two things left to me now. Keep myself fit and do my job. Serve my country."

Weldon's growing passion for Williams climaxes when he discovers him creeping into the house one night. Believing Williams is coming to him, he sits on the edge of his bed, straightens his hair, and waits longingly—only to be stunned when Williams goes into his wife's room instead. Outraged that the reviled Leonora, if unknowingly, has beaten him even here, he storms into her room and shoots Williams dead.

As more than one reviewer noted, the murder itself comes as sort of an anti-climax, but that's relatively unimportant because the murder, and our foreknowledge of it, is mainly a device to keep us watching and listening to the characters, most of whom threaten each other's life at one point or another. *Reflections* is not so much a whodunit as a why-did-it-have-to-happen-at-all? As Montgomery Clift says in *Freud*, "From error to error, one discovers the entire truth." *Reflections* reveals a progression of errors, committed by a fumbling cast of characters who are psychologically prone to them because they never communicate with each other and continually misinterpret one another's words and actions. The theme of watching, yet not really seeing, runs throughout the film. Weldon deceives himself into believing that Williams is coming to him because that's what he wants to believe—a belief fostered when, following a jeep accident, a group of soldiers, including Williams, turns around to see what happened, and Weldon, who has been following Williams, perceives the boy's staring at him as sexual interest. When Mrs. Langdon sees Williams creep into the Penderton home, she convinces herself he's her husband, goes to investigate, and, discovering that he isn't, tells Langdon that Leonora is deceiving *him* by having an affair with an enlisted man. Her husband ridicules the idea that Leona is having an affair with him or anyone else, and later, when Mrs. Langdon spots Williams again from her window, she persuades herself that he isn't really there.

All the characters in *Reflections* are quintessential

162

Huston setting a scene with Brian Keith, Julie Harris and Zorro David.

Huston losers in that they engineer the misfortunes that befall them. There isn't a winner in the bunch—except, perhaps, for Anacleto, though we don't know for sure as we never learn what happened to him. Still, just having gotten away from this nest of obsessive and self-destructive people can be seen as a positive step. At the very least, he takes himself out of the running as either murderer or victim.

To emphasize the film's psychological oppressiveness and find a visual equivalent for the novel's brooding, interior spirit, Huston, together with cinematographers Aldo Tonti and Oswald Morris (who took over halfway through but accepted no screen credit), evolved a costly and complicated process of desaturating the film's color until only a gold and slightly pinkish image emerged. Morris called the effect on the film's mood "quite extraordinary." Warner Brothers didn't agree, however, and released the film in full Technicolor, which made the film pictorially striking and quite beautiful to look at, but decidedly worked against the emotional impact Huston wanted *Reflections* to have. John Russell Taylor, one of the few contemporary critics to have seen the film in its desaturated process, summed up the effect of this switch when he wrote: "…atmosphere is obviously very important to such a subject, and the ghostly, tantalizing look of the original contributed a lot. The film still works well enough, but the images of Private Williams lurking by Leonora's bedside in a room colored only by the faint, almost unnoticeable pink glow from a negligee hung behind the door, or of Anacleto painting for his mad mistress's pleasure a curious, almost indecipherable image of a cockerel with one great glittering eye…remain indelible from the first version, reduced as they are in the second to a relative commonplace."

Sinful Davey (1969)

A MIRISCH PICTURE
Released through United Artists
DeLuxe Color/95 minutes

CREDITS:

Director: John Huston; *Producers:* Walter Mirisch and William N. Grof; *Screenplay:* James R. Webb, based on the autobiography *The Life of David Haggert* by David Haggert; *Cinematographers:* Freddie Young and Ted Scaife; *Editor:* Russell Lloyd; *Music:* Ken Thorne; *Art Director:* Carmen Dillon; *Videocassette source:* Not Available.

Davey (John Hurt) and his accomplice, MacNab (Ronald Fraser), are caught in the act of bodysnatching, Davey's latest criminal enterprise.

CAST:

Davey Haggert: John Hurt; *Annie:* Pamela Franklin; *Constable:* Nigel Davenport; *McNab:* Ronald Fraser; *Duke of Argyll:* Robert Morley; *Jean:* Fidelma Murphy; *Duchess of Argyll:* Maxine Audley; *Penelope:* Fionnuala Flanagan; *Sir James:* Donal McCann; *Captain Douglas:* Allan Cuthbertson; *Bill:* Eddie Byrne; *Boots:* Niall MacGinnis; *Jock:* Noel Purcell; *Andrew:* Francis De Wolff; *Mary:* Judith Furse.

* * *

Contemporary Reviews

"…a movie of no discernible style, notable only for the artistic and physical resources it squanders."— *The New York Times*

* * *

Beautifully photographed in Ireland, *Sinful Davey* is another of John Huston's *films manqué*—the others being *The Red Badge of Courage*, *The Barbarian and the Geisha*, and *Phobia*. It tells the story of a young Nineteenth-century Scottish thief (whose father was hanged by the Crown for similar offences) who sets out

Davey Haggert (John Hurt) performs a delicate balancing act to elude capture by Army officers. He has just deserted to "fulfill his destiny."

165

*Sinful Davey (John Hurt) comes to the rescue of Sir James
Campbell (Donal McCann), who has been attacked by
hoodlums.*

166

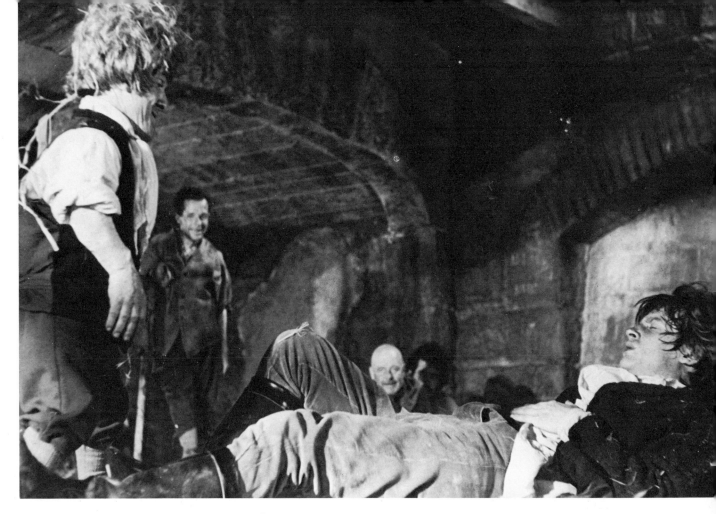

Davey (John Hurt), newly arrived in prison, is greeted and taught a lesson by fellow inmate Billy the Goat (Mickser Reid), the man with the head of iron.

to exceed his late father's reputation for outlawry before he too is brought down by the authorities. The film was made almost back to back with Huston's *A Walk with Love and Death*; both were released the same year. Taken together, they reflect two different, though not necessarily opposing, views of youth during the turbulent sixties.

In *A Walk with Love and Death*, two youthful lovers (Anjelica Huston and Assaf Dayan) are swept away by a ravaging and seemingly unending war they fail to comprehend, want no part of, but simply cannot escape. Davey on the other hand is a reckless youth and an army deserter who determines to fly in the face of authority at every opportunity—a sort of Nineteenth-century Yippie. *A Walk with Love and Death*, befitting its theme, is the more somber of the two films, whereas *Sinful Davey* is a mordant black comedy about crime and criminals that harks back to Huston's *Beat the Devil* and looks forward to *Prizzi's Honor*. As with *Beat the Devil*, the subtlety of the film's humor seemed to escape contemporary audiences and critics—the few, that is, who got a chance to see *Sinful Davey*.

Pulled from release after an unsuccessful one-week run in New York City, the film has seldom re-surfaced, not even on television, and remains one of Huston's premier box office flops.

Prior to its short-lived release, *Sinful Davey* was also heavily re-cut (by producer Walter Mirisch), who restructured the film so that its story became a flashback. Mirisch also added an unnecessary narration (shades of *Red Badge*). "I was aghast!" Huston remarked upon seeing it. "Like *The Barbarian and the Geisha*, it had been ruined after I delivered my final cut."

Ever since *The Red Badge of Courage* debacle with MGM, Huston's studio contracts have stipulated that he be given a 16mm print of *his* cut of any film he makes for them. This stipulation came too late to save the original cut of *The Red Badge of Courage* from oblivion, but not, it would appear, *The Barbarian and the Geisha* and *Sinful Davey*. Enterprising videocassette distributiors should take note of this if they are considering releasing either of these two films on tape. By releasing Huston's original versions rather than the tampered-with theatrical prints now extant, they would be providing audiences and Huston fans with a rare opportunity to view these two films exactly as John Huston intended them to be seen.

167

A Walk with Love and Death (1969)

A 20th CENTURY-FOX PRODUCTION
DeLuxe Color/90 minutes

CREDITS:

Director: John Huston; *Producer:* Carter De Haven; *Screenplay:* Dale Wasserman and Hans Koningsberger, based on the novel *A Walk with Love and Death* by Hans Koningsberger; *Cinematographer:* Ted Scaife; *Editor:* Russell Lloyd; *Music:* Georges Delerue; *Art Director:* Wolf Witzemann; *Videocassette source:* Not Available.

CAST:

Claudia: Anjelica Huston; *Heron:* Assaf Dayan: *Robert:* Anthony Corlan; *Sir Meles:* John Hallam: *Pilgrim Leader:* Robert Lang; *Priest:* Guy Deghy; *Monk:* Michael Gough; *Robert the Elder:* John Huston.

* * *

Contemporary Reviews

''No historical data could explain the pervasive terror of that tiny fragment of the Hundred Year War that John Huston treats in his beautiful and under-rated *A Walk with Love and Death*. . . . Huston starts with the ordinary reality of this war—the bewildering way that enemies and friends become interchangeable—and works towards more universal overtones of doom and fear. His style is simple and low-keyed, but there is never any question of linkage between his medieval world and the modern *zeitgeist.* ''—*Film Heritage*

''…one feels that Huston is no longer doing what's close to him—that he's looking for subjects…the movie lacks urgency. One fears that it will be pretentious, but it isn't, and it's continually compell-ing. But it's too remote, and, maybe because it's so restrained—almost reserved—it never fully releases the lyricism of its conception.''—*The New Yorker*

''So much of what succeeds in *A Walk with Love and Death* resembles what fails in other recent John Huston movies that it is tempting to label this film a lucky accident. But luck in the arts is rarely accidental, and Huston's tendency to idealize, soften and generalize the action of the Hans Koningsberger novel upon which his movie is based contributes to real and intelligent artistic achievement.''—*The New York Times*

* * *

The violence of the Hundred Years War. From John Huston's A Walk with Love and Death.

Anjelica Huston as Claudia, one of the doomed lovers in her father's A Walk with Love and Death.

169

With tongue not completely in cheek, Huston says he took on *A Walk with Love and Death* in order to give his then sixteen-year-old actress daughter, Anjelica, her first big break on the screen. The producers of the film, 20th Century-Fox, agreed to finance the project—a period piece about two doomed young lovers surrounded by war—because they saw in it an opportunity to cash in on the success of Franco Zeffirelli's *Romeo and Juliet* (1968), which was doing "boffo biz" with the youth market all over the world. The film that Huston went on to make, however, was by no means the lavish romantic costumer that Fox expected. Nor did it make a star out of daughter Anjelica—*Prizzi's Honor* would accomplish that. Except in France, the film was a box office failure and is today considered one of Huston's biggest flops. In terms of

Heron (Assaf Dayan) exhibits his innate compassion to another victim of the war.

financial return—the film is still seldom shown—it may well be, but *A Walk with Love and Death* is also quite remarkable on a number of levels. One of them is that unlike most Huston films it intentionally reflects the times in which it was made, the turbulent sixties. The film is also an example of the director's technique at its most ascetic. Though a medieval war film full of knights, castles and battles, *A Walk with Love and Death* is resolutely no-epic.

The story takes place in France during the Peasant's Revolt of 1358, the beginning of the period more commonly known as the Hundred Years War. Heron, an expelled university student, heads for the sea to escape his war-ravaged homeland and along the way meets and falls in love with Claudia, the daughter of a nobleman who has been murdered by uprising peasants. The vengeful Claudia encourages Heron to make war on the peasants who killed her father, but his already pacifistic consciousness is

Her father dead, Claudia (Anjelica Huston) finds herself alone and an outcast.

raised even more by an encounter with another nobleman, Robert the Elder, who has joined the peasants because he considers their cause just. Robert and his son are slain by mercenary knights, and the two lovers flee once more. Seeking refuge in an abbey fortress, they decide to marry, but the righteous clergymen urge them to renounce the "ways of the flesh" or be expelled. They refuse, however, and after the nuns and monks flee the soon-to-be-attacked fortress to save their skins, Heron and Claudia marry one another in a private ceremony under the eyes of God. As the film ends, they await their fate at the hands of either the peasants or the knights, for, whichever faction ar-

rives to assault the fortress, the two lovers are doomed.

Huston intended to shoot this tragic story in France, but his plans were interrupted by the 1968 student riots there that threw Paris, indeed the whole country, into tumult. His second option was Czechoslovakia, but when Russian tanks moved in to quell the 1968 Czech Uprising, he was forced to move his unit to Austria and then Italy, where the film was completed.

The impact of all this political turmoil and violence—which was taking place not only in Europe, but in America as well—on the viewpoint of the film is unmistakable. Koningsberger's original novel sought to draw a direct parallel between the political unrest of medieval and modern times. Huston's film not only retains this parallel, but emphasizes it even more. "It is an abstract of our time with a Middle Age frame around it," he told the press.

Indeed it is. Essentially, Heron and Claudia are two flower children, who would prefer to make love, not war. But the politics of the age are against them and they are destroyed. Still, they meet their end with courage and a strong commitment to one another. Huston had made a "youth movie" alright, but one that didn't pander to its audience.

The lovers (Anjelica Huston and Assaf Dayan) take refuge in an abbey.

172

The Kremlin Letter (1970)

A 20th CENTURY-FOX PRODUCTION
DeLuxe Color/113 minutes

CREDITS:

Director: John Huston; *Producers:* Carter De Haven and Sam Wiesenthal; *Screenplay:* John Huston and Gladys Hill, based on the novel *The Kremlin Letter* by Noel Behn; *Cinematographer:* Ted Scaife; *Editor:* Russell Lloyd; *Music:* Robert Drasnin; *Art Director:* Elven Webb; *Videocassette source:* Not Available.

The efficient Whore (Nigel Green), leaning over crate, disposes of some recent victims.

CAST:

Ward/Sturdevant: Richard Boone; *Erika:* Bibi Andersson; *Whore:* Nigel Green; *Highwayman:* Dean Jagger; *Sophie:* Lila Kedrova; *Sweet Alice:* Michael MacLiammoir; *Rone:* Patrick O'Neal; *B.A.:* Barbara Parkins; *Potkin:* Ronald Radd; *Warlock:* George Sanders; *Kosnov:* Max Von Sydow; *Puppetmaker:* Raf Vallone; *Bresnavitch:* Orson Welles; *Erector Set:* Niall MacGinnis; *Priest:* Marc Lawrence; *Admiral:* John Huston.

* * *

Contemporary Reviews

"No doubt, as serious people say, we should expect more of Huston. *The Kremlin Letter* comes at you in a breathless rush, and carries you off on a switchback course of comedy, satire, irony and deeper meaning. Even if we forget the meaning and concentrate on the fun—as Huston himself has done for long stretches— the eventful trip through Hustonland should leave us with little cause for complaint."—*Sight and Sound*

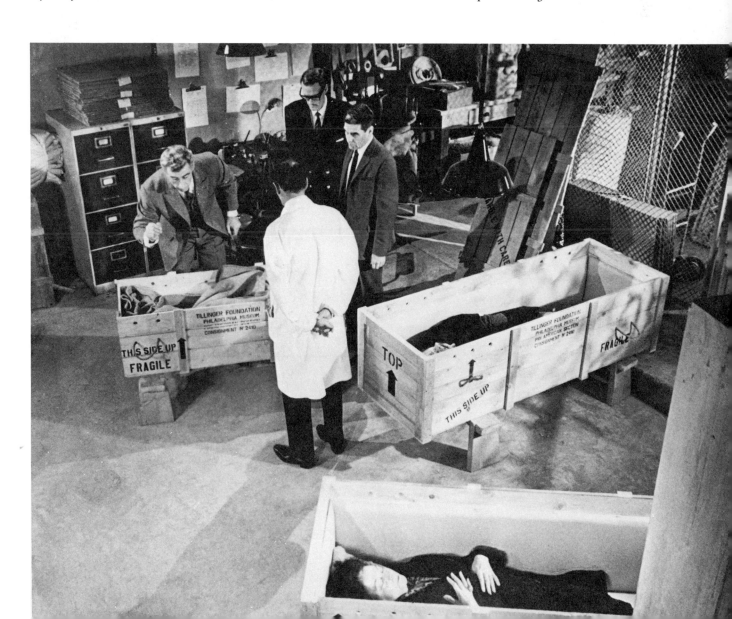

The Warlock (George Sanders) made up for his job as a female impersonator.

"*The Kremlin Letter* carries a foul load of script, full of exposition, and a complicated plot that loses one at the outset. The picture is visually undistinguished, and the sound is badly recorded.... *The Kremlin Letter* has a trick, unresolved ending that is miscalculated, because we don't give a damn. The publicity says, 'Be on time...for, if you miss the first five minutes, you miss one suicide, two executions, one seduction, and the key to the plot.' If you don't go at all, you can miss that and a lot more."—*The New Yorker*

"As with so many recent Huston films, the scale of everything—geography, sets, absurdities, misanthropies, running time—has been enlarged as if to disguise what looks to be the director's awful boredom with movies."—*The New York Times*

* * *

Barbara Parkins as B.A., who unlocks safes with her toes, but whose main job is to solicit information by making friends and sleeping with enemy agents.

When his plans to bring Brian Moore's prize-winning novel *The Lonely Passion of Judith Hearne* to the screen collapsed due to a lack of financing, and creative disagreements with producer Ely Landau over *The Madwoman of Chaillot* (1969) led to his walking off the project and being replaced by Bryan Forbes, Huston retrenched and turned to a quite different type of source material: Noel Behn's currently best-selling novel *The Kremlin Letter*. A spy thriller with echoes of *The Maltese Falcon* (its hero, Rone, is a linear descendant of the morally uncertain and potentially self-destructive Sam Spade) and *The Asphalt Jungle* (with its air of no honor among spies), it offered Huston yet another opportunity to explore his view of how poorly the world has fared—morally, politically, spiritually—since World War II, a recurring theme of Huston's evident in his work as early as *Key Largo* (1946), and, with its reverberations of the destructive Vietnam conflict, as recently as *A Walk with Love and Death* (1969). It would pop up again as an important subtheme in *Under the Volcano* (1984).

Orson Welles heads an all-star cast in Huston's The Kremlin Letter. *To his immediate right, Bibi Anderson, who plays the wife of sadistic K.G.B. agent Max von Sydow—seated second from Welles's left.*

Huston also admits to having chosen this for his next film because, after the poor box office showings of *Sinful Davey* and *A Walk with Love and Death,* he very much needed a hit, and *The Kremlin Letter,* a James Bond-like tale of espionage, kinky sex and sadistic violence, seemed a likely candidate. He was wrong. The film flopped—possibly for reasons having to do with the overall seriousness of the director's viewpoint, which contrasted greatly with the satiric tone he also brought to the film. Another possible reason for the film's failure with audiences was Patrick O'Neal's colorless performance as Rone. Like Sam Spade, Rone is a reckless adventurer who gets in over his head with a bunch of conniving, self-deluded cutthroats. As he lacks Spade's energy and wit, however, one tends not to care very much whether or not he comes out on top. And, in fact, he doesn't.

Because of his keen intelligence, photographic memory, and aggressive self-confidence, Rone, a lieutenant commander in the U.S. Navy, is discharged to undertake a top-secret mission to reclaim a stolen government letter declaring war on China that fell into the hands of the Russians years before. His chief contact is an abrasive but fatherly operative named Ward, who spells out the details of the scheme, trains him, then lets Rone go. His first step is to locate a group of former top spies (a sort of dirty quarter-dozen of espionage), who once worked together under the tutelage of a maverick spy named Sturdevant (who has since undergone plastic surgery and dropped out of sight), and enlist them in the cause. Each is known only by a bizarre code name—the Whore, the Erector Set, the Warlock,

Rone (Patrick O'Neal) gets out of this scrape but finds himself trapped in a moral dilemma at the film's conclusion.

etc.—and posseses a particular underhanded talent essential to the operation. Rone effortlessly accomplishes all this and sets the plot in motion. He even falls in love with the Erector Set's virginal protégé, a gorgeous thief named B.A. who unlocks safes with her toes, but whose main job is to solicit information by sleeping with enemy agents.

The Kremlin Letter turns out to be another of Huston's black birds, however. The scheme to reclaim it is entirely a bogus one cooked up by the legendary Sturdevant, disguising himself as Ward, in order to revenge himself against a brutal KGB officer named Kosnov. One by one the spies, who have been used only to smoke Kosnov out, are killed until only Rone and B.A. are left. She, however, has been kidnapped by the mercenary Sturdevant, who agrees to let her go only if Rone will undertake one more job for him—the execution of a pair of political undesirables. At the end

of the film, Rone, who is totally in over his head by now, is left to ponder his moral dilemma. Whichever way he chooses to act, someone innocent must die. The film concludes on this bleak note.

As is apparent, the plot of *The Kremlin Letter* is fairly convoluted and even confusing—a shortcoming Huston admits himself. This is another probable reason for its failure at the box office. But the film's main flaw is Rone. He's simply much less interesting than the cast of weird characters that surround him. Although he's the protagonist, he fairly slips into the background—unlike Sam Spade, who keeps pace with his colorful adversaries every step of the way. The *Mission Impossible*-like tone of the film (Robert Drasnin's score even sounds like Lalo Schifrin's theme for the then popular TV series) also works against it. Huston's aural experiment with having the foreign actors speak their dialogue entirely in Russian while simultaneously dubbing over the English translation in their own voices is yet another confusing element that fails to come off.

Fat City (1972)

A COLUMBIA PICTURE
Eastman Color/100 minutes

CREDITS:

Director: John Huston; *Producers:* John Huston and Ray Stark; *Screenplay:* Leonard Gardner, based on the novel *Fat City* by Leonard Gardner; *Cinematographer:* Conrad Hall; *Editor:* Marguerite Booth; *Music:* Marvin Hamlisch; *Art Director:* Richard Sylbert; *Videocassette source:* Not Available.

John Huston's gallery of losers in Fat City.

CAST:

Tully: Stacy Keach; *Ernie Munger:* Jeff Bridges; *Faye:* Candy Clark; *Oma:* Susan Tyrell; *Ruben:* Nicholas Colosanto; *Babe:* Art Aragon; *Earl:* Curtis Cokes; *Lucero:* Sixto Rodriguez; *Wes:* Billy Walker; *Buford:* Wayne Mahan; *Fuentes:* Ruben Navarro.

* * *

Contemporary Reviews

''Technically the film is efficient, with good use of locations in and around Stockton, California. There is useful depth of field in an early shot in a gymnasium where Bridges is punching a bag close to camera, while further back in the same composition Keach begins to shadowbox. Then comes a reverse shot of the same set-up. The ironic age gap and the contemplation of things to come have already

started to impinge: the fresh-faced boy will turn into the split-lip punk, sure as you're born. Huston, in a marked change from the merriment of some of his recent acting roles, has plunged into this downbeat parable with plenty of his well-known persuasion.''—*Films and Filming*

''The good news for those who have admired Huston's truest work (or for those who couldn't care less but who like engrossing movies) is that in *Fat City* Huston has confronted a piece of material and a milieu perfectly suited to his insights and talents. The result is his best film in years, and one of the best he has ever done: a lean, compassionate, detailed, raucous, sad, strong look at some losers and survivors on the side streets of small-city Middle America.''—*Los Angeles Times*

Tully (Stacy Keach) slugs it out with his Mexican opponent (Sixto Rodriguez).

''Nowadays, when so many filmmakers are free and so many audiences are unhappy, it is a positive virtue for a director to avert disaster. Huston might have tried to get more out of *Fat City*, but at the very considerable risk of ending up with much less, and being the old poker player that he is, he decided not to bluff with a middling hand. The result is a modest success that the esthetic poverty of the season has elevated into a major triumph.''—*Village Voice*

* * *

Huston drew substantially upon his own experiences as a club fighter on the California circuit in the making of *Fat City*. He even went so far as to look up some old acquaintances from his early days as a boxer and cast them in small roles. As a result, *Fat City* has an ultra-realistic feel to it which is enhanced by Conrad Hall's cinema-verité photography.

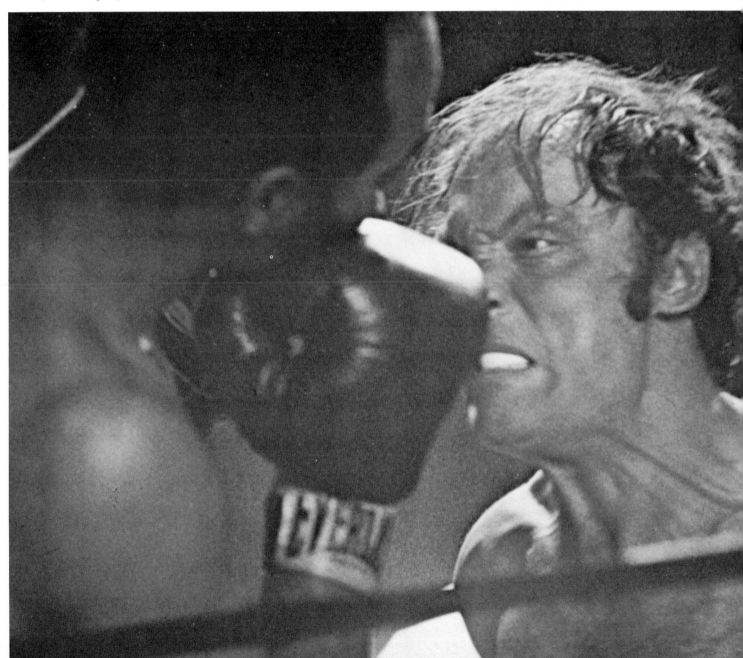

As the film is about losers who spend much of their time hanging around indoors, in gyms and bars, Hall chose to shoot mostly under available light conditions, thereby eliminating any surface prettiness or gloss to the locations. Remarking on the film's realistic photography, Huston said, "When you go into a bar it's like stumbling into a theater. You can't find your way until your eyes adjust themselves. There you reach around and try and find a barstool the same way you try to find a seat in a theater. That is what led Conrad and me to do the exteriors with explosive skies and the background and interiors, which were all on the spot, almost in silhouettes." Hall's technique adds immeasurably to the film's stark, documentary-like atmosphere. Once again, however, the experimental palette of a Hus-

ton film went unnoticed by the Academy of Motion Picture Arts and Sciences, for Conrad Hall received no nomination for his outstanding and innovative work.

Huston adapted the film from a widely praised first novel by Leonard Gardner. Gardner alone is credited for the screenplay, but Huston and Gladys Hill contributed largely to it as well. Shot on location in Stockton, California, *Fat City* marked the first time the director had made a full-length feature wholly in America since *The Misfits*.

Once again, Huston focuses his and our attention on a group of dreamers and self-deceivers, led by an over-the-hill (at age 29!) pug named Tully. Once a small-time champion, Tully is now a broken-down wreck of a man, and an alcoholic to boot. Divorced from his wife, he continues to dream about settling down once again and being back on top in the ring, though he is now hardly equipped to rise to either challenge. Like one of the self-deluded cus-

Tully (Stacy Keach) after his victorious fight. He hardly looks the winner, though.

Tully (Stacy Keach) and Ernie (Jeff Bridges) earn a few extra bucks outside the ring.

tomers of Harry Hope's bar in Eugene O'Neill's *The Iceman Cometh* (which *Fat City* resembles in a number of ways), Tully survives on pipedreams; without them, he wouldn't last through the day.

Tully's not alone. He befriends a younger fighter, Ernie Munger, who fancies himself an up-and-comer. While Tully dreams of a comeback, Ernie dreams of his first big win, though Huston makes it quite clear that the kid's chances for a future in the fight game are little better than Tully's. Tully, in fact, could be Ernie just a few years down the road if the kid doesn't smarten up. Huston drives

this home when, at one point, Ernie is knocked out in the ring before his trainer even finishes folding up the kid's robe.

The drama's other chief loser is Oma, a barfly whom Tully briefly moves in with after her present old man, Earl, gets busted for assault and sent to prison. The scenes between Stacy Keach as Tully and Susan Tyrell as Oma are funny, pathetic and stingingly real as the two of them, both losers, ramble on, argue with each other at cross-purposes, and finally drive each other nuts. Tyrell, who has since fashioned a career out of playing emotional basket cases like Oma, won an Oscar nomination for Best Supporting Actress (she lost to Eileen Heckart for *Butterflies are Free*), though her part is really a lead. The

181

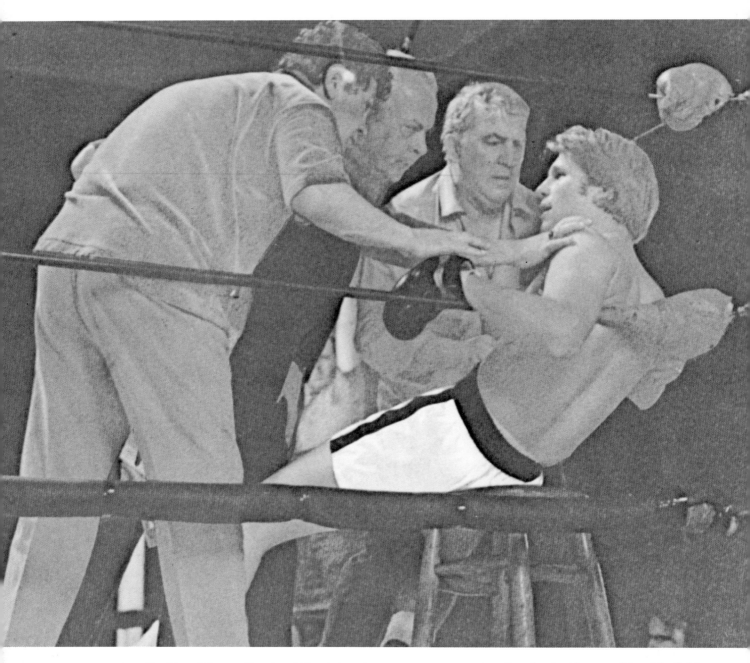

Ernie (Jeff Bridges) follows Tully's downhill path into the ring.

only other significant female role is that of Ernie's wife, Faye, but her appearances are brief.

Huston doesn't deny that *Fat City* (a slang term for "making it") is a downbeat story and attributes its poor showing at the box office mainly to that fact. Even when Tully wins his comeback bout, it's on a technicality. And he takes such a battering that at first he doesn't even realize he has won. His Mexican opponent enters the ring just because it's a job, fights even though he's ill, and when the fight is over and Tully is basking in all the makebelieve hoopla, collects his share of the gate and leaves the stadium alone, his feet firmly on the ground.

Tully's manager cautions him to stay sober, keep fit, and he'll soon be on the comeback trail for real. But Tully dismisses his winnings for the night as too small and rejects the manager's offer. It's clear that for Tully, the pipedream has become a lot easier to live with than the terrifying prospect of turning that dream into a reality.

182

The Life and Times of Judge Roy Bean (1972)

A NATIONAL GENERAL PICTURE
Technicolor/123 minutes

CREDITS:

Director: John Huston; *Producer:* John Foreman; *Screenplay:* John Milius; *Cinematographer:* Richard Moore; *Editor:* Hugh S. Fowler; *Music:* Maurice Jarre; *Art Director:* Tambi Larsen; *Videocassette source:* Warner Home Video.

CAST:

Judge Roy Bean: Paul Newman; *Lillie Langtry:* Ava Gardner; *Maria Elena:* Victoria Principal; *Reverend LaSalle:* Anthony Perkins; *Sam Dodd:* Tab Hunter; *Bad Bob:* Stacy Keach; *Grizzly Adams:* John Huston; *Frank Gass:* Roddy McDowell; *Rose Bean:* Jacqueline Bisset; *Tector Crites:* Ned Beatty; *Bart Jackson:* Jim Buck; *Nick the Grub:* Matt Clark; *Whorehouse Lucky Jim:* Steve Kanaly; *Fermilee Parlee:* Bill McKinney.

* * *

Contemporary Reviews

"Instant folklore from John Huston. A two-hour Western burlesque, strongly reminiscent of *The Ballad of Cable Hogue* but overblown and self-indulgent.

Bean (Paul Newman) gets his revenge on those who hanged him and left him for dead. Once again, Huston indulges his penchant for recreating, or at least recalling, celebrated paintings. The scene recalls Frederick Remington's famous oil of an Old West saloon shoot-out titled "A Miss Deal."

The director as Grizzly Adams in The Life and Times of Judge Roy Bean.

The title role looks a little heavy on Paul Newman, who gets upstaged by a bear.''—*Sight and Sound*

"Newman's twittering and Huston's small jokes with the famous performers making cameo appearances are just stardust they're throwing in their own eyes—maybe so they won't have to see the ugly right-wing fantasy they've trapped themselves in. Their only achievement is in blunting the impact of the material: the audience, trying desperately just to have a good time, takes its cues from the tacky genial tone and reacts as if it were watching a more violent version of a spoofy James Garner TV show, until the snarled point of view locks the audience out al-

together. It might have been better if Huston and Newman hadn't softened the viciousness; then they'd have had to face the disgrace of what they were working on. Of course, if they hadn't tampered with it, it might have been a hit, and then maybe they wouldn't have been ashamed at all.''—*The New Yorker*

* * *

John Huston says that what attracted him to John Milius's script for *The Life and Times of Judge Roy Bean* was its "...splendid feeling for the Old West." Yet the film he made from it could scarcely be called a western in the purest sense of the term. Actually, it is more of a satire—a sort of *Beat the Devil* on horseback—in which the director spoofs everything from western genre clichés to star Paul Newman's big box

Bean (Paul Newman) and the approving townsfolk look over the corpse of Bean's latest victim, flamboyant albino gunfighter Bad Bob (Stacy Keach), with approval.

Bean (Paul Newman) officiates at the funeral of yet another breaker of ''The Law West of the Pecos.'' The woman is Bean's Indian common law wife, Maria Elena (Victoria Principal).

office hit *Butch Cassidy and the Sundance Kid*. Like *Butch, Roy Bean* even includes a tacky, out-of-place song (''Marmelade, Molasses and Honey'' sung by Andy Williams), but in this case the director sends the interlude up by having the sequence played not for wistfulness but for foolishness in which Newman and his Indian ''wife'' cavort with a bear.

And yet the film is also serious. When the town Judge Bean has built grows into an oil-rich empire run by the power-mad lawyer, Gass, conniving politicians, and a strong-arm police force (called ''brown shirted bastards'') whose job it is to extinguish any lingering flames of ''Beanism,'' Huston also links the film to a theme that has run throughout much of his work ever since *Key Largo:* America's loss of innocence and its ideals. The film also serves as a warm-up to *The Man Who Would Be King*—which may well have been the real reason why Huston was attracted to it in the first place. Like *King,* the film

186

Bean (Paul Newman) tries to string up Frank Gass (Roddy McDowell) for trying to usurp his power.

switches back and forth from broad comedy to seriousness and culminates in an elegy for the late hero whose story has been told. In many ways, it is the same story. Like Dravot, Roy Bean carves out his niche in a benighted land, sets himself up as almighty ruler and dispenses justice with an iron (though not nearly as equitable) hand. Dravot loses his kingdom because he deludes himself into believing that he's a god and pushes his luck too far. Bean has a similar fantasy obsession (with actress Lillie Langtry) that takes him away from his empire just long enough for others to assume power there. When he returns, he finds his omnipotence questioned, so he packs up and slips away—though his spirit eventually returns to rescue the town from the corruption that has engulfed it.

While there are obvious parallels between *The Man Who Would Be King* and *The Life and Times of Judge Roy Bean,* there are differences too, the most important one being the character of Bean himself, who is not nearly so well drawn (or likable) a rogue as Daniel Dravot. Both are equally larger than life. But Bean

Lillie Langtry (Ava Gardner) surveys the historical weaponry housed in the Judge Roy Bean Memorial Museum as she passes through Vinegaroon.

remains only a caricature of the rough and ready frontiersman whose idea of justice is to hang everybody who disagrees with him. In this regard, it's difficult to separate him from the "brown shirts" who take over Vinegaroon after his departure, and all but impossible to mourn the passing of his type of "rugged individualist." In contrast, we *do* mourn the loss of Dravot, who, for all his failings, does make Kafiristan a better place to live.

John Milius insists that his original script for *Roy Bean* was less of a cartoon and that on paper Bean was a more multi-faceted character. "There were dark, evil sides to that man, as well as funny, charming sides," he says. "You saw that the evil was necessary at first, but that, as time progressed, it was no longer needed….The whole thing was horribly mangled." The elements Milius wanted to stress aren't exactly missing from the film, but are definitely suppressed due to Huston's contrasting desire to make a wild and extravagant satire on the Old West rather than a bona fide genre piece. Milius might better have directed the film himself, which he attempted to do, but was voted down by producer John Foreman and his partner, Paul

Newman, in favor of the more experienced Huston. In a sense though, the film Milius wanted to make had already been done as Sam Peckinpah's *The Ballad of Cable Hogue* (1970), a film to which even Huston's lampooning version of the tale bears a very striking resemblance—particularly in its opening scenes where Bean is left to die, but survives to build a lucrative business out of nothing, aided by an itinerant preacher.

Milius's anger with Huston over the latter's comic treatment of his *Roy Bean* script proved short-lived, however. A year later he finally did make his directorial debut with *Dillinger* and in 1975 cast Huston the actor as John Hay in his epic *The Wind and the Lion*. In fact, Milius now admits that he learned a great deal from watching Huston direct *The Life and Times of Judge Roy Bean*. "He was like a drill instructor at boot camp," he says. "Now I'm a real marine [myself] and I can like my D.I."

The Mackintosh Man (1973)

A WARNER BROTHERS PICTURE
Technicolor/105 miinutes

CREDITS:

Director: John Huston; *Producer:* John Foreman; *Screenplay:* Walter Hill, based on the novel *The Freedom Trap* by Desmond Bagley; *Cinematographer:* Oswald Morris; *Editor:* Russell Lloyd; *Music:* Maurice Jarre; *Art Director:* Alan Tomkins; *Videocassette source:* Warner Home Video.

CAST:

Reardon: Paul Newman; *Mrs. Smith:* Dominique Sanda; *Sir George Wheeler:* James Mason; *Mackintosh:* Harry Andrews; *Slade:* Ian Bannen; *Brown:* Michael Hordern; *Brunskill:* Peter Vaughan; *Soames:* Nigel Patrick; *Judge:* Roland Culver; *Taafe:* Percy Herbert; *Jack Summers:* Robert Lang; *Gerda:* Jenny Runacre; *Buster:* John Bindon; *Prosecutor:* Hugh Manning; *Police Commissioner:* Wolfe Morris; *O'Donovan:* Noel Purcell; *Tervis:* Donald Webster; *Palmer:* Keith Bell; *Warner:* Niall MacGinnis.

* * *

Contemporary Reviews

"A curiously dishevelled script provides ground-work for one of Huston's more blarneying entertainments, veering from simple-mindeness to sophistication according to the mood of the moment."—*Sight and Sound*

"*The Mackintosh Man*, as melodrama, ranks somewhere between Huston's *The Kremlin Letter* and *Beat the Devil* (at least it's almost as confusing as *Beat the Devil*, if not as funny)."—*The New York Times*

"…no one is better than Huston at using 'background' to propel—rather than merely support—the main action. Only he could convey so much impending danger in an Irish pub drink-'em-up or register such maddening futility in a Maltese functionary's clammy response to a cry for help. Aristocrat that he is, Huston achieves such effects with a nonchalance bordering on carelessness. His latest film is glaringly full of plotholes, but if you fall into them, he seems to be saying, it's your own damn fault."—*Newsweek*

* * *

Huston admits that he has done some films "…just for the money." He also admits that he's usually regretted it afterwards. *The Mackintosh Man* is a good case in point.

The director says that the project grew out of a commitment Paul Newman had with Warner Brothers to appear in one more film in order to fulfill a contract with them. Desmond Bagley's spy novel *The Freedom Trap* was the property the studio offered. Newman and his partner, John Foreman, took it on and approached Huston to direct. He agreed. "The three of us had had a fine time on *Roy Bean* and were reluctant to go our separate ways," Huston says, adding that the money offered to him proved a strong incentive as well. As did the location: his home turf of Ireland.

The script by Walter Hill, who has since become a director himself *(The Warriors, 48 Hours)* centers around the efforts of an undercover agent named Reardon to infiltrate and expose a covert group that is springing security risk prisoners out of jail and spiriting them to the Soviet Union. To do this, Reardon snatches some diamonds, is caught, and lands in prison with a twenty-year sentence. Having received a certain amount of notoriety over the lucrative theft, he is quickly approached by one of the group's jailhouse insiders and offered a chance to escape along with a man named Slade, the security risk next in line for springing. After he agrees to turn over half of his profits

Paul Newman as undercover agent Reardon, also known as The Mackintosh Man.

Reardon (Paul Newman) gets his instructions from
Mackintosh (Harry Andrews) as Mrs. Smith (Dominique
Sanda), Mac's assistant—and daughter—listens in.

Mackintosh (Harry Andrews) reveals details of the plan to
double agent Sir George Wheeler (James Mason).

Reardon (Paul Newman) makes a break for it and gets revenge in the bargain: he kicks the amazon Gerda (Jenny Runacre) in the crotch, where she once kicked him.

from the diamond theft, the escape is successfully engineered and he and Slade are bound over at a safe house in the remote Irish countryside.

At this point, however, the plan—Reardon has been assigned to not only smoke out the villains but to kill Slade, if necessary—starts to unravel. Reardon's boss, Mackintosh, has revealed details of the plan to a right-wing member of Parliament, Sir George Wheeler, who turns out to be a double agent and the mastermind of the covert group. Mackintosh is summarily killed in a hit and run accident. Reardon is unmasked and almost beaten to death. But he

manages to escape, and, with the help of Mackintosh's daughter, Mrs. Smith, sets out to track down Wheeler and Slade and bring them to justice. In the final confrontation, however, the two Soviet agents, knowing their jig is up, convince Reardon that the game has ended in a draw and that nothing is to be gained by the three of them shooting each other down. Deciding to let each other live and go their separate ways, they all set aside their weapons, but in a last-minute turnabout, Mrs. Smith scoops up one of the guns and shoots Wheeler and Slade down to avenge her father's death. Spurning Reardon for what she considers his act of bad faith, she walks off into the night.

Huston confesses that the film's ironic conclusion was the last scene written and the last shot. "All the time we were filming we were casting about

Reardon (Paul Newman) and Mrs. Smith (Dominique Sanda) lay plans to snare Wheeler now that her father has been put out of commission.

frantically for an effective way to bring the picture to a close,'' he says. ''Finally...an idea for an ending came to us. It was far and away the best thing in the movie, and I suspect that if we had been able to start shooting with it in mind, *The Mackintosh Man* would have been a really good film.'' He's right in that the last-minute ending establishes a dramatic sense of inner conflict within the character of Reardon that the rest of the film fails to justify. Reardon's decision to let Wheeler and Slade go rather than lose his own life in a pointless gun duel with them is contrary to his orders and thus an act of defiance against the government agency that employs him. Yet nowhere in the film's earlier scenes is there even the slightest hint of discontent in his mind. Even when he realizes that Mackintosh has duped him by revealing only part of the overall plan (almost costing him his life), he dutifully sets about finishing the job exactly as the late Mackintosh would have wished. The last-minute transformation of Reardon into a complex Huston hero simply comes too late to generate much interest in either the character or the film.

Regardless of the film's script problems, Huston's direction is sharp and inventive throughout. The starkly photographed scenes of prison life are quite effective, as are Oswald Morris's atmospheric shots of the craggy Irish countryside. But as one critic aptly noted of the film's basically tired espionage plot, ''It's all been done just too many times before.''

193

The Man Who Would Be King (1975)

AN ALLIED ARTISTS PICTURE
Technicolor/129 minutes

CREDITS:

Director: John Huston; *Producer:* John Foreman; *Screenplay:* John Huston and Gladys Hill, based on the short story "The Man Who Would Be King" by Rudyard Kipling; *Cinematographer:* Oswald Morris; *Editor:* Russell Lloyd; *Music:* Maurice Jarre; *Production designer:* Alex Trainer; *Videocassette source:* CBS/Fox Home Video.

John Huston on location in Morocco with The Man Who Would Be King.

CAST:

Daniel Dravot: Sean Connery; *Peachy Carnehan:* Michael Caine; *Rudyard Kipling:* Christopher Plummer; *Billy Fish:* Saeed Joffrey; *District Commissioner:* Jack May; *Roxanne:* Shakira Caine; *Kafu-Selim:* Karrovin Ben Bouih; *Ootah:* Doghmi Larbi; *Babu:* Mohammed Shamsi; *Mulvaney:* Paul Antrim; *Ghulam:* Albert Moses.

* * *

Contemporary Reviews

"Not in a very long while has Mr. Huston, who wrote the screenplay with Gladys Hill and also directed the film, been so successfully lighthearted and so consistently in command of his subject. The movie...has just enough romantic nonsense in it to enchant the child in each of us."—*The New York Times*

"As long as [Kipling] is on hand to lend an air of wide-eyed disbelief to the strange account of how two British con men nearly conquered the never-never highlands of Kafiristan, the movie is an engaging realization of Kipling's wonderful schoolboy tale. But once the caper itself takes over, the movie

Peachy (Michael Caine) and Danny (Sean Connery) gather the warring tribes around them as their first step in becoming kings of Kafiristan.

loses its way, meandering uncertainly from high, bloody adventure to Stingmanship, British style, between the two con men to intimations of what Kipling's story really was—a satirical tour-de-force of British imperialism at its most horrific and absurd.''—*Newsweek*

* * *

John Huston had read Rudyard Kipling's cautionary tale ''The Man Who Would Be King'' when he was a boy, and wanted to make a film of it as early as the fifties. He envisioned it as a solid action

vehicle for his close friends Humphrey Bogart and Clark Gable, but other commitments delayed the project, which Huston shelved indefinitely when Bogart died. Following production of *The Night of the Iguana*, however, he resurrected the idea, hoping to secure Richard Burton and Peter O'Toole as the stars, but this time financing proved a problem and Huston's plans once again fell through. Having enjoyed a good working relationship with producer John Foreman on *The Life and Times of Judge Roy Bean* and *The Mackintosh Man* (Foreman would go on to produce Huston's award-winning *Prizzi's Honor* as well), Huston again brought up the subject in 1973 and Foreman was later able to arrange a co-production deal with Allied Artists and Columbia Pictures. Foreman's business partner, Paul Newman, was initially suggested to play one of the film's two leads, but it was Newman himself who vetoed the idea, rightfully thinking that he would be totally miscast as a British soldier and adventurer, and he suggested Sean Connery and Michael Caine instead. Connery and Caine, who were fast friends in real life but had never co-starred with each other in a film before, accepted enthusiastically and Huston's long-dreamed-of film of *The Man Who Would Be King* was finally underway. Location shooting was set for Morocco, doubling as India of the 1880s, and the Atlas Mountains of Marrakesh, where Huston's production designer, Alex Trainer, constructed the mythical city of Sikandergul where Danny and Peachy meet their fate.

The script had been written at Huston's home in Las Caletas, Mexico—he had sold his Irish estate some years before—by the director himself together with his longtime associate Gladys Hill, who later described their working methods this way:

"I…first break the novel down, scene by scene. I then memorize the book, so when John and I are discussing a scene, action or sequence, I can say, 'Remember,

The aging priest crowns Danny (Sean Connery) king of Kafiristan.

John, such and such happened.' He may say, 'Where is it?' and then I find it in the book and read it to him. From there we talk about it and then I write it. I put in the description and the dialogue. Then I take it to Mr. Huston to read. And if it has to be redone, it's redone and we discuss it again. Then Mr. Huston will, if he wishes, change the dialogue. We don't give any unnecessary camera directions. The screenplay we do is the shooting script, but when Mr. Huston sets up a shot, he does it the way he wishes."

Typically, though sticking fairly closely to Kipling's original novella, Huston altered it in important ways. For example, in Kipling's story, Peachy becomes a king of Kafiristan as well. He and Danny rule together and are both killed when the priests discover the truth of Danny's deception—though it is implied that Peachy, who is tortured for his transgression rather than executed outright like Danny, dies some days later from his wounds. In the film, he survives as a cripple to return to India and relate the tale of his and Danny's sad but grand adventure to the astonished Kipling. Danny himself thus becomes the film's central focus—much like Dobbs in *Sierra Madre* and Ahab in *Moby Dick.* Huston also expanded upon the mystical elements of Masonry

present in Kipling's story by making Danny and Peachy's membership in the Masonic Order a key reason why they are initially accepted by the otherwise suspicious Kafiri priests. The priests also worship the "All Seeing Eye," a Masonic symbol (Danny wears one on his chest) dating back to Alexander the Great, the first white ruler of Kaifiristan from whom the priests believe Danny to be descended.

Peachy and Danny are a pair of rascals, two British soldiers of fortune who swear off drink and take a mutual vow of celibacy so as not to be distracted from their latest scheme, which is to journey to the remote land of Kafiristan, rally its warring tribes around them, and set themselves up as monarchs. They are, in effect, two small-time imperialists with big-time ideas. They are also a very winning pair, and quite lucky in the bargain. As they set out on their adventure, Kipling gives Danny a Freemason medal that saves the latter's life at a crucial moment when the Kafiri priests, who are about to kill Danny, spot the emblem hanging from his neck and identify it as one of their own holy insignias.

Danny (Sean Connery) and Peachy (Michael Caine) discover the riches left behind by Alexander the Great, all theirs for the taking.

In an earlier battle, Danny is hit by an enemy arrow but is unharmed because the point pierces only his bandolier. The enemy interprets the lucky accident as a sign that Danny is impervious to death and lays down its arms in surrender. Due mainly to luck, Danny is enthroned as king and pronounced by the priests rightful heir to all the riches left behind centuries ago by Alexander the Great. Danny and Peachy start marking time until the monsoon season is over so that they can make off with their haul. But as time passes, Danny starts believing that more has been at work here than simple luck and convinces himself that he really is Alexander's heir, and thus a god.

Over his pragmatic partner's strong objections, Danny decides to marry, a decision even the priests object to, for in their eyes it is unseemly for a god to take a mortal wife. Danny's luck begins to go wrong when an ominous blight descends upon his once prosperous kingdom. At the marriage ceremony, the bride, Roxanne, convinced she will go up in smoke if mated with a god, scratches Danny on the cheek, making him bleed. Seeing that Danny is mortal after all and that they have been duped, the priests and villagers turn on their former king and execute him while Peachy is forced to watch. Summarily tortured for his complicity in the deception, Peachy survives

to tell the tale to Kipling, and, as proof, leaves behind his friend's decomposed head, still wearing its crown.

It would be interesting to see what kind of film Huston would have made of this same material if he had been able to shoot it back in the fifties when the idea first occurred. One suspects that that film might have been more of a sweeping adventure in the tradition of George Stevens's *Gunga Din* (1939) than this one is. Though perhaps not, for Huston has always emphasized characters and theme in his films over scenery and thundering action. And *The Man Who Would Be King* is no exception. But there is also a distinctly melancholy flavor to the film, which may have been due not only to the subject's long incubation period, but to Huston's own advancing years. The director quite obviously grew to love the characters of Peachy and Danny as he thought about them over the years, and, despite their failings, came to view them as essentially admirable men with great courage and

God/King Danny (Sean Connery) commits a fatal mistake by taking the beautiful Roxanne (Shakira Caine), a mortal woman, for his bride.

devotion to one another.

The film contains all the recognizable Huston elements and is far from pessimistic because Danny does indeed become king—and a responsible and just one at that. He simply loses his grip on himself and pushes his luck too far. Yet even in death, he achieves mythical status, which is certainly no small achievement.

There is also underlying anti-imperialist message to the film, for both Kipling and Huston see Peachy and Danny as, in critic Charles Champlin's words, ''...advance scouts of an exploitative society invading an older and more primitive culture with no wish to stay, understand or share but only to grab and split.'' But the theme upon which Huston places the greatest emphasis is that of friendship. Peachy and Danny have been everywhere together. They are bound to one another. And in Huston's view, Danny's major transgression is not that he attempts to assume godhood, but that, in doing so, he breaks his contract with Peachy and temporarily ruptures their friendship. It is no small matter that when confronted with the probability of execution, Danny, realizing what he's done, considers death

The jig up, Danny (Sean Connery), Peachy (Michael Caine) and a few loyal followers make a hopeless attempt at escape.

less important than Peachy's forgiveness. And when he gets it, he greets his fate with, "Everything's all right then." In turn, the anguished expression on Peachy's face as he watches his friend fall to his death from a collapsed bridge is absolutely heart-wrenching. The scene is played to perfection by Michael Caine.

Some have called Huston's *The Man Who Would Be King* the ultimate "buddy movie," which it may well be. But this frivolous description denies the film its substantial emotional power. Peachy and Danny aren't just pals, they're kindred spirits, two halves of the same whole. And their remarkable tale is a moving tribute to the deathless nature of friendship.

In my view, Huston's very personal and magnificent *The Man Who Would Be King* should have swept the Oscars in 1975, but, alas, the film received only one nomination—for best screenplay adaptation. It lost (to *One Flew Over the Cuckoo's Nest.*) But surely the director must have been used to this by now.

Wise Blood (1980)

AN ITHACA–ANTHEA CO-PRODUCTION
Released through New Line Cinema
Technicolor/108 minutes

CREDITS:

Director: John Huston; *Producers:* Michael and Kathy Fitzgerald; *Screenplay:* Benedict and Michael Fitzgerald, based on the novel *Wise Blood* by Flannery O'Connor; *Cinematographer:* Gerry Fisher; *Editor:* Roberto Silvi; *Music:* Alex North; *Videocassette source:* MCA Home Video.

"Nobody ever escapes from Jesus!" the bogus blind preacher, Asa Hawks (Harry Dean Stanton), tells the skeptical Motes (Brad Dourif).

CAST:

Hazel Motes: Brad Dourif; *Asa Hawks:* Harry Dean Stanton; *Hoover Shoates:* Ned Beatty; *Enoch Emory:* Dan Shor; *Preacher:* William Hickey; *Sabbath Lily:* Amy Wright; *Landlady:* Mary Nell Santacroce; *Grandfather:* John Huston.

* * *

Contemporary Reviews

"Wise Blood is the most eccentric American movie in years.…The cast, including even bit players who appear as cops, used-car salesmen and townsfolk, enough oddballs to staff a Tennessee Williams repertory company.…Huston's only lapses are a few purple flashback sequences.…Still, those moviegoers who have a taste for *Wise Blood* are not going to cavil about flaws. It is enough to ride the wild imaginative waves of this singular artistic adventure."—*Time magazine*

"John Huston has wandered off the beaten track many times in the course of his long, bumpy and prodigious career, and at 73 he is as uncompromis-

Enoch (Dan Shor), left, and Motes (Brad Dourif) encounter Sabbath Lily (Amy Wright) peddling her religious tracts on the street.

ing a maverick as ever. *Wise Blood,* a virulently comic, grotesquely unforgettable adaptation of Flannery O'Connor's celebrated novel of customized redneck religion and redemption, is as strange and original a movie as Huston has ever made.''—*Newsweek*

* * *

John Huston returned briefly to the short subject to make *Independence,* a dramatized documentary about events leading up to the signing of the Declaration of Independence. Financed by the National Park Service, the 30-minute color film was put into limited release by 20th Century-Fox on the 200th birthday of the Declaration and featured Eli Wallach as Ben Franklin, Anne Jackson as Abigail Adams and Patrick O'Neal as George Washington. E.G. Marshall served as narrator. (Unavailable to the general public for a decade, *Independence* has recently made it to cassetts via M.P.I. Home Video.) A severe bout with emphysema then laid the director up for a time.

While he was recuperating at his home in Las Caletas, Mexico, he received a copy of the Flannery O'Connor novel, *Wise Blood,* from an aspiring producer named Michael Fitzgerald, whose family served as executors of the late novelist's literary estate. Fitzgerald wanted Huston to direct the film and insisted that financing was forthcoming, though, in fact, more than a year would pass before the young producer was able to scrape up the required $2 million budget.

Huston had not read the book before, but when he did, he quickly realized that the material was right up his alley. The novel's brooding, repressive Southern Gothic atmosphere was strikingly similar to *Reflections in a Golden Eye,* and its characters were the most offbeat collection of losers and lost souls the director had contemplated dealing with since *Fat City.* In the book's obsessive hero, Hazel Motes, Huston found a self-destructive protagonist whose messianic fervor, Godlessness and capacity for violence almost equalled that of Captain Ahab in *Moby Dick.* O'Connor's co-mingling of broad comedy with scenes of stark, and sometimes horrific, drama also appealed to the director's sensibilities, for he had been experimenting along these same lines many years himself.

Huston agreed to do the film and selected newcomer Brad Dourif for the lead, and very difficult, role of Hazel Motes. Other professionals in the cast included Harry Dean Stanton, Ned Beatty, Amy Wright, Mary Nell Santacroce, Dan Shor, and, in a small role, the skeletal William Hickey, who would

Motes (Brad Dourif) rejects con man Hoover Shoates's (Ned Beatty) scheme to promote the ''Church of the Truth Without Christ'' into a money-making operation.

later earn an Oscar nomination for his performance in Huston's equally offbeat *Prizzi's Honor.* Huston also took a small part as Motes's grandfather, who appears in a series of flashbacks. The remainder of the cast, however, was made up of non-professionals selected from among the residents of Macon, Georgia, where the film was shot.

Huston completed the film ahead of schedule and substantially under budget, convinced that he had a critical winner on his hands, if not a commercial one. His judgment as to the film's commercial possibilities seemed to be borne out when every major Hollywood studio declined to distribute the film due to its offbeat and, in their view, ''unmarketable'' nature. Eventually, the film was picked up by Bob Shaye's independent company, New Line Cinema, and secured limited release around the country, mostly on the strength of Huston's name. As Huston hoped, the film earned him his best reviews in years. And it also made back its small cost. ''I'm intensely proud of it,'' he told the press. ''As proud of as anything I've ever done.''

Of all previous Huston protagonists, Hazel Motes bears the most striking resemblance to Captain Ahab. Like Ahab, Motes has been spiritually wounded (as well as physically, he implies). He no

Shoates (Ned Beatty) outfits a ne'er-do-well (William Hickey)
to look like Motes and attempts to promote his own "Church
of the Truth Without Christ."

longer believes in the redemptive powers of Christ for he no longer believes in sin ("It's a trick on niggers," he mumbles to himself and anyone else who'll listen). Upon being discharged from the army, he returns home to spread The Truth as he now sees it by establishing his own religion, the "Church of Truth Without Christ." Having been around the world and experienced much, he now believes in nothing, except himself. His grandfather was a preacher and drummed the concept of sin into him at an early age. He now seeks to cast off this concept, repudiate religious guilt, and get everyone else to do the same.

His first crusade is to debunk an intinerant preacher named Asa Hawks, who purportedly blinded himself to demonstrate his faith in Jesus, thus earning himself hundreds of converts. Motes proves Hawk's blindness to be fraudulent, but also discovers that Hawks was once an iconoclast too.

The lonely, sex-starved Sabbath Lily (Amy Wright) seduces Motes (Brad Dourif).

Hawks says he "learned," however, and finally gave up fighting against the mainstream because, he admonishes Motes, "Nobody ever escapes from Jesus."

Motes later meets up with a con man, Hoover Shoates, who sees in Motes's new religion an opportunity ripe for exploitation. Motes rejects the promotional scheme, however, because Shoates doesn't really believe and is only looking to make money. Shoates dresses up a bum to look like Motes and goes into competition, but Motes trails the bum in his car and mercilessly runs him over for "mocking him."

Eventually, Motes decides to move to a different city and spread his gospel anew, but on the way, he is stopped by a cop who pushes his ramshackle car into a lake. Defeated, Motes returns to his lodging house, and, in imitation of Hawks, proceeds to blind himself with quick lime, only he does it for real. He also fills his shoes with stones to make walking painful and straps wire around his body to make himself bleed—all in an effort to make himself *pay,* as he explains it; to make himself *clean.*

He finally expires from his self-inflicted wounds, a martyr to his own benighted cause.

As played by Brad Dourif, Hazel Motes is a man obsessed—wild-eyed, impatient, and violent. When the lonely, simpled-minded Enoch, whose only quest is friendship, says he'll guide Motes to Hawks's house, then can't find it, Motes punches him to the ground "for lying." Motes's murder of the bum is another expression of his violent nature. Like Ahab, Motes is a "right man" (in writer A.E. Van Vogt's phrase) on a righteous crusade. He will not be dissuaded, challenged, or mocked. "I'd strike the sun if it insulted me!" Ahab roars in *Moby Dick.* Motes is the same way, and when his quest fails, his violence turns inward and he sickeningly mutilates himself precisely because he has failed—though, in a way, his martyrdom to his own cause turns him into the human savior he has been searching for to replace Jesus in his new church.

Wise Blood is a complex, challenging, and unquestionably grim work—though it is frequently quite funny, too. Motes's path to self-destruction is painful and often uncomfortable to watch. He is, like Ahab, a desperately sick man, but, and this is important to note, not necessarily wrong. His message is more humanistic than punishing, and in the end it is his own "wise blood"—his gift of the prophets, an ability to read signs that no one else can—that mostly gets spilled. Huston and composer Alex North's use of Aaron Copland's "Fanfare for the Common Man" over Motes's deathbed scene is not meant to be satiric. For like Ahab, there is a sense of grandeur to the preacher's grim but purposeful fall.

Phobia (1980)

A PARAMOUNT PICTURE
Technicolor/90 minutes

CREDITS:

Director: John Huston; *Producer:* Zale Magder; *Screenplay:* Lew Lehman, Jimmy Sangster and Peter Bellwood, from a story by Gary Sherman and Ronald Shusett; *Cinematographer:* Reginald H. Morris; *Editor:* Stan Cole; *Music:* Andre Gagnon; *Production designer:* Ben Edwards; *Videocassette source:* Not Available.

CAST:

Dr. Peter Ross: Paul Michael Glaser; *Inspector Barnes:* John Colicos; *Jenny St. Clair:* Susan Hogan; *Barbara Grey:* Alexandra Stewart; *Bubba King:* Robert O'Ree; *Henry Owen:* David Bolt; *Johnny Venuti:* David Eisner; *Laura Adams:* Lisa Langlois; *Sergeant Wheeler:* Kenneth Walsh; *Dr. Clegg:* Neil Vipond; *Dr. Alice Toland:* Patricia Collins.

* * *

Contemporary Reviews

"With credibility strained from the very beginning, *Phobia* doesn't stand a chance. The hoariest of twist endings…buries any hope remaining in this limp and predictable 'psychological thriller.' One of the dreariest films of the year."—*Cinefantastique*

"Absolutely terrible film about psychiatrist whose patients, all suffering from various phobias, are being murdered one by one. Relentlessly stupid, illogical, and unpleasant."—Leonard Maltin's *TV Movies*

* * *

In October, 1979, Huston flew to Toronto to begin shooting his first full-fledged horror movie, *Phobia,* though he preferred to call it a mystery. "It's a little like Agatha Christie's *Ten Little Indians,*" he told the press. "Everybody gets killed, except the killer, of course. We're not discovering any new ground here. It's a conventional murder mystery. They all have a form. They're supposed to. And I'm not going to change that."

Based on an original story by director Gary Sherman and Ronald Shusett (co-author of *Alien*), the screenplay was worked on by three writers, including Britisher Jimmy Sangster, whose series of "mini-Hitchcock" thrillers for England's Hammer Films in the sixties (*Paranoia, Nightmare, Hysteria*) were very much in the same vein as *Phobia.* Like the earlier Hammers and the Hitchcock masterpiece, *Psycho,* that inspired them, *Phobia* was a psychological shocker designed to play a game of cat-and-mouse with the audience. "It's an interesting story," Huston said. "A psychiatrist is treating people who are suffering from various phobias and they begin to die violently. The psychiatrist sets out to find the culprit and therein lies the twist." Reportedly, the director kept his cast and crew in the dark as to the identity of the killer as well, hoping that the on-set suspense would transfer to the screen. So no one was ever given a beginning-to-end script.

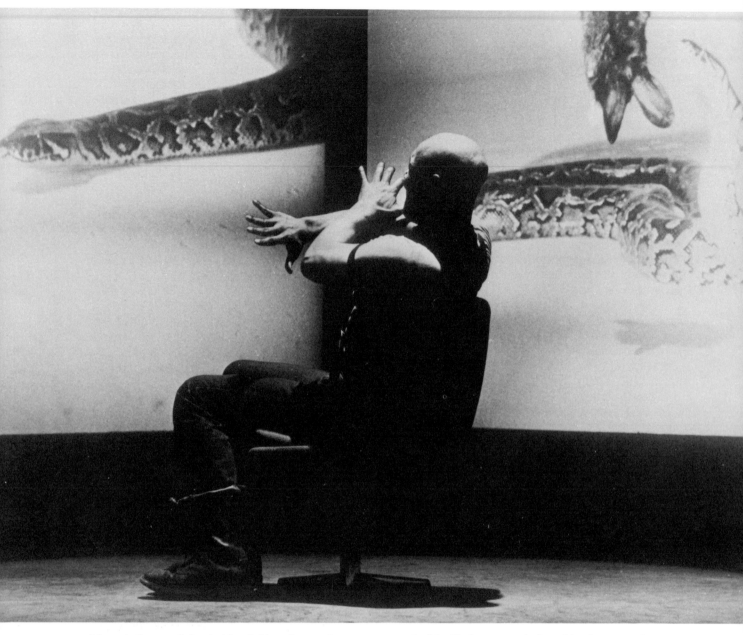

Through the use of visual aids, phobic patients such as Bubba King (Robert O'Ree), who's terrified of snakes, are forced to confront the fears that drive them to commit violent and destructive acts.

On a superficial level, the film is similar to the work of Canadian shockmaster David Cronenberg, but it is also very much in keeping with Huston's own themes and interests, particularly his interest in hysterical neuroses and the use of hypnotherapy as a dramatic method of treatment. Though he viewed the film as a flat-out entertainment ("It's a broad thriller," he said. "The premise is barely con-

ceivable."), he nevertheless hired a consultant, Dr. Melvyn Hill, to keep a close eye on the film's treatment scenes to assure as much medical accuracy and authenticity as possible.

Paul Michael Glaser stars as Dr. Peter Ross, a controversial Canadian psychotherapist who is convinced that he can cure the murderers and other mentally disturbed patients in his care by probing their individual phobias. He believes these private fears govern their lives and are the cause of their problems with the law.

Ross's patients include a girl named Barbara, who suffers from agoraphobia, a fear of open spaces;

206

Pronounced cured, Barbara (Alexandra Stewart) is released but discovers her agoraphobic fears returning and panics.

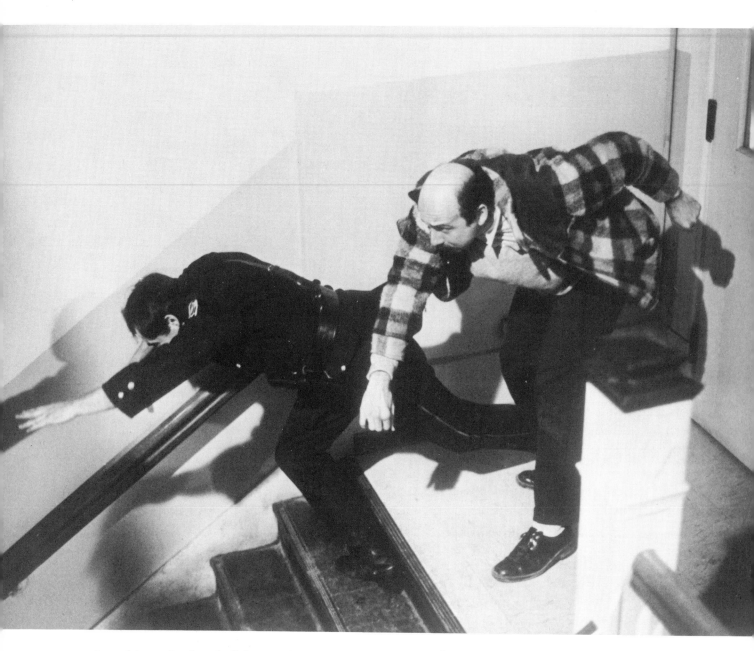

Some violent action from the little-seen John Huston production of Phobia.

a punk rocker and car thief with claustrophobia; a man who is terrified of snakes; another man with acrophobia, a fear of heights; and a woman named Laura, whose fear of men stems from her having been raped as a child. Ross uses group and individual counseling sessions to help treat them. More dramatic, however, is his *Clockwork Orange*-like use of visual aids whereby each patient is forced to confront images of his or her phobia flashing upon a giant movie screen.

The hospital is divided in its support of Ross's ideas for treatment. The police on the other hand believe Ross's methods are not only unsound but dangerous, and will result in madmen and women being let loose on the streets.

As a test, Barbara is allowed to go downtown and buy herself a pocketbook. But when she finds herself in a crowd, she panics and returns to Ross's apartment for help. He is out at the time. While waiting for him, she decides to take a look at her file and when she opens the drawer is killed by an exploding bomb. Suspicion immediately falls on one of the other patients, but then, one by one, they too begin to die violently by means of the thing they fear most. The acrophobe falls to his death from a girder; the punk rocker is trapped in an elevator shaft and crushed; Laura is attacked in a bathtub and drowned; and the last victim is killed by a rattlesnake. The police are baffled until finally their suspicions fall on Ross himself, who, in a not very surprising twist, does indeed turn out to be the killer, suffering from his own psychological conflict. As a youth, Ross had a phobia himself—fear of the water—and his inability to save his little sister from drowning resulted in severe punishment from his father. All along, Ross has been killing his patients because of their failure to be cured.

Upon completing the film, Huston dubbed it "quite well done, technically" and expressed hopes for it success. Those hopes were dashed, however, when the film's distributor, Paramount, pronounced the film not worthy of general release because of some negative reactions at advance screenings and sold it outright to television, where it has appeared uncut on pay cable's The Movie Channel and in an "edited for television" version on NBC. Despite Huston's esteemed reputation in Europe, *Phobia* has not been released theatrically there either. For all intents and purposes, it remains essentially a "lost" Huston film.

I don't really agree with the studio's assessment of the film as "unreleasable." It is well done technically. But Huston is certainly correct in describing the film's premise as barely conceivable. In fact, it is barely credible and has more holes in it than a slab of Swiss cheese. Perhaps because Jimmy Sangster was involved with the script, my suspicions fell on Ross during the first ten minutes and never wavered from then on. *Phobia* offers very little in the way of surprise or suspense.

Victory (1981)

A PARAMOUNT PICTURE
Metrocolor/110 minutes

CREDITS:

Director: John Huston; *Producer:* Freddie Fields; *Screenplay:* Evan Jones and Yabo Yablonsky, from a story by Yabo Yablonsky, Djordje Milicevic and Jeff

Maguire; *Cinematographer:* Gerry Fisher; *Editor:* Roberto Silvi; *Music:* Bill Conti; *Art Director:* J. Dennis Washington; *Videocassette source:* MGM/UA Home Video.

CAST:

Robert Hatch: Sylvester Stallone; *John Colby:* Michael Caine; *Luis Fernandez:* Pélé; *Terry Brady:* Bobby Moore; *Major Karl von Steiner:* Max Von Sydow; *Chief Commentator:* Anton Diffring; *Rose:* Tom Pigott-Smith; *Colonel Waldron:* Daniel Massey; *Coach Mueller:* Gary Waldhorn; *Renee:* Carole Laure; *Shurlock:* Julian Curry.

* * *

Contemporary Reviews

"*Victory* is a crowd pleaser, no doubt about it. After his risky, uncommercial *Wise Blood* and the still unreleased *Phobia,* it probably made commercial sense for Huston to shoot for mass popularity with *Victory.* He's a sly old pro, and once again he'll land on his feet, but this renowned gambling man is at his most interesting when he's playing against the odds. He wins the game in *Victory,* but you can't help feeling he's playing with a stacked deck."—*Newsweek*

"With Pélé doing wondrous tricks on field, and Bill Conti's huge score blasting away underneath John Huston's superb blending of game action with the stadium's increasingly delirious response to it, *Victory* achieves its goal. Anyone who does not find himself yelling along with the extras should probably have stayed home with his Proust and bitters."—*Time* magazine

* * *

By 1980, John Huston had been writing and/or directing motion pictures for half a century. Shortly after celebrating his 74th birthday, the press asked him if he ever thought about retiring. "I've had lots of fun making films," he told them. "The time to quit is when it is no longer fun. I can't see that happening soon. Every new picture is a delight."

Delights for him they may well have been, but Huston's last two pictures had not exactly been blockbusters, and he now needed a hit. The old Hollywood axiom of "you're only as good as your last picture" held as true for John Huston—despite his prestige in the industry and overall impressive track record—as it did for any up-and-comer. And so it was quite fortuitous when producer Freddie Fields approached him with the script for an offbeat war film called *Escape to Victory.* The title was later changed

Producer Freddie Fields confers with director John Huston on the set of Victory, *the story of a soccer match between a group of desperate Allied prisoners and a German team during World War II.*

to *V for Victory,* then, finally, just *Victory.*

"I had a good feeling about this film from the first day when Freddie Fields talked to me about it and gave me a script to read," Huston said. "It wasn't really a sports picture and it wasn't a war picture. It had some of the moral themes of *The Bridge on the River Kwai,* with a great deal more action. In it a simple brown ball took the place of guns and bombs in a battle between two sides with opposing philosophies. I thought audiences had seen quite enough war films with people shooting one another."

Rightly sensing the commercial hit he needed, Huston quickly signed on. Sylvester Stallone, fresh from his smash success with *Rocky,* Michael Caine and international soccer star Pélé were selected for the film's main leads, a trio of Allied prisoners of war who go to Paris for a propagandistic soccer match with the Germans, hoping to escape during half-time.

The film was shot entirely on location in Hungary, utilizing a three-acre prison set built on the grounds of the Allag Riding Stables not far from Budapest. Another major set was Budapest's MTK Stadium, home of one of Hungary's best known soccer clubs, which posed as the Paris Colombes Stadium, where similar sporting events were staged in 1943, the period of the film. Five interior sets were also constructed at Mafilm Studio, home base for the Hungarian film company that provided Huston with much of his crew and production staff. More than 250,000 extras were used during the 53 days of

Michael Caine is an imprisoned English officer and former star soccer player, and Max von Sydow a German propaganda official.

International soccer great Pélé demonstrates his wizardry to the Allied prisoner-of-war team forced into a match against the Germans.

shooting, most of them as cheering fans in the lengthy and exciting soccer sequence that concludes the film.

Readily admitting that he was no authority on soccer, Huston left the design and choreography of the game sequences to Pélé and second unit director

Robert Riger. Other world-famous soccer stars appearing in these sequences along with Pélé were England's 1966 World Cup Champion Bobby Moore; Argentina's 1978 World Cup Champion Osvaldo Ardiles; American Werner Roth, three-time captain of both the U.S. National Team and the championship New York Cosmos; and a host of other players from Scotland, Ireland, Belgium, Poland and Norway.

The film opens in Gensdorf Prison in southern

Goalie Sylvester Stallone scuffles with the opposition during the climactic game in Paris.

Germany, where British, American, Canadian, Australian, French, Dutch, Belgian, and Anzac officers have been lumped together as prisoners of war. Bored from the seemingly endless days and months of confinement, many of them take to playing soccer to pass the time. These games are supervised by Captain Colby, a professional soccer player before the war, who keeps having run-ins with a hot-headed American, Captain Hatch, who insists on tackling his opponents American-style. A visiting German Intelligence Officer, Major von Steiner, notices the games and approaches Colby with the idea of arranging a friendly match between the Allied POWs and a unit of German soldiers stationed nearby. Colby sees a chance to better the men's lot and agrees, provided von Steiner comes up with the necessary uniforms and equipment. Colby's fellow officers see in the plan a possibility for escape, whereas von Steiner's superiors envision a great propagandistic coup and enlarge the game into a much publicized contest to be staged in Paris, involving professional footballers from both sides.

Hatch wants no part of the game, however, because he's bent on escaping beforehand and has already developed a workable plan. He makes his break and arrives in Paris, where he's contacted by the French underground and persuaded to be recaptured and returned to Gensdorf with plans for a mass break by all the Allies who are to take part in the game. The idea is for the group to escape during half-time by means of a tunnel that runs beneath the stadium. Confronted by the brutal and unfair tactics of the German players and officials during the first half of the game, the Allied players reconsider, however, and decide to forego their escape and win the match instead. When they do, the throngs of cheering Frenchmen in the stands swarm the field and sweep the victorious Allied players out of the stadium, allowing them to escape after all.

Though written by others, *Victory* was a project made to order for Huston. In Captain Hatch, he had his characteristically adventurous, easily bored and thus impetuous hero whose inner conflict stems from a desire to go through with his solitary escape or allow himself to be recaptured and returned to prison so that he can help others to escape as well. Hatch is equally in conflict with himself on the playing field, where he prefers his showy brand of one-upsmanship to team play even though it may cost his side a game. In this regard, he is a danger not only to himself but to everyone else as well. By the climactic game, however,

213

Caine and his teammates begin a daring escape attempt beneath the soccer stadium during halftime.

Pélé is lifted aloft by fellow members of the victorious Allied team.

he has resolved these conflicts and become part of the Allied group. He even saves the day when, as goalie, he prevents the Germans from making a winning score.

In *Victory,* the escape plan of the footballers goes awry due to their own choosing. Winning the game— and winning it fairly at that— becomes more important to them than escaping, for the German propaganda machine has transformed the contest in the eyes of the world (and the Allied players) from a mere game into a major skirmish that the Allies are bent on winning. Not only do they win, they win *big.* And succeed in escaping in the bargain via a route no one had even considered—through the tumultuous crowds.

Critics were quick to take note of the film's passing resemblance to John Sturges's *The Great Escape* (1963), though that film ended on a much bleaker note, as well as Stallone's own *Rocky,* which also championed victory for the underdog. But surely the scriptwriters also had in mind Robert Aldrich's *The Longest Yard* (1974), another football story in which a group of prison inmates led by con Burt Reynolds, who is a former pro like Colby, takes on the prison's guards in a game that is likewise ballyhooed into a major, existential contest.

Annie (1982)

A COLUMBIA PICTURE
Technicolor/128 minutes

CREDITS:

Director: John Huston; *Producer:* Ray Stark; *Screenplay:* Carol Sobieski; *Cinematographer:* Richard Moore; *Editor:* Michael A. Stevenson; *Music:* Charles Strouse; *Lyrics:* Martin Charnin; *Music Staging and Choreography:* Arlene Phillips; *Music Arranged and Conducted By:* Ralph Burns; *Videocassette source:* RCA/Columbia Pictures Home Video.

CAST:

Annie: Aileen Quinn; *Miss Hannigan:* Carol Burnett; *Daddy Warbucks:* Albert Finney; *Grace Farrell:* Ann Reinking; *Lily:* Bernadette Peters; *Rooster:* Tim Curry;

Punjab: Geoffrey Holder; *F.D.R.:* Edward Herrmann; *Sandy:* Himself.

* * *

Contemporary Reviews

"For a production that means to bring children back to the movies, dragging their parents with them, *Annie* has a dark, dour meanspirited tone—*Oliver Twist* as retold by Fagin....Director John Huston offers production numbers full of empty extravagance, a host of familiar characters (like Punjab and Asp) with little to do—and a chorus of baby Mermans knowingly strutting their stuff, breaking the sound and charm barriers."—*Time* magazine

"This is a very big, loud, overbearing musical comic strip which tries so hard at getting you to like it, you might eventually cave in from sheer exhaustion. Musical-haters won't be converted, but the film has a crusty tone that tempers the saccharine nicely. Credit that to veteran director John Huston's sensibilities and a very good cast working at peak form."—*Cinefantastique*

* * *

John Huston directing a musical? Leapin' lizards!

Actually, the idea isn't so farfetched as it may seem. "I have always wanted to do a musical," Huston has said. "Even back in my early days at Warner Brothers when Dick Powell and Ruby Keeler were making three or four every year. But no one at the studio would let me try my hand at it."

In 1982, the director finally got the chance to try his hand when old friend and frequent collaborator Ray Stark offered him the helm on Columbia's multi-million dollar production of *Annie.* The result was one of the spriteliest movie musicals in years, though the film did fail to perform up to expectations at the box office and was not the blockbuster everyone assumed it would be.

Annie had been an unexpected smash hit on the Broadway stage, where it premiered in 1976. Mike Nichols and Lewis Allen were the show's producers. Charles Strouse composed the music and Martin Charnin wrote the lyrics. Charnin also directed the show, which swept that year's Tony Awards, earning a total of seven, including Best Musical. Thomas Meehan's book was based on the enduring Harold Gray comic strip about a feisty, Depression-era orphan with red hair (and no discernible eyes), who becomes the ward of one of America's wealthiest and most influential

Carol Burnett, Bernadette Peters, and Tim Curry with an ebullient Huston outside the Hudson Street Home for Girls set for Annie.

financiers, Oliver "Daddy" Warbucks.

Columbia President Alan Hirschfield paid a whopping $9.5 million for the film rights to the show, the highest ever for the motion picture rights to a Broadway musical. The amount even eclipsed the $5.5 million fee Lerner and Loewe had charged Warner Brothers for the rights to their hit musical *My Fair Lady* back in 1962. Also negotiated into the contract was a clause that the film version would not be made until the Broadway show had closed. By the time *Annie* went dark on the stage, however, Columbia was in the throes of the notorious David Begelman check-forging scandal of the late seventies. As a result

of the scandal, Begelman, who would have been in charge of putting *Annie* into production, was removed as studio chief, Alan Hirschfield went to 20th Century-Fox and Frank Price was elected the new president of Columbia Pictures. Price assigned *Annie* to producer Ray Stark, who, in turn, signed John Huston to direct.

Though Huston had never made a musical before, he was in many ways ideally suited to the project. Huston's overall body of work is quite remarkable in its consistency. The same themes, or variations on them, pop up again and again. And *Annie* is no exception. The feisty Annie is herself yet another incarnation of the typical Huston adventurer who has a tough time sitting still and rushes headforth into action with an almost reckless abandon. Annie's "dream" is to escape from the orphanage where she is constantly running afoul of the boozy headmistress,

216

Miss Hannigan (Carol Burnett) and Grace Farrell (Ann Reinking), secretary to Daddy Warbucks, engage in a tug of war over Annie (Aileen Quinn), who has won the opportunity to spend a week at the fabulous Warbucks estate.

Eleanor Roosevelt (Lois DeBanzie), Daddy Warbucks (Albert Finney), F.D.R. (Edward Herrmann) and Annie (Aileen Quinn) break into the showstopper "Tomorrow."

*Lily (Bernadette Peters) and Rooster (Tim Curry) pose as
Annie's long lost parents in order to collect the reward
Warbucks has offered.*

Lily (Bernadette Peters), Rooster (Tim Curry) and Miss Hannigan (Carol Burnett) tunefully toast their scheme to bilk Daddy Warbucks out of $50,000.

Miss Hannigan, and be reunited with her long-lost parents. To foster a more humanitarian image, billionaire businessman Oliver Warbucks agrees to let one of Miss Hannigan's charges move into his home and live for a week in wealth and splendor. Over Hannigan's protestations, Annie is selected and she soon warms Warbucks's heart so much that he decides to adopt her. Though Annie suspects her parents may, in fact, be dead, she refuses to let go of her illusion of being reunited with them, and Warbucks reluctantly offers a $50,000 reward for information as to their whereabouts. Two con artist friends of Miss Hannigan, Lily and Rooster, scheme with the headmistress to collect the reward by posing as Annie's parents. When the crooks take Annie away with them, the orphan finally realizes that it is Warbucks whom she now considers her real "Daddy" and the pair is warmly reunited at the musical's cheerful conclusion.

Though Annie does overcome her false illusions and win out handsomely in the end, it would be a mistake, I think, to read too much of a message into the film's sunny optimism. Musicals, after all, are not known for being downbeat—except, perhaps, for *Cabaret*. And yet the New Deal era in which the film is set surely appealed to Huston precisely for its sense of hope and optimism. "What Roosevelt was doing with the New Deal seemed to hold [a lot of] promise," Huston has said, and he still refers to F.D.R., who figures prominently in the film's showstopping number, *Tomorrow,* as "...the only President in my time I thoroughly approved of."

Under the Volcano (1984)

A UNIVERSAL PICTURE
Technicolor/109 minutes

CREDITS

Director: John Huston; *Producers:* Moritz Borman and Wieland Schulz-Kiel; *Screenplay:* Guy Gallo, based on the novel *Under the Volcano* by Malcolm Lowry; *Cinematographer:* Gabriel Figueroa; *Editor:* Roberto Silvi; *Music:* Alex North; *Production designer:* Gunther Gerzso; *Videocassette source:* MCA Home Video.

CAST:

Geoffrey Firmin: Albert Finney; *Yvonne Firmin:* Jacqueline Bisset; *Hugh Firmin:* Anthony Andrews; *Senora Gregoria:* Katy Jurado; *Brit:* James Villiers; *Dr. Vigil:* Ignacio Lopez-Tarzo; *Quincy:* Dawson Bray; *Gringo:* Jim McCarthy; *Dwarf:* Rene Ruiz; *Diosdado:* Emilio Fernandez.

* * *

Contemporary Reviews

"With nothing to prove (he's now 77), he [Huston] has turned to difficult works by major writers: in 1979 he made a surprisingly effective film of Flannery O'Connor's *Wise Blood,* and now he's made an even more surprising movie based on a much more difficult work....Huston is helped by the Goya-like cinematography of Gabriel Figueroa, one of the world's great camera artists, and by the electrifying acting of the Mexicans in the cast, notably actor-director Emilio Fernandez....Finney is remarkable. He plays Geoffrey like a ham actor, but a perpetual drunk *is* a ham actor: histrionics is the pathology of his sloshed behavior."—*Newsweek*

"Somber but striking adaptation of Malcolm Lowry's novel about alcoholic diplomat in Mexico during the late 1930s; rich in atmosphere and texture, with a great performance by Finney."—Leonard Maltin's *TV Movies*

* * *

In *Under the Volcano,* Huston's straightforward adaptation of Malcolm Lowry's dizzying 1947 cult novel about the final day in the life of an alcoholic British ex-consul bent on self-destruction, the director invites us to examine yet another group of characters whose faults lie not in their stars, but in themselves.

Heading the list is the consul himself, Geoffrey Firmin, an extreme alcoholic plagued by guilt over a wartime incident in his past and revolted by the current (1938) moral state of the world, which is once more heading towards war. Estranged from his actress wife, Yvonne, who joins him for an attempted reconciliation on the inauspicious occasion of the Mexican Day of the Dead, Firmin has resigned from his post as British consul to Cuernavaca and committed himself to the bottle. He and Yvonne are joined on this climactic day by Geoffrey's half brother, Hugh, a sometime journalist recently returned from the Spanish Civil War who is presently hunting down a story about a Mexican Nazi Party rumored to be growing among the peasants and bandidos in the nearby hills. Hugh and Yvonne once had a brief fling, and the trio's knowledge of the affair only adds to the mounting tension between them.

At the conclusion of both novel and film, Geoffrey bitterly turns on Yvonne and Hugh at the height (or nadir, if you will) of his drunken despair and rejects them both. "Hell is my natural habitat!" he shouts self-pityingly. And hell is precisely where he winds up: a seedy cantina called "El Farolito," where he encounters a band of fascist-minded Mexican cutthroats (they call him a "Jew") who playfully shoot him to death for ostensibly trying to steal a horse that belongs to one of them. The gunfire frightens the horse, which bolts and fatally injures Yvonne, who, with Hugh, has lucklessly tracked her wayward husband to the bar.

Huston had wanted to film Lowry's book for

John Huston on the set of Under the Volcano, *which he'd wanted to film since first reading the novel in 1947.*

Yvonne (Jacqueline Bisset) and the Consul (Albert Finney) walk through a plaza in Cuernavaca, Mexico, during the Day of the Dead celebration.

many years. The $4 million production was eventually co-financed by the Mexican government, 20th Century-Fox and Universal studios. Michael and Kathy Fitzgerald, with whom Huston had been associated on *Wise Blood,* executive-produced. The entire film was shot on location in the Mexican state of Morelos and bears an obvious kinship to Huston's previous films with a Mexican locale, *The Treasure of the Sierra Madre* and *The Night of the Iguana.*

Firmin, like Fred C. Dobbs, literally goes to hell under the heat of the Mexican sun. As already noted, he believes hell to be his natural habitat. At one point in *Sierra Madre,* Dobbs is viewed through the flames of a campfire, which appear to engulf him like hellfire as he too is overwhelmed by the dark

forces within him. Like Dobbs also, Firmin finds himself surrounded at the conclusion of the film by a murderous band of Mexican criminals, all of whom could well be described as second cousins to *Sierra Madre's* Gold Hat and his violent gang. In the evil dwarf who runs the cantina (played chillingly by Rene Ruiz), Huston etches his most memorable portrait of absolute villainy since Gold Hat.

Like the Reverend T. Lawrence Shannon in *Iguana,* Firmin has become addicted to the bottle as an antidote to his despair. Yvonne, like Maxine, represents the drunkard's last hope for salvation. But Firmin is far more advanced on his path to self-destruction than Shannon and so rejects the life-affirming alternative she represents in favor of total oblivion.

In Lowry's book, Yvonne and Hugh emerge as potent characters. (Screenwriter Guy Gallo eliminates a fourth important character, Firmin's boyhood friend Jacques Laruelle, whose betrayal of the consul by having an affair with Yvonne is attributed

222

in the film to Hugh instead.) In Huston's film version, however, Yvonne and Hugh remain somewhat vague characters who are not nearly so well drawn as the consul. Both are equally self-deluded, but in Yvonne's case particularly, we never really know why. After a year of being separated from her husband, whom she has just recently divorced, she suddenly returns in an attempt to revive their relationship, though it's clear from the start the consul is now much too far gone for such a possibility to exist. For Huston, she seems to serve mostly as a symbol (like Maxine in *Iguana* and Roslyn in *The Misfits)*, whose return on the Day of the Dead—when, according to Mexican folklore, the dead come alive for a day to be celebrated—forces Firmin to finally take stock of

himself. Unlike Maxine and Roslyn, however, Yvonne's man fails her, for the stuff Yvonne's dreams are made of—Firmin—is hopelessly lost to alcoholism, self-hatred and shattered idealism.

Hugh's self-delusion on the other hand is that he is, or should be, some kind of Hemingwayesque hero. He sings of gallantry and revolution, regretting that he too did not receive a red badge of courage on the battlefields of Spain like the many men whose heroic deeds he covered there. At one point when this regret overwhelms him, he jumps into a ring and fights a bull to prove his courage to himself. Hugh is a soldier without a war, searching for, but not finding, the very ideals his half-brother has lost.

The consul self-pityingly equates his inner conflict with that of the tormented lead character in the Peter Lorre film *Los Manos de Orlac (The Hands of Orlac,* a.k.a. *Mad Love)*, which he sees a clip from early on. A poster for the film also appears prominently in the background of the seedy cantina where the consul

223

The Consul (Albert Finney), his estranged wife, Yvonne (Jacqueline Bisset), and his half-brother, Hugh (Anthony Andrews), are each wrapped up in private reveries as they travel to nearby Tomalin for a bullfight.

The Consul (Albert Finney) questions Dona Gregoria (Katy Jurado) about a packet of letters he thinks he may have left in her cantina.

The Consul (Albert Finney) brandishes a machete during the film's climax in a dingy bar/brothel called El Farolito.

meets his dramatic, and perhaps even heroic, end. In the film, Lorre plays a deranged surgeon who grafts the hands of an executed mad slasher onto a concert pianist named Orlac, who recently lost his own hands in a train accident. Orlac is thereafter compelled to kill, even though he doesn't understand why. Firmin views his compulsive mistreatment of Yvonne and his own self-abuse as similar. Orlac's hands kill, but his heart does not, the consul insists apologetically, comparing Orlac's plight to his own.

Essayists on Malcom Lowry (Lowry was an alcoholic who died from drink in 1957) have often described the consul as an "epic alcoholic." Huston sees him the same way and does not dismiss the character's failed struggle with his inner demons lightly. Yvonne at one point tells her husband that he has a great soul. Huston too mourns the consul's shattered idealism and defeated spirit and in the cantina scene portrays him as a sort of white knight, or innocent, who, perhaps because he *is* drunk, unwisely but heroically takes on the villains as his last act on earth.

In his documentary *Notes from Under the Volcano,* a behind-the-scenes chronicle of the making of the film, producer Gary Conklin asked Huston about this

225

very point. The director's reply was not only revealing of his attitude toward Geoffrey Firmin, but apropos to a theme he has expressed in many of his films since World War II. "I've often been asked by journalists what was behind his drunkenness," Huston said. "There's been speculation on the part of those who've written about Lowry that perhaps it was the consul's court martial, the event that led to his court martial when he was supposed to have put German officers into the fiery furnace of his Q ship—or rather his crew did that and he had to answer for it. Did this lead to his drunkenness? I prefer to think not. I prefer to think of his drunkenness as rather God-like. And along those lines, I wonder where God has been since World War II? If one can judge by the state of affairs on the planet earth, why He's not in strict attendance? He's away on some other constellation. Probably on a bat Himself."

Prizzi's Honor (1985)

AN ABC MOTION PICTURES
PRESENTATION
Released through 20th Century-Fox
Technicolor/130 minutes

CREDITS:

Director: John Huston; *Producer:* John Foreman; *Screenplay:* Richard Condon and Janet Roach, based on the novel *Prizzi's Honor* by Richard Condon; *Cinematographer:* Andre Bartkowiak; *Editors:* Rudi and Kaja Fehr; *Music:* Alex North; *Production designer:* Dennis Washington; *Videocassette source:* Vestron Video.

CAST:

Charley Partanna: Jack Nicholson; *Irene Walker:* Kathleen Turner; *Eduardo Prizzi:* Robert Loggia; *Angelo "Pop" Partanna:* John Rudolph; *Don Prizzi:* William Hickey; *Dominic Prizzi:* Lee Richardson; *Maerose Prizzi:* Anjelica Huston.

* * *

Contemporary Reviews

"...the duplicitous dame has been close to Huston's heart ever since *The Maltese Falcon,* and the endearingly cynical Prizzis fall somewhere between the absurdist crooks of *Beat the Devil* and the connivers of *The Asphalt Jungle.* The man is clearly in his element, and he spins out his byzantine fable...with unhurried and supremely confident aplomb."—*Newsweek*

"This project obviously stirred the 78-year-old Huston's wise old blood. He has never offered his bleak view of human nature with more slyness or style, and in Nicholson he has an actor whose subtlety and nerve match his...a shrewd and entertaining fable told out of the corner of cynical mouths."—*Time* magazine

* * *

The greatest irony in John Huston's ironic black comedy *Prizzi's Honor* is that while all the characters—mobsters and cops alike—talk incessantly about "honor," none of them knows the meaning of the word.

What they're really talking about is power and territoriality—vested interests. But they have deceived themselves into thinking otherwise. And their, as well as our, world, Huston and writer Richard Condon satirically observe, is not a better place for their self-deception. The film's focal character, Charley Partanna, a slow-witted Brooklyn hitman for the powerful Prizzi Family, sums up the film's damning message best when he falls for the beguiling Irene, another "hitter" who has been contracted to kill him, and intuitively remarks, "I look at you, I see what I wanna see." This goes for most everyone else in the film as well.

At Charley's birth, Don Prizzi agrees to become the boy's godfather (in more ways than one) and pledges to his close ally, "Pop" Partanna, that from then on he'll look out for the man's son as if he were his own. After Charley grows up, the Don compels him to take a blood oath to uphold Prizzi's Honor at any and all costs. Engaged to marry Maerose, daughter of the Don's son, Dominic, Charley is stood up by the girl, however, and out of honor to him, the Prizzis disown her until such time as Charley either agrees to take her back or marries someone else.

At a wedding of another Prizzi granddaughter, Charley meets the beautiful but mysterious Irene and falls instantly in love with her, as she does with him, not realizing at first that she too is a professional hitman and the brains behind a recent scam of the Prizzis' Las Vegas operation that Charley has been assigned to put right. After Charley and Irene

Director John Huston on the set of Prizzi's Honor, *listening to a dialogue recording.*

The wily Maerose (Anjelica Huston) makes overtures to the slow-witted Charley (Jack Nicholson), her former beau whom she's determined to get back.

marry, Maerose is accepted back into the family. This is but the first step, however, in regaining her lost honor as she sets about scheming to win Charley back. To accomplish this, she blows the whistle on Irene's involvement in the Las Vegas scam. Because Irene is Charley's wife, the Prizzis agree to take no action against her provided she returns the money she stole. Over Charley's initial objections ("We'd rather eat our children than part with money"), Irene agrees to return the money, in exchange for the insurance claim on the stolen loot.

Later, during an entreprenurial kidnapping engineered by herself and Charley, the luckless Irene shoots a police officer's wife. To preserve their own honor, the once-crooked but now righteous cops start putting the heat on the Prizzi mob. To take the heat off, the Don orders Irene to be sacrificed. The job of killing her and handing her body over to the police is given to Charley himself, whose reward for his allegiance to the Prizzis will be to replace Dom-

228

"Pop" Partanna (John Rudolph), Charley's dad, expresses joy at the news of Charley's (Jack Nicholson) upcoming wedding to Irene.

inic as the mob's top man. Unknown to Charley, Dominic puts a contract out on him, hiring Irene as the hitman. The final confrontation takes place in Irene's Los Angeles apartment where she attempts to shoot Charley in bed but winds up getting knifed by him instead.

As the film ends, Charley gets back together with the wily Maerose, her honor now fully re-stored. He has learned an important lesson about the perils of trying to marry and work outside The Family, which has always owned him lock, stock and barrel.

Despite its serious subtext and resonances of *The Godfather* ("It's only business," is how the Don describes the death warrant he assigns Irene), *Prizzi's Honor* is a delightful comedy in the mold of Huston's earlier *Beat the Devil,* though it is not as free-wheeling as that film was. In Richard Condon, who has fash-ioned a career out of writing dark contemporary thrillers *(The Manchurian Candidate, Winter Kills)* with a

Irene (Kathleen Turner) and Charley (Jack Nicholson) dispose of their latest "hit"—actually, her *latest.*

230

Portrait of two hitmen in love. Charley (Jack Nicholson) and Irene (Kathleen Turner) in Huston's crime comedy, Prizzi's Honor.

Jack Nicholson, Kathleen Turner, and Anjelica Huston with their director on the set of the multi-award-winning Prizzi's Honor.

satiric bite, Huston found an ideal collaborator, and his film (scripted by Condon and Janet Roach) follows Condon's original fairly closely. Both book and film are essentially a romance about two mis-matched lovers swallowed up in a game of mob power and politics that each of them comes to understand much too late. The film's irony and humor emerge mostly through the performances of its stars, although Alex North's satiric score with its repeated refrains of Rossini's *The Thieving Magpie* contributes strongly as well.

As the befuddled Charley, Jack Nicholson gives a masterful performance that is both hysterically funny and quite touching in equal measure. His scenes with the sultry, deceptively innocent Turner rank among the funniest Huston has given us since *Beat the Devil*. All the cast is first rate. But the film's revelation is Huston's daughter, Anjelica, whose performance as the low-key spiderwoman, Maerose, won her a well-deserved Oscar as the year's Best Supporting Actress. Nicholson was also nominated as Best Actor, but he lost to William Hurt for *Kiss of the Spider Woman*, which, ironically, would be a very good title for a sequel to *Prizzi's Honor* about Charley's relationship with Maerose.

Though John Huston won the New York Film Critics Award and earned a variety of other accolades for his direction of *Prizzi's Honor*, he once again failed to take home the Oscar. Though nominated, he lost to Sydney Pollack for *Out of Africa*.

Huston returned to Las Caletas following the Academy Award celebration and, virtually without a pause, announced plans to shoot a documentary about the breathtaking Sea of Cortez off the coast of Mexico, near his home. But the project was stalled when, in the spring of 1986, Cannon Films and producer Martin Poll approached Huston to direct the film version of Anne Edwards' novel *Haunted Summer*, an historical romance about the incident that gave rise to Mary Shelley's writing *Frankenstein*. A script had been written by Lewis John Carlino and production was set to begin in Europe practically on the eve of Huston's 80th birthday. Coincidentally, director Ken Russell, a filmmaker with whom Huston shares a great deal thematically (though not stylistically), began shooting a quite similar project, *Gothic*, on location in England that May. Due to ill health, however, Huston was compelled to bow out of the project at the last minute and Ivan Passer was signed to direct instead.

Huston, whose emphysema had become quite debilitating, announced no future filmmaking plans. He continued to remain active though and was particularly involved in the Directors' Guild of America's ongoing protests against the "colorization" of classic black-and-white movies by broadcast mogul Ted Turner and others.

The Dead (1987)

Vestron Pictures/Zenith
A Wieland Schulz-Kiel and Chris Sievernich
Production
Color/82 minutes

CREDITS

Director: John Huston; *Producers:* Wieland Schulz-Kiel and Chris Sievernich; *Screenplay:* Tony Huston, based on the short story by James Joyce; *Cinematographer:* Fred Murphy; *Editor:* Roberto Silvi; *Music:* Alex North: *Production Designers:* Stephen Grimes and Dennis Washington; *Videocassette Source:* Vestron Video.

CAST:

Gretta Conroy: Anjelica Huston; *Gabriel Conroy:* Donal McCann; *Lily:* Rachel Dowling; *Aunt Julia Morkan:* Cathleen Delaney; *Aunt Kate Morkan:* Helena Carroll; *Mary Jane:* Ingrid Craigie; *Mr. Browne:* Dan O'Herlihy; *Bartell D'Arcy:* Frank Patterson; *Freddy Malins:* Donal Donnelly; *Mrs. Malins:* Marie Kean.

* * *

Contemporary Reviews:

"In the context of Huston's long and unpredictable career, *The Dead* adds yet another wrinkle. His work as a director confounds all the leading theories of cinematic authorship—for a helmsman with such a strong presence on film, he was as protean as could be. *The Dead*, a work that is both extremely personal and strangely formal, further strengthens that paradox."—*Premiere*

* * *

"Assembling a cast of great Irish actors, he's made a movie of astonishing warmth and humor, which then deepens to produce breathtaking emotional music. You hang on every word and observed gesture, every perfectly calibrated performance. *The Dead* is 75 [sic] minutes long; there's not a frame you'd want to change. What a swan song."—*Newsweek*

* * *

Producer Wieland Schulz-Kiel first approached John Huston about *The Dead* while they were making *Under the Volcano* together in Mexico. The idea appealed strongly to Huston for a number of reasons, many of them personal and quite nostalgic.

The concluding tale in a volume of Irish short stories called *Dubliners*, *The Dead* was a longtime favorite of Huston's, as was the story's author, James Joyce, whom Huston always acknowledged as a major influence on his work. "Mother went to Europe and, upon her return, smuggled in a copy of Joyce's *Ulysses*,

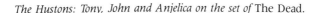
The Hustons: Tony, John and Anjelica on the set of The Dead.

Anjelica Huston as Gretta, who is haunted by an old love, in John Huston's The Dead, *based on a story by James Joyce.*

which was banned in the United States," he wrote in his autobiography. "It was probably the greatest experience that any book has ever given me. Doors fell open." Adapting the Joyce story to the screen would allow Huston to not only pay formal hommage to one of his artistic mentors, but permit him to draw on important, albeit challenging, literary source material for his cinematic inspiration, a favored Huston modis operandi throughout the director's career.

There were other reasons too. Huston had lived in Ireland for twenty-five years, had become an Irish citizen, and though he now resided in Mexico, he retained his Irish passport and still considered himself to be an Irish country squire through and through. Two of his children, Tony and Anjelica, had spent their formative years growing up on Huston's sprawling Irish estate, St. Clarens, and though the estate had long since been sold, they continued to view St. Clarens as the one place they would always call "home." Always regretting the loss of St. Clarens (Huston had been forced to sell the place to climb out from under a mountain of debt), the director saw *The Dead* as an opportunity to express his longing and affection for that part of his past, and for the Irish people who had played such a large part in it—an important motivation behind Joyce's writing of the short story as well. Now nearing the end of his career and his life, Huston told his daughter, Anjelica, "We must do this one for Ireland."

It was Schulz-Kiel who suggested that Huston's son, Tony, an aspiring screenwriter, would be the ideal choice to do the screenplay. John Huston quickly agreed. "James Joyce had long been a common bond between us," Tony Huston wrote in *American Film*. "During my school days, I'd become something of a Joyce aficionado, while *Ulysses* had had the most profound effect on Dad as a young man. In our many discussions, *The Dead* occupied a special place, not merely as a potential film, but as a reference to which we compared our experiences in the way others resort to the Bible. Consequently, when Wieland broached the subject, I virtually had a sense of predestination, that all the time I'd spent thinking about the story had inevitably led to Dad's request that I write the screenplay." Though the elder Huston contributed to the screenplay as well, he took no screen credit, preferring to let his son's name stand alone. Tony Huston's screenplay subsequently earned a well deserved Oscar nomination, but did not win.

The Dead became even more of a family affair when Anjelica Huston, fresh from winning the Best Supporting Actress Oscar for her father's last film, *Prizzi's Honor,* signed on to play the pivotal role of Gretta, the film's female lead. Many of the extended family of artists and technicians who had contributed so much to Huston's work in the past were drawn into the project as well, including production assistant Tom Shaw, production designers Stephen Grimes and

234

Dennis Washington, composer Alex North, editor Roberto Silvi, and others.

It had taken a number of years for Schulz-Kiel to muster financial support for the film's proposed $3.5 million budget—most of which was acquired on the strength of Huston's name and agreed-upon participation. By that time, however, the director was in exceedingly poor health due to his emphysema, and he seemed to be growing worse. Forced to bow out of a previous film commitment for health reasons, Huston was now considered uninsurable. *The Dead* was given the green light only when it was agreed that another director, Karel Reisz, would stand ready to step in should Huston's health deteriorate and he be unable to complete the picture.

With that established, shooting began in January of 1987 in a warehouse in Valencia, California, not far from Los Angeles, that had been reconverted into a soundstage. Though chairbound and hooked up to an oxygen machine throughout the shoot, Huston remarkably appeared to grow healthier as each day progressed and he was able to complete the film on his own, on time and on budget. More remarkable still, *The Dead* would turn out to be one of the finest achievements of the director's career— arguably even *the* finest, a gentle summing up, and final commenting upon, the central themes that had run throughout his work with such remarkable consistency right from the very beginning.

As the film commenced production, the director described *The Dead's* prototypical Huston theme to the press this way. "The story's about a man being revealed to himself," he said, "and while we're watching that, I think we're revealed to ourselves. What we are and what we think we are are really two different things. And the discovery of who one is is a soul-shaking experience."

The person who undergoes this soul-shaking experience is Gabriel Conroy, a somber, middle class Dublin journalist whose announced "boredom with Ireland" and subtly expressed contempt for the foibled and sometimes foolish people surrounding him mask his own emotional emptiness. Gabriel's deluded self-view is that he thinks more, feels more, knows more, in short possesses a secret, more complicated and richer inner life than anyone around him, including his own wife, Gretta, a girl of the peasant class. The revelation that the emotional lives of his friends and, especially, his wife, are, in fact, vastly more complicated than his own not only shakes him to the core, but fills him with a compassion for "all the living and all the dead" that he'd never known before.

The film unfolds in two acts. The first takes place at a dinner party hosted by Gabriel's Aunts Julia and Kate on the Twelfth Night of Christmas, the Feast of the Epiphany, a time when, according to Christian custom, the Lord reveals Himself and His Truth to His flock.

Aunt Julia (Cathleen Delaney) and Aunt Kate (Helena Carroll) welcome Gretta (Anjelica Huston).

This first act is essentially a comedy of manners during which Gabriel's character and the characters of those around him to whom he feels superior are revealed in a series of humorous, sometimes embarrassing, and often touching moments of subtle interaction. Gretta remains somewhat of a cypher, however, a quiet presence throughout the proceedings whom Gabriel ignores most of the time as he is so caught up in his own reactions to the affair. This situation reverses completely during the film's concluding act when Gretta and Gabriel take a room at a local hotel rather than braving the winter elements to make their way home. As the party concludes, one of the guests, tenor Bartell D'Arcy, is persuaded to sing, and he performs a moving ballad about lost love. The song rivets Gretta's attention as she and her husband are leaving and she becomes subdued and uncommunicative during the carriage ride to the hotel. In the quiet of their room, Gabriel presses her for an explanation as to why the song had such an emotional impact on her.

In a brilliantly acted scene of confession that should have earned Anjelica Huston her second Academy Award nomination, Gretta tells of a young man named Michael Furey who used to sing that same song. The two were lovers, but their affair came to an end when Furey died of tuberculosis in his seventeenth year. Gabriel is not only astonished by the revelation that his wife had a former lover but is brought up short by the fact that her still ardent feelings for her long dead suitor stand their own loving but rather passionless marriage out in cold relief. What follows, as Gabriel is forced to take stock of himself, his wife and everyone else he thought he'd known but hadn't, is one of the most mesmerizing sequences in Huston's entire body of work—indeed, in the history of the movies themselves.

Standing at the window and gazing out at the falling snow, Gabriel reflects on his past and as the camera shifts from one breathtaking view of the Irish landscape to another—including the graveyard where Michael Furey is buried—he is confronted by a broad vision of mortality, the richness of life, and his own real place in the scheme of things that transforms him. It is truly an epiphantic, life affirming moment in which one can't help but see shades of the characters in Huston's past films—the heroes and losers, the triumphant and the damned—and share the love, understanding, and compassion he so obviously had for them all.

For a filmmaker to exit the stage at the top of his form is an uncommon enough experience. For him to exit with a masterpiece—and his own cinematic epitaph to boot—is somewhat of a miracle. But the old man did it.

What a swan song, indeed!

Gabriel Conroy (Donal McCann, back to camera) gives a loosely prepared speech to his fellow dinner guests.

An exuberant Huston with producers Wieland Schulz-Kiel (left) and Chris Sievernich (right) on the set of The Dead, *the director's final and, arguably, best film.*

Huston the Actor

TODAY'S FILMGOERS know John Huston as much for his acting as his directing—in some quarters, perhaps even moreso. Huston had already done much acting on the stage in the early days of his career, of course, and had even sought work as an extra upon his arrival in Hollywood in the late twenties. Reputedly, he had very small roles in three early William Wyler films: *The Shakedown* (1929), a part-talkie with a boxing milieu starring the ill-fated James Murray; *Hell's Heroes* (1930), Wyler's all-talkie remake of the oft-filmed Pete B. Kyne story, *The Three Godfathers*, starring Charles Bickford; and *The Storm* (1930), a disaster film starring William "Hopalong Cassidy" Boyd. Huston's first known screen performance, however, was with his father in the 1929 Paramount short *Two Americans*, directed by John Meehan.

After deciding to become a writer and then a director, Huston never seriously contemplated a return to acting as a secondary career. "There was one actor in my family, and that was my dad," he proclaimed. "I could never top him and I don't want to try." That conviction, however, did not prevent him from performing uncredited cameos à la Hitchcock in three of his own early films, *The Treasure of the Sierra Madre, We Were Strangers* and *The Red Badge of Courage*. In *Sierra Madre*, where he appears as the man in the white suit who repeatedly slips the down-on-his-luck Dobbs some pesos, the director actually gave himself a speaking part. In *We Were Strangers*, however, he appears silently in a brief scene as a love-sick Cuban bank clerk whose prospects for a date with the delectable China (Jennifer Jones) are dashed because the girl has other, more revolutionary, plans. The director also gave himself a small part as a soldier in *The Red Badge of Courage*, but his cameo was subsequently cut from the film.

For his cameo as Lord Acton, leader of the climactic fox hunt that concludes *The List of Adrian Messenger*, Huston finally decided to take a screen credit and had his name listed with the rest of the cast. While finishing *Messenger*, he was contacted by director Otto Preminger, then casting *The Cardinal*, and asked to play a major supporting role in the film, that of a crusty but politically savvy Cardinal of Boston who assists an idealistic young priest, Father Fermoyle (Tom Tryon), in his rise to the upper echelons of the Roman Catholic Church. "I didn't want to use any of the established character actors because they would bring too much of their familiar image to the role," Preminger said later.

Huston being made up (by Jennifer Jones) for his cameo as a Cuban bank teller in We Were Strangers.

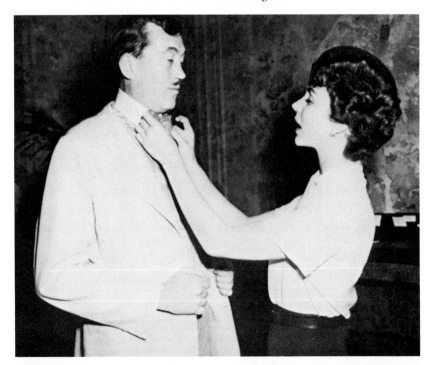

238

As the grandfather of the imprisoned Robert Duvall in Breakout.

239

As Cardinal Glennon in The Cardinal, *the role which earned him an Oscar nomination as Best Supporting Actor.*

"I wanted someone new, but also impressive, and it occurred to me that John Huston would be perfect."

Preminger himself occasionally took on small roles for other directors, notably Billy Wilder, for whom he appeared (memorably) as the natty but vile Nazi prison camp commander, Oberst von Scherbach, in Wilder's *Stalag 17* (1953), opposite William Holden. He now hoped that Huston would do the same for him. After some persuasion, Huston accepted the part for the agreed-upon price of two paintings which Preminger would purchase for the director's ever-expanding private collection. Though Preminger was known as somewhat of a tyrant on his sets, Huston found working with him to be an agreeable experience. "He didn't roar at me, or if he did, it was a muted roar," Huston reported in his autobiography.

Of working with Huston, Preminger later said, "[He] was a joy to direct. He behaved as we both want actors to behave: he came to the set on time knowing his lines. He rehearsed and did the role without the slightest critical comment about the direction or even a hint of professional advice. *Perfect.*" Huston's working method with other directors in subsequent films would proceed along this same line. "Although I feel at times I could tell the director how to do something," he has said, "I close that gate immediately."

Though *The Cardinal* was a big box office hit for Preminger, it did not fare well with many of the nation's film critics, not a few of whom labelled it one of the year's (1963) ten worst films. Not so Huston's performance, however, which was almost unanimously singled out as the film's high point. *Time* magazine's review was not untypical. "John Huston, with rip snorting vitality, all but steals the show," it wrote. "Huston is superb." The Academy of Motion Picture Arts and Sciences, lately and all too frequently lacking in its recognition of Huston the writer-director, thought so too, and nominated him for the 1963 Best Supporting Actor Oscar, though he lost to Melvyn Douglas for *Hud.*

Much to Huston's surprise, the success of his performance in *The Cardinal* led to offers to appear before the camera in a host of other films as well. He was approached to narrate documentaries and do voice-overs for commercials and public service announcements. Thus he finally found himself embarking on that acting career that he had always scoffed at. Nevertheless, he still considers acting to be just a divertissement. "It's a nice way to make a buck," he says. "It's a lark, and a very well paid one. But I don't take acting seriously. I don't put any great store in my skills as an actor. Always and forever, I'm a director."

Huston is quite forthright about his methods of selecting the roles he undertakes, readily admitting that he accepts them indiscriminately. "Whether the pictures were good or bad or indifferent was of no consequence," he says. "I liked myself in *Chinatown.* And when I saw the picture about the Kennedys, *Winter Kills,* I thought that was amusing. But not much else. I just spoke my lines." One wonders if the director

240

includes the increasing number of cameos and speaking parts he has taken on in his own films in this appraisal of his acting work. His delightful performance as Noah in *The Bible* was surely more than "just speaking lines." In addition to *The Bible*, other Huston-directed films where he has appeared before the camera include: *Casino Royale*, *A Walk with Love and Death*, *The Kremlin Letter*, *The Life and Times of Judge Roy Bean*, and *Wise Blood*.

Huston is quite right in considering his performance in *Chinatown* one of his best. As the unctuous, land-grabbing Noah Cross, who commits adultery with his own daughter (Faye Dunaway), then tries to steal the child of their incestuous union away from her, Huston, under Roman Polanski's precise direction, is subtly but thoroughly loathsome, and chillingly real.

Perhaps one of Huston's most intriguing performances, however, is one that we'll probably never see. In 1970, Orson Welles, who had acted in three of Huston's films, asked him to star in what would turn out to be Welles's final, and unfortunately unfinished, work as a director, *The Other Side of the Wind*, a tale of the "New Hollywood." In the film, which Welles shot off and on from 1970 to 1975, Huston plays a legendary, Welles-like filmmaker, Jake Hannaford, who returns to the Hollywood that has always scorned him in an attempt to make a comeback. Most of the film centers around a gala but soulful birthday party given for Hannaford that's attended by a host of Hollywood luminaries, as well as critics, reporters, assorted well-wishers, hate-mongers, and other hangers-on. Appearing in the film along with Huston are director Peter Bogdanovich, the late actress Lilli Palmer, Susan Strasberg, and Bob Random. Huston completed his scenes in Los Angeles and Arizona, having had, in his words, "a marvelous time." When

Welles died in 1985, however, the film was still unfinished. In 1975, with only a few additional scenes remaining, Welles ran out of completion money. Worse still, the main investors were all Iranian businessmen, and when the Shah was deposed, their assets, including the negatives of *The Other Side of the Wind*, were frozen. Those who saw an early rough cut of the uncompleted picture call it a *knockout*, Huston says, admitting that he himself hasn't seen it and isn't likely to, for every scrap of footage is now tied up in a vault somewhere in the benighted city of Tehran.

Huston's voice is so distinctive that even under layers of make-up, which he often dons for his film roles, he can't help but be identified. This was surely the case with one of his most unusual film appearances, that of the simian lawgiver in the 1973 *Battle for the Planet of the Apes*, the final installment of the epic science-fiction series that began in 1968 with *Planet of the Apes*. For this same reason, Huston is equally recognizable in the animated features *The Hobbit* (1977) and *Return of the King* (1980), both based on the works of fantasist J.R.R. Tolkien, to which Huston (as well as Otto Preminger!) contributed impressive vocal characterizations.

In the syndicated television mini-series *American Caesar*, based on William Manchester's prize-winning biography of General Douglas MacArthur, Huston contributed both face (sans make-up) and voice to play the part of MacArthur himself, reciting the late warrior's words on camera and over rare archival footage chronicling the general's career. John Colicos, whom Huston had recently directed in *Phobia*, served as the series' narrator. Around the same time (1982), Huston also narrated a fiction film, *Cannery Row*, reading the words of John Steinbeck upon whose novel of the same name the film, starring Nick Nolte, was based.

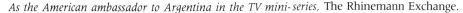

As the American ambassador to Argentina in the TV mini-series, The Rhinemann Exchange.

In addition to the PBS documentaries *Hollywood on Trial* and *John Huston: A War Remembered*, both mentioned earlier in this book, Huston has participated in the biographical documentaries *Agee* (1980) and the Oscar-nominated *George Stevens: A Filmmaker's Journey* (1985). In each, however, he appears neither as actor nor narrator, but as himself, recounting personal memories of his two former friends and colleagues: writer James Agee in the first film, director George Stevens in the latter.

Other documentaries where Huston appears as himself (because they are *about* him) include the 1966 BBC, NET, and CBS co-production, *The Life and Times of John Huston, ESQ*, which features interviews with Huston's daughter Anjelica and son Tony, his former wife Evelyn Keyes, long time associate Gladys Hill, and stars with whom the director has worked such as Elizabeth Taylor and Marlon Brando. Prior to selling his Irish estate, Huston also served as host and narrator for an intimate travelogue about his former home called *John Huston's Dublin* (1980), another European-made film which has been little shown in this country.

The Screen Directors Guild, for which Huston once served as treasurer, has also made a documentary film about his career as part of an on-going series on the work of American filmmakers. The title of the film, which is available mainly to educational institutions, is simply *John Huston*. And for PBS again, Huston figured prominently in *Lights! Camera! Annie!*

As Professor Moriarty in Sherlock Holmes in New York, *with Charlotte Rampling as Irene Adler, Geoffrey Moore as her son, and Roger Moore as Sherlock Holmes. In background, left to right: David Huddleston as Inspector Lafferty, Gig Young as Mortimer McGraw, and Patrick McNee as Dr. Watson.*

As yet another perverted character, the evil uncle of the Marquis De Sade in Cy Endfield's DeSade, *with Senta Berger.*

(1982), a behind-the-scenes account of the making of his only musical.

At 80, John Huston appeared to slacken off somewhat from his acting career in favor of directing.

At 80, John Huston appeared to slacken off somewhat from his acting career in favor of directing. "I have no intention of acting at the expense of directing," he said. That seemed to be the case, for after 1985, he appeared on screen very infrequently. One of his most memorable turns, however, was in the pilot telefilm for NBC's revival of the *Alfred Hitchcock Presents* television series (1955-1965). In the pilot, remakes of four dramas culled from the earlier series, Huston appeared as the title character of the segment titled *Man From the South*, playing an inveterate gambler (type casting?) who challenges a young man to ignite his lighter ten times in a row. If the man "I have no intention of acting at the expense of directing," he said. That seemed to be the case, for after 1985, he appeared on screen very infrequently. One of his most memorable turns, however, was in the pilot telefilm for NBC's revival of the *Alfred Hitchcock Presents* television series (1955-1965). In the pilot, remakes of four dramas culled from the earlier series, Huston appeared as the title character of the segment titled *Man From the South*, playing an inveterate gambler (type casting?) who challenges a young man to ignite his lighter ten times in a row. If the man wins the wager, he gets Huston's expensive car. If he loses, Huston gets his little finger, which he is prepared to chop off with a meat cleaver the second the lighter misfires. Huston had a high old time with the part, playing it with gusto and ghoulish relish. The part, incidentally, was played originally by Peter Lorre, co-star of Huston's very first feature film as a director, *The Maltese Falcon*, thus drawing the circle nicely closed.

As the unctuous and evil Noah Cross in Roman Polanski's Chinatown.

The Films of John Huston - Actor

(Minor or uncredited roles)

1929

The Shakedown (UNIVERSAL)

Director: William Wyler; *Producer:* Carl Laemmle; *Cast:* James Murray, Barbara Kent, George Kotsonaros, John Huston (uncredited). *Videocassette source:* Not available.

Two Americans (PARAMOUNT)

Director: John Meehan; *Cast:* Walter Huston, John Huston; *Videocassette source:* Not available.

1930

Hell's Heroes (UNIVERSAL)

Director: William Wyler; *Producer:* Carl Laemmle; *Cast:* Charles Bickford, Raymond Hatton, Fred Kohler, John Huston (uncredited); *Videocassette source:* Not available.

The Storm (UNIVERSAL)

Director: William Wyler; *Producer:* Carl Laemmle; *Cast:* Lupe Velez, William Boyd, Paul Cavanaugh, John Huston (uncredited); *Videocassette source:* Not available.

As a pleasure-loving tycoon (Joe Kennedy?) in Winter Kills.

1948

The Treasure of the Sierra Madre (WARNER BROS.)

Director: John Huston; *Producer:* Henry Blanke; *Cast:* Humphrey Bogart, Tim Holt, Walter Huston, John Huston (uncredited); *Videocassette source:* Key Video.

1949

We Were Strangers (COLUMBIA)

Director: John Huston; *Producer:* S.P. Eagle; *Cast:* John Garfield, Jennifer Jones, Gilbert Roland, John Huston (uncredited); *Videocassette source:* Not available.

1963

The List of Adrian Messenger (UNIVERSAL-INTERNATIONAL)

Director: John Huston; *Producer:* Edward Lewis; *Cast:* George C. Scott, Dana Wynter, Kirk Douglas, John Huston; *Videocassette source:* MCA Home Video.

1967

Casino Royale (COLUMBIA)

Director: John Huston, et. al.; *Producers:* Charles K. Feldman and Jerry Bresler; *Cast:* David Niven, Deborah Kerr, William Holden, John Huston; *Videocassette source:* RCA/Columbia Home Video.

1970

The Kremlin Letter (20TH CENTURY-FOX)

Director: John Huston; *Producers:* Carter De Haven and Sam Wiesenthal; *Cast:* Richard Boone, Patrick O'Neal, Orson Welles, John Huston; *Videocassette source:* Not available.

1972

The Life and Times of Judge Roy Bean (NATIONAL GENERAL)

Director: John Huston; *Producer:* John Foreman; *Cast:* Paul Newman, Ned Beatty, Ava Gardner, John Huston; *Videocassette source:* Warner Home Video.

1980

Wise Blood (NEW LINE CINEMA)

Director: John Huston; *Producers:* Michael and Kathy Fitzgerald; *Cast:* Brad Dourif, Harry Dean Stanton, Ned Beatty, John Huston; *Videocassette source:* MCA Home Video.

(Major roles)

1963

The Cardinal (COLUMBIA)

Director: Otto Preminger; *Producer:* Otto Preminger; *Cast:* Tom Tryon, Carol Lynley,, Romy Schneider, John Huston; *Videocassette source:* Not available.

1966

The Bible (20TH CENTURY-FOX)

Director: John Huston; *Producer:* Dino De Laurentiis; *Cast:* George C. Scott, Ava Gardner, Richard Harris, John Huston; *Videocassette source:* CBS/Fox Home Video.

1968

Candy (CINERAMA RELEASING)

Director: Christian Marquand; *Producer:* Robert Haggiag; *Cast:* Marlon Brando, Ewa Aulin, Richard Burton, John Huston; *Videocassette source:* Not available.

1969

A Walk with Love and Death (20TH CENTURY-FOX)

Director: John Huston; *Producer:* Carter De Haven; *Cast:* Anjelica Huston, Assaf Dayan, John Huston; *Videocassette source:* Not available.

De Sade (AMERICAN-INTERNATIONAL)

Director: Cy Endfield; *Producers:* Samuel Z. Arkoff and James H. Nicholson; *Cast:* Keir Dullea, Senta Berger, Lilli Palmer, John Huston; *Videocassette source:* Not available.

1970

Myra Breckinridge (20TH CENTURY-FOX)

Director: Michael Sarne; *Producer:* Robert Fryer; *Cast:* Raquel Welch, Rex Reed, Mae West, John Huston; *Videocassette source:* Not available.

The Bridge in the Jungle (INDEPENDENT)

Director: Pancho Kohner; *Producer:* Pancho Kohner; *Cast:* Charles Robinson, Katy Jurado, John Huston; *Videocassette source:* Not available.

The Other Side of the Wind (INDEPENDENT)

Director: Orson Welles; *Producer:* Orson Welles; *Cast:* John Huston, Peter Bogdanovich, Lilli Palmer; *Unfinished.*

1971

The Deserter (PARAMOUNT)

Director: Burt Kennedy; *Producers:* Norman Baer and Ralph Serpe; *Cast:* Bekim Fehmiu, John Huston, Richard Crenna; *Videocassette source:* Not available.

Man in the Wilderness (WARNER BROS.)

Director: Richard C. Sarafian; *Producer:* Sandy Howard; *Cast:* Richard Harris, John Huston, Henry Wilcoxon; *Videocassette source:* Not available.

1973

Battle for the Planet of the Apes (20TH CENTURY-FOX)

Director: J. Lee Thompson; *Producer:* Arthur P. Jacobs; *Cast:* Roddy McDowall, John Huston, Claude Akins; *Videocassette source:* Playhouse Video.

1974

Chinatown (PARAMOUNT)

Director: Roman Polanski; *Producer:* Robert Evans; *Cast:* Jack Nicholson, Faye Dunaway, John Huston; *Videocassette source:* Paramount Home Video.

1975

Breakout (COLUMBIA)

Director: Tom Gries; *Producers:* Robert Chartoff and Irwin Winkler; *Cast:* Charles Bronson, Robert Duvall, Jill Ireland, John Huston; *Videocassette source:* RCA/Columbia Home Video.

The Wind and the Lion (MGM/UA)

Director: John Milius; *Producer:* Herb Jaffe; *Cast:* Sean Connery, Candice Bergen, Brian Keith, John Huston; *Videocassette source:* MGM/UA Home Video.

1976

Sherlock Holmes in New York (20TH CENTURY-FOX TELEVISION)

Director: Boris Sagal; *Producer:* John Cutts; *Cast:* Roger Moore, John Huston, Patrick MacNee, Charlotte Rampling; *Videocassette source:* Not available.

Circasia (INDEPENDENT)

Director: Kevin McClory; *Producer:* Kevin McClory; *Cast:* Sean Connery, Shirley MacLaine, John Huston, Eric Clapton; *Videocassette source:* Not available.

1977

Tentacles (AMERICAN-INTERNATIONAL)

Director: Oliver Hellman; *Producer:* Enzo Doria; *Cast:* John Huston, Shelley Winters, Bo Hopkins, Henry Fonda; *Videocassette source:* Vestron Video.

The Rhinemann Exchange (NBC-TV)

Director: Burt Kennedy; *Producer:* Richard Collins; *Cast:* Stephen Collins, Larry Hagman, Lauren Hutton, John Huston; *Videocassette source:* Not available.

The Hobbit (RANKIN-BASS PRODUCTIONS AND NBC-TV)

Directors: Arthur Rankin, Jr. and Jules Bass; *Producers:* Rankin and Bass; *Voices:* John Huston, Orson Bean, Richard Boone, Otto Preminger; *Videocassette source:* Not available.

As Buck Loner in Myra Breckinridge.

With karate champion Joe Lewis in the chop-socky melodrama Jaguar Lives!

1978

The Word (CBS-TV)

Director: Richard Lang; *Producer:* David Manson; *Cast:* David Janssen, James Whitmore, Eddie Albert, John Huston; *Videocassette source:* USA Home Video.

The Bermuda Triangle (INDEPENDENT)

Director: Rene Cardona, Jr.; *Producer:* Rene Cardona, Jr.; *Cast:* John Huston, Gloria Guida, Claudine Auger; *Videocassette source:* VidAmerica.

Angela (INDEPENDENT)

Director: Boris Sagal; *Producer:* Zev Braun; *Cast:* Sophia Loren, Steve Railsback, John Huston; *Videocassette source:* Embassy Home Video.

1979

Jaguar Lives! (AMERICAN-INTERNATIONAL)

Director: Ernest Pintoff; *Producer:* Derek Gobson; *Cast:* Joe Lewis, Christopher Lee, Donald Pleasance, John Huston; *Videocassette source:* Not available.

Winter Kills (AVCO-EMBASSY)

Director: William Richert; *Producer:* Fred Caruso; *Cast:* Jeff Bridges, John Huston, Anthony Perkins, Sterling Hayden; *Videocassette source:* Embassy Home Video.

The Greatest Battle (INDEPENDENT) A.K.A. BATTLE FORCE

Director: Hank Milestone; *Cast:* John Huston, Henry Fonda, Stacy Keach, Samantha Eggar; *Videocassette source:* Continental.

Head On (INDEPENDENT) A.K.A. FATAL ATTRACTION

Director: Michael Grant; *Producer:* Alan Simmonds; *Cast:* Stephen Lack, Sally Kellerman, John Huston, Laurence Dane; *Videocassette source:* Vestron Video.

The Visitor (INDEPENDENT)

Director: Michael J. Paradise; *Producer:* Ovidio Assonitis; *Cast:* Mel Ferrer, Glenn Ford, John Huston, Sam Peckinpah, Shelley Winters; *Videocassette source:* Embassy Home Video.

As a priest in A Minor Miracle.

As a psychiatrist in Lovesick *with Dudley Moore.*

The Return of the King (ABC-TV)

Directors: Akiyuki Kubo, Arthur Rankin, Jr. and Jules Bass; *Producers:* Rankin and Bass; *Voices:* Orson Bean, Theodore Bikel, John Huston, Roddy McDowall; *Videocassette source:* Not available.

1983

Lovesick (WARNER BROS.)

Director: Marshall Brickman; *Producer:* Charles Okun; *Cast:* Dudley Moore, Elizabeth McGovern, Alec Guinness, John Huston; *Videocassette source:* Warner Home Video.

Mr. Corbett's Ghost (INDEPENDENT)

Director: Danny Huston; *Producer:* Barry Navid; *Cast:* Paul Scofield, Burgess Meredith, John Huston; *Videocassette Source:* Not available.

A Minor Miracle (INDEPENDENT)

Director: Terry Tanen; *Producer:* Tom Moyer; *Cast:* John Huston, Pélé, David Ruprecht; *Videocassette source:* Embassy Home Video.

1985

Alfred Hitchcock Presents (UNIVERSAL/NBC-TV)

Man from the South segment
Director: Steve De Jarnatt; *Producers:* Stephen Cragg and Alan Barnette; *Cast:* John Huston, Steven Bauer, Melanie Griffith, Kim Novak; *Videocassette source:* Not available.

1986

Momo (INDEPENDENT)

Director: Johannes Schaaf; *Producer:* Horst Wendlandt; *Cast:* Radost Bokel, Leopoldo Trieste, Bruno Stori, Ninetto Davoli, Mario Adorf, John Huston; *Videocassette source:* Not available.

The youthful John Huston, circa 1923.

The Final Fade Out

Buoyed by the experience of making *The Dead*, which was scheduled for release in late 1987, and somewhat on the rebound physically, John Huston sought refuge from his infirmities during the last months of his life in work, work and more work.

With son Tony, he adapted a Jim Harrison novel called *Revenge* for a proposed film to star Kevin Costner and Anthony Quinn. As with *The Dead*, Huston wanted the project to be another family affair, this time with son Danny forming the third part of the triumverate, as director. Huston had been encouraging Danny's directorial aspirations for some time. Danny had been given the responsibility for directing the opening title sequence of his father's *Under the Volcano*, and, on his own, had directed an hour-long film called *Mr. Corbett's Ghost* in which John Huston had acted a lead role. Despite John Huston's name and clout in the industry, however, Danny failed to get the *Revenge* assignment. The film went to director Tony Scott instead. Prior to production, the Hustons' script went through so many rewrites (by author Jim Harrison and others) that when the film finally reached the screen in early 1990, neither John nor Tony's name appeared in the credits.

Undaunted, John Huston considered directing another film himself. The proposed project was yet another literary masterpiece for which Huston had a special fondness—Herman Melville's novella, *Benito Cereno*. But plans for the project, a large budget adventure film to be shot in the Caribbean, collapsed due to Huston's uninsurability.

Again he began searching for another project that might serve equally well as Danny's feature film directorial debut, and found one in Thornton Wilder's whimsical novel, *Theophilus North*, which, at one time, Huston had considered turning into a film himself. He set about writing the script with his *Prizzi's Honor* collaborator, Janet Roach (writer James Costigan contributed to the script as well). Financial backing was secured from an independent production company, Heritage Entertainment, when it was agreed that Huston would act in the film, serve as its executive producer, and help Danny out behind the scenes as well. Ensuring that Danny would be given the best shot possible, longtime Huston associates Tom Shaw and Roberto Silvi signed on as co-producer and editor, respectively. Likewise, Danny's low budget, debut feature, retitled *Mr. North*, was to be bolstered by considerable star power. Tammy Grimes, Harry Dean Stanton, David Warner and Lauren Bacall agreed to appear in the film. Maintaining the family affair spirit of the enterprise, Anjelica Huston accepted a small but important role, and Huston's other daughter, Allegra (Danny's half sister), flew in from England to appear in a cameo as well. Because of the elder Huston's uninsurability, it was agreed that another actor be made available to step in and play Huston's part should he become incapacitated during shooting. Huston turned to his old friend Robert Mitchum, who flew to the film's location, Newport, Rhode Island, to stand ready.

As shooting on *Mr. North* proceeded in the late spring of 1987, it became eminently clear that the rejuvenation John Huston had experienced while making *The Dead* was fast waning. In fact, his physical condition, triggered by his longtime bout with emphysema, was deteriorating rapidly. As arranged, Robert Mitchum took over Huston's role as the invalided millionaire James McHenry Bosworth, who is given a new lease on life due to the intervention of Mr. North. At one point in the film, Bosworth says to North: "I've lived a very adventurous life. My daughter tells me I should be grateful for that and not be greedy for more. But oh how I do long sometimes to breathe the sweet air of freedom." The line very likely summed up John Huston's own feelings at the time.

Shortly before his 81st birthday, Huston's condition worsened when his weakened lungs filled with pneumonia. He was rushed to a hospital in nearby Fall River, Massachusetts, where his condition was pronounced "critical." Miraculously, he seemed to improve and he was later moved to a private house in Newport Harbor, near the *Mr. North* location.

But the die was clearly cast. In the early hours of August 28, 1987, as he lay alone in bed with his longtime companion and nurse, Marciela (to whom he had lovingly dedicated *The Dead*), by his side, John Huston made his final fade out. That same day, his body was flown to California, and following a memorial service on August 31, his ashes were layed to rest next to the grave of his mother, Rhea Gore Huston, in Hollywood Memorial Park.

Of the many tributes that poured in at the time of his death, one (as recounted in Lawrence Grobel's massive biography of the entire Huston clan, *The Hustons*) stands out to me as the most moving and astute. It was written by directors Fred Zinneman and George Stevens, Jr., who called Huston "...[among] the last vanishing breed of men who were great filmmakers and whose work illuminated the richness of their life experiences." That message should be taken to heart by everyone who sees film as an art form capable of the kind of personal expression inherent to all the other arts, yet who persist in lionizing the empty but estimably cinematic extravaganzas of today's "movie brat" generation.

With John Huston's passing, more than a great filmmaker exited the stage. A great American artist did as well.

John Huston, shortly before his death on August 28, 1987, at age 81.

John Huston, age 57, on the set of Freud *(1963).*

Bibliography

Periodicals

Bachmann, Gideon: "Huston in Morocco," *Sight ana Sound,* Summer, 1975, pp. 161-165

Champlin, Charles: "Huston Wartime Films on KCET," *Los Angeles Times,* April 30, 1981.

Corliss, Richard: "The Disasters of Modern War," *Time,* January 19, 1981, pp. 80

Dempsey, Michael: "A Walk with Love and Death," *Film Heritage,* Winter 1970-71, pp. 14-18.

Drew, Bernard: "John Huston: At 74 No Formulas," *American Film,* September, 1980, pp. 38-45, 66-67.

Egger, Urs: "John Huston Interview," *Cinema Papers,* October, 1977, pp. 138-141, 185.

Eyles, Allan: "Behind the Camera, Oswald Morris," *Focus on Film,* No. 8, pp. 28-37.

Grobel, Lawrence: "Interview with John Huston," *Playboy,* Fall, 1985, pp. 63-65, 68-72, 178-182.

Huston, Tony: "Family Ties," *American Film,* September, 1987, pp.16–19, 49.

Kakutani, Michiko: "John Huston's Last Legacy," *The New York Times,* Dec. 31, 1987, pp. 1, 50.

Koningsberger, Hans: "From Book to Film—Via John Huston," *Film Quarterly,* Spring, 1979.

McGuigan, Cathleen: "Huston's Volcanic Vision," *Newsweek,* October 31, 1983, pp. 79-83.

Millar, Gavin: "John Huston," *Sight and Sound,* Summer, 1981, pp. 203-205.

Schary, Dore: "Heyday in Hollywood," *American Film,* November, 1979, pp. 50-55, 78-79.

Taylor, John Russell: "John Huston and the Figure in the Carpet," *Sight and Sound,* Spring, 1969, pp. 70-73.

Walsh Michael: "John Huston Raises *The Dead,*" *Time,* March 16, 1987, pp. 92-93.

Books

Agee, James: *Agee on Film,* Beacon Press, 1964.

Bosworth, Patricia: *Montgomery Clift,* Bantam Books, 1979.

Callan, Michael Feeney: *Sean Connery,* Stein and Day, 1983.

Eames, John Douglas; *The MGM Story,* Crown, 1982.

Fitzgerald, Michael G.: *Universal Pictures,* Arlington House, 1977.

Grobel, Lawrence: *The Hustons,* Scribners, 1989.

Gussow, Mel: *Zanuck: Don't Say Yes Until I Finish Talking,* Pocket Books, 1972.

Hall, William: *Raising Caine,* Prentice-Hall, 1982.

Higham, Charles: *Orson Welles,* St. Martin's Press, 1985.

Hirschhorn, Clive: *The Universal Story,* Crown, 1983.

Hirschhorn, Clive: *The Warner Bros. Story,* Crown, 1979.

Huston, John: *An Open Book,* Alfred A. Knopf, 1981.

Kaminsky, Stuart: *John Huston, Maker of Magic,* Houghton Mifflin Company, 1978.

LaGuardia, Robert: *Monty,* Arbor House, 1977.

McCarty, Clifford: *The Films of Humphrey Bogart,* Citadel Press, 1975.

McClintick, David: *Indecent Exposure,* Dell, 1983.

Meyer, William R.: *The Making of the Great Westerns,* Arlington House, 1979.

Mosley, Leonard: *Zanuck: The Rise and Fall of Hollywood's Last Tycoon,* Little, Brown and Company, 1984.

Negulesco, Jean: *Things I Did and Things I Think I Did,* Linden Press, 1984.

Nolan, William F.: *John Huston, King Rebel,* Sherbourne Press, 1965.

Pye, Michael and Myles, Lynda: *The Movie Brats,* Holt, Rinehart and Winston, 1979.

Ross, Lillian: *Picture,* Dolphin Books, 1962.

Rubin, Steven Jay: *The James Bond Films,* Arlington Preminger, Otto: *An Autobiography,* Doubleday & Company, 1977.

Sarris, Andrew: *Interviews with Film Directors,* Bobbs-Merrill, 1967.

Steinberg, Cobbett: *Film Facts,* Facts on File, 1980.

Viertel, Peter: *White Hunter, Black Heart,* Doubleday, 1953.

Vizzard, Jack: *See No Evil,* Pocket Books, 1971.

Youngkin, Stephen D., Bigwood, James and Cabana, Raymond: *The Films of Peter Lorre,* Citadel Press, 1982.